JAM JAM JAM
with
THE EAGLES

CONTENTS

Introduction	4
Performance Notes	5
Tablature Explanation	8
Hotel California	9
Life In The Fast Lane	29
One Of These Nights	49
Tequila Sunrise	65
New Kid In Town	76
Lyin' Eyes	98
Take It Easy	122
Best Of My Love	142

 To download the online audio scan the QR code or go to fabermusic.com/audio.

The audio is split into two sections; section 1 (tracks 1–8) is the backing tracks to the titles listed above. Section 2 (tracks 9–16) is each of the backing tracks listed above with all the lead guitar parts included for your reference, played by Stuart Bull.

Music arranged & produced by Stuart Bull and Steve Finch.
Recorded at the TOTAL ACCURACY SOUNDHOUSE, Romford, England.

Stuart Bull: guitar & drums, Gerry Cunningham: bass, Pete Adams: keyboards.

Professional Guitar Workshops

© International Music Publications Ltd
First published in 1996 by International Music Publications Ltd
International Music Publications Ltd is a Faber Music company
Brownlow Yard, 12 Roger Street, London WC1N 2JU
Printed in England by Caligraving Ltd
All rights reserved

ISBN10: 0-571-53178-4
EAN13: 978-0-571-53178-3

Reproducing this music in any form is illegal and forbidden by the Copyright, Designs and Patents Act, 1988.

To buy Faber Music publications or to find out about the full range of titles available,
please contact your local music retailer or Faber Music sales enquiries:

Faber Music Ltd, Burnt Mill, Elizabeth Way, Harlow, CM20 2HX England
Tel: +44(0)1279 82 89 82
fabermusic.com

Introduction

The TOTAL ACCURACY 'JAM WITH...' series, is a powerful learning tool that will help you extend your stockpile of licks and fills and develop your improvisational skills. The combination of musical notation and guitar tablature in the book together with backing tracks on the CD gives you the opportunity to learn each track note for note and then jam with a professional session band. The track listing reflects some of The Eagles' most popular recordings, providing something for guitarists to have fun with and improvise with, as well as something to aspire to.

The first eight tracks on the CD are full length backing tracks recorded minus lead guitar. The remaining tracks feature the backing tracks with the lead guitar parts added. Although many of you will have all the original tracks in your own collection, we have provided them in the package for your reference. The 'JAM WITH...' series allows you to accurately recreate the original, or to use the transcriptions in this book in conjunction with the backing tracks as a basis for your own improvisation. For your benefit we have put definite endings on the backing tracks, rather than fading these out as is the case on some of the original recordings. The accompanying transcriptions correspond to our versions. Remember, experimenting with your own ideas is equally important for developing your own style; most important of all however is that you enjoy JAM with THE EAGLES and HAVE FUN!

From the Mid-1970s to the start of the 1980s The Eagles held sway as one of the great rock bands of the decade. But while rock was the group's forte, they blended elements of folk and country into many of their songs. The Eagles evolved from the folk and countryrock movement that sprang up in Southern California in the late '60s and early '70s. None of the four founding members were native Californians, but all eventually settled in Los Angeles because of the musical environment.

Bernie Leadon had a huge interest in folk music which caused him to learn guitar and banjo before he reached his teens. Leadon played with local groups in Florida in the mid-1960s before heading to Los Angeles in 1967, where he worked with a series of groups in the late '60s. Rand Meisner's career began in his teens with local groups in the Midwest. Later, in Los Angeles, he was a founding member of Poco with Richie Furay and Jim Messina.

Glenn Frey grew up in the more frenetic pace of urban Detroit and after dropping out of college, he moved to Los Angeles. Hanging out at the Troubadour club, he became acquainted with Don Henley. Henley liked to play drums, but wasn't sure of his career direction. He finally heeded the advice of an English teacher that music suited him best and he headed for the 'big time' in Los Angeles. Frey meanwhile was trying to use some of his songs as a wedge for a solo career and got the chance to play some to David Geffen, then manager of Joni Mitchell and Crosby, Stills, Nash & Young. Geffen discouraged the solo approach and told Frey to join a band. Heeding this, Frey accepted a job with Linda Ronstadt, and as the band needed a drummer he looked up Henley. The two proved highly compatible, and on the first night of the Ronstadt tour they agreed to start their own band. The band, in effect, took shape around them. Ronstadt's manager, John Boylan, brought in Randy Meisner on bass guitar and also recruited Bernie Leadon on lead guitar.

Helped by strong recommendation from Jackson Browne, the group got Geffen as their first manager and he financed the band so they could move to Aspen, Colorado, to rehearse, write songs, and polish their act in local clubs. Meanwhile, Geffen managed to get Frey a release from Amos Records and lined up a recording contract with Asylum. In early 1972, he arranged for the band to go to England to work on their debut LP under the direction of veteran producer Glyn Johns. The first fruit of that was the hit single "Take It Easy", written by Browne and Frey and issued in early summer 1972. In July 1972 their first album, EAGLES, was released.

In 1973, the band went back into London's Olympia studios to work on their second album. It was an ambitious project, a concept album with all the songs tied into the theme of the rise and·fall of the Doolin-Dalton gang of Wild West fame. Called DESPERADO it came out in the spring of 1973 and was only moderately successful. The lukewarm reception to the LP stirred unease among some admirers, fearing The Eagles might go the way of Poco and the Burritos. Adding to that were reports of internal dissension and later, of arguments with Johns about the next LP. The band decided to switch from Geffen to Irving Azoff for management, with Bill Szymczyk moving in as producer. In the process the band found a fifth member, Don Felder - one of the best slide guitarists in pop music. When the album ON THE BORDER was released it was announced that Felder had become The Eagles' fifth member.

Rumours persisted about internal problems as the months went by. In 1975 "One of These Nights" was released and went well past platinum levels. By the end of 1975, Leadon indicated he had become tired of the touring grind and the pressures of band life and wanted out. His place was taken in early 1976 by Joe Walsh. Also managed by Azoff, Walsh was an excellent guitarist, singer and songwriter, who had been a member of the James Gang and later a successful solo artist.

The LP HOTEL CALIFORNIA combined unique insights with first-rate musicianship on every track. Among the singles hits culled from it were gems such as the title song and "New Kid In Town". But another personnel shift was on the agenda: Randy Meisner departed during 1979 to seek a solo career - his place was taken by bass guitarist Timothy B Schmidt, a former member of Poco. The new line-up completed the next album, THE LONG RUN, in the autumn of '79. The LP went platinum and provided three top 10 singles, "Heartache Tonight", the title song, and "I Can't Tell You Why". In the early 1980s, the two prime writing forces, Henley and Frey, began work on solo albums and due to their efforts towards these projects, The Eagles was disbanded in May 1982.

In the spring of 1987 there were rumours about a reunion, but that didn't happen until early 1994 when Henley, Frey and Walsh met to talk about this possibility. The result was a world tour and a new album HELL FREEZES OVER, with four new songs and 11 live tracks including a superb acoustic version of "Hotel California".

Performance Notes

Hotel California

A seventies classic, renowned for its multiple of layers of guitar, which build more and more as the song progresses. At the beginning, the main part is taken by a twelve string acoustic with a capo at the seventh fret. This is soon joined by a quieter melody, played on six string guitar and by the time the first chorus comes around there are more still. Each verse and chorus brings a new part.

The climax of the song is when the first solo begins, using a natural sounding valve overdrive - probably a Fender Twin reverb. The two lead guitars swap solos using several interesting tricks such as bending two strings at once to achieve the sound of one note raising up then another coming down - also sliding along one string to make whole segments of the melody.

Like many seventies records, some of the solo work here is played through a phase-shifter giving some of the playing a very liquid sound.

The solo work is all based around the B minor pentatonic scale (B,D,E,F#,A) incorporating occasional notes to fit with certain chords; eg when the F# major chord comes in for the first time the solo guitar plays a Bb to fit perfectly over the chord which contains a Bb. This approach is known as 'playing over the changes' and involves thinking not so much what key you are in, but what chord you are in, using the overall context of the B minor pentatonic. The famous harmonies follow the harmony of the backing chords very closely, but great care should be taken to keep the phrasing 'tight' between the two harmony guitars.

Life In The Fast Lane

This song is played with an overdrive sound - though not too over driven - and was probably played on a Gibson Les Paul through one of Joe Walsh's hot-rodded Fender Twin Reverb amplifiers. The main theme is introduced, then doubled an octave higher. As with all harmony or doubling work it is important to keep the phrasing identical on the two guitars.

During the verse a multitude of guitars play different parts. The key to using this approach is not to allow any one part to be too loud in the nix, but to link with the others equally in the listener's mind. Later in the song some heavy riffing happens, based around an E chord - accented by the drums and the rest of the band. The solo is played using a slide or bottleneck - remember when using a slide to play directly above the fret required and always mute behind the slide, to stop the sound from becoming messy. The solo work is based around the B major pentatonic scale, but uses several 'chromatic passing tones' - notes which fit in a faster context to join ideas but not when sustained individually.

One Of These Nights

An atmospheric introduction on bass and guitar, layering up different parts leads to a sudden harmony part played on another pair of guitars (this part could be played on one guitar). The general feel of the track is very funky, with minimalistic work from a clean rhythm guitar. The harmony guitars join in occasionally for an embellishment.

The solo is played with an overdriven sound and a funky style again. It may take some practice to execute some of these phrases perfectly at first, especially in succession, or even two bent notes as happens quite early in the solo which uses the E minor pentatonic scale (E,G,A,B,D), however to follow a more melodic path some notes are added especially to fit with certain chords; eg a C is used over the A minor chord which contains A,C and E. It would be possible to solo over the chords without adding these extra notes, but would not sound as interesting. Overall, it's important to keep short notes and chords in this track percussive - maybe even exaggerating this until it comes naturally.

Tequila Sunrise

Beginning with acoustic guitar - soon joined by a clean electric playing bent notes and double stops through a slight tremelo effect - this part is quite inventive in it's use of string bends and though it requires practice to play this kind of part smoothly, it is very rewarding. The solo section is played on acoustic guitar using double stops over open strings making this a solo that could possibly stand on its own with no backing! It is based around the G major scale (G,A,B,C,D,E,F#,G) with some chromatic movement (movement by steps) between the notes of the scale.

New Kid In Town

Played on both 'clean' and 'distorted' guitars, with back up from a strummed acoustic, there are a variety of different parts here. The clean guitar plays a mixture of double stops and arpeggiated chords (probably a Fender Telecaster through a Fender Twin Reverb amp). While the distorted guitar joins with some surprise accents in the chorus. Interestingly, the song is in the key of E major for the verse, and E minor for the chorus. Fills are based around the E major pentatonic scale (E,F#,G#,B,C#).

As with "One Of These Nights" there are occasions when the chord work needs to be really crisp, in this case a direct contrast from the flowing arpeggiated chords. Towards the end of the track, the clean guitar plays a chiming part which stays constant over changing chords. Generally speaking, a versatile approach is required for this versatile song.

Lyin' Eyes

A mellow sounding track, with acoustic guitar backing throughout, punctuated with various fills on electric guitar. Many of the fills use the double-stop and string bending techniques, to create a sound not unlike a pedal steel guitar. This is probably better described as 'warmth' almost certainly the result of playing a clean valve amplifier (probably a Fender Twin Reverb) at volume.

The solo guitars also descends chromatically from one chord to another - a fret at a time - on occasion. This lends a country feel to the overall sound. Generally this songs needs to sound as effortless as possible! This track is in the key of G.

Take It Easy

This track is underpinned by acoustic guitar throughout - later being joined by banjo, in the country tradition! but one thing that is very noticeable about this song is the chiming, chorused embellishment probably played on a Fender Telecaster, through a Fender Twin Reverb amplifier. Another traditional country trick to appear in this song are the 'double-stops' frequently used by the lead guitar. The important thing to remember about these, if one of the notes is to be bent, is to keep the other note or notes absolutely static rather than allowing them to drift sharp. This is particularly relevant to the fill which joins the track with the drums, making it a great exercise for building fretting hand strength. This part is based around the G major pentatonic scale (G,A,B,D,E). In the main part of the song the lead guitar plays arpeggiated chords along with the strummed acoustic - this was probably improvised originally, but is reproduced note for note here. If you do decide to play this part in an improvised manner, take care not to let it become too busy.

Best Of My Love

Performed over a lush backing of acoustic twelve-string, the solo guitar part was originally played on a pedal steel guitar, which is often heard in country music. However, it can be played on electric guitar using a bottleneck or slide, to almost identical effect. The scale used is the C major pentatonic (C,D,E,G,A). An important ingredient of the sound here is lots of reverb, and as always when playing slide, mute behind the slide - positioning it directly over the required frets. Also try keeping the guitar's tone knob down low. This should be played with a warn, clean tone.

Notation & Tablature explained

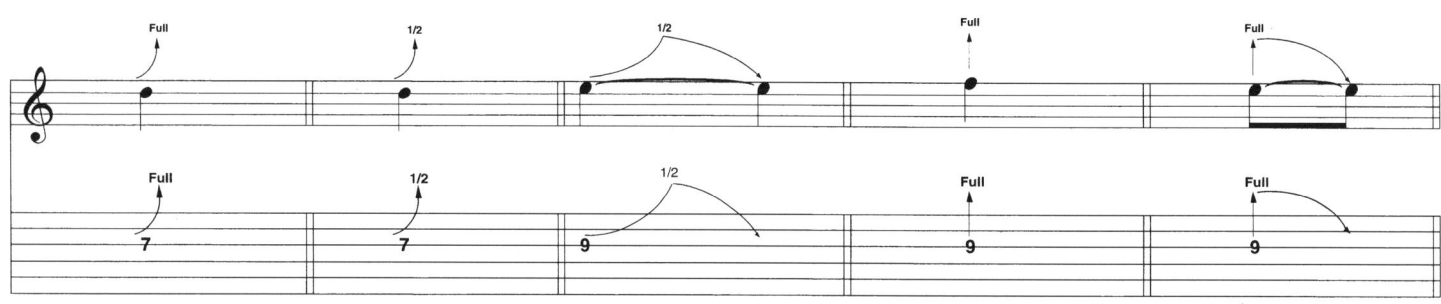

BEND: Strike the note and bend up a whole step (two frets)

BEND: Strike the note and bend up a half step (one fret)

BEND AND RELEASE: Strike the note, bend up a half step, then release the bend.

PRE-BEND: Bend the note up, then strike it

PRE-BEND AND RELEASE: Bend up, strike the note, then release it

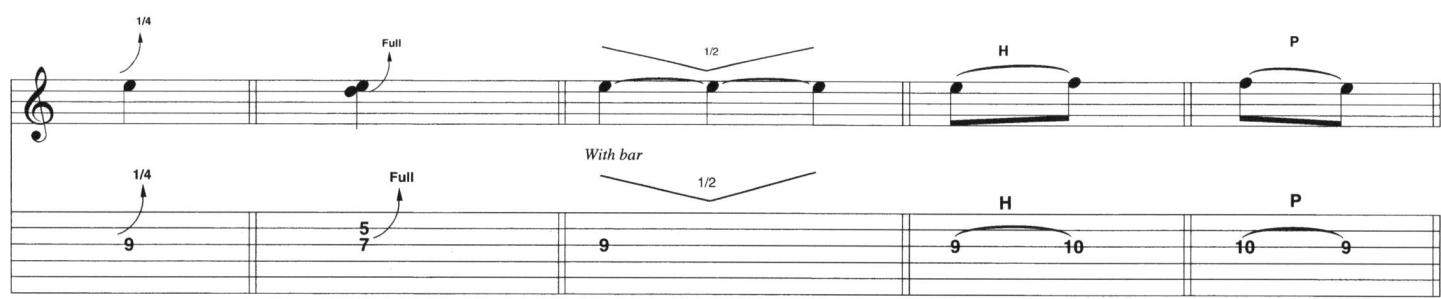

QUARTER-TONE BEND: Bend the note slightly sharp

UNISON BEND: Strike both notes, then bend the lower note up to the pitch of the higher one

TREMOLO BAR BENDS: Strike the note, and push the bar down and up by the amounts indicated

HAMMER-ON: Strike the first note, then sound the second by fretting it without picking

PULL-OFF: Strike the higher note, then pull the finger off while keeping the lower one fretted

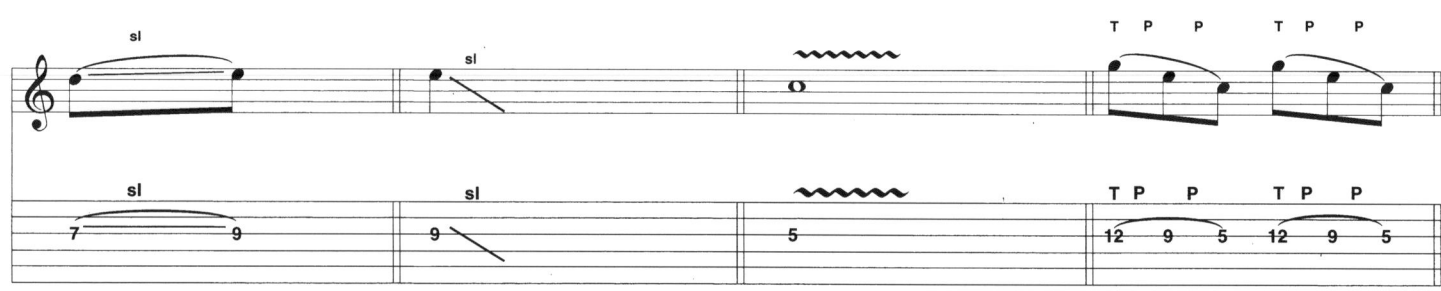

SLIDE: Slide the finger from the first note to the second. Only the first note is struck

SLIDE: Slide to the fret from a few frets below or above

VIBRATO: The string is vibrated by rapidly bending and releasing a note with the fretboard hand or tremolo bar

TAPPING: Hammer on to the note marked with a T using the picking hand, then pull off to the next note, following the hammer-ons or pull-offs in the normal way

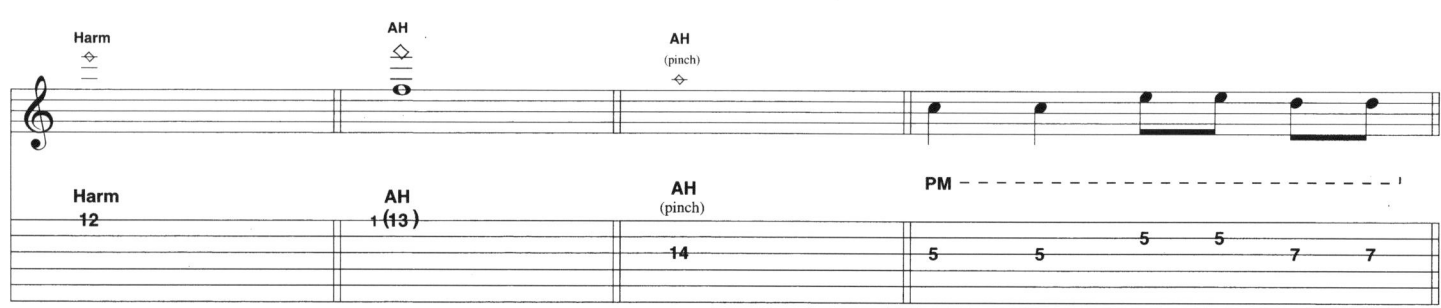

NATURAL HARMONIC: Lightly touch the string directly over the fret shown, then strike the note to create a "chiming" effect

ARTIFICIAL HARMONIC: Fret the note, then use the picking hand finger to touch the string at the position shown in brackets and pluck with another finger

ARTIFICIAL HARMONIC: The harmonic is produced by using the edge of the picking hand thumb to "pinch" the string whilst picking firmly with the plectrum

PALM MUTES: Rest the palm of the picking hand on the strings near the bridge to produce a muted effect. Palm mutes can apply to a single note or a number of notes (shown with a dashed line)

Hotel California

Words and Music by DON FELDER, DON HENLEY and GLENN FREY

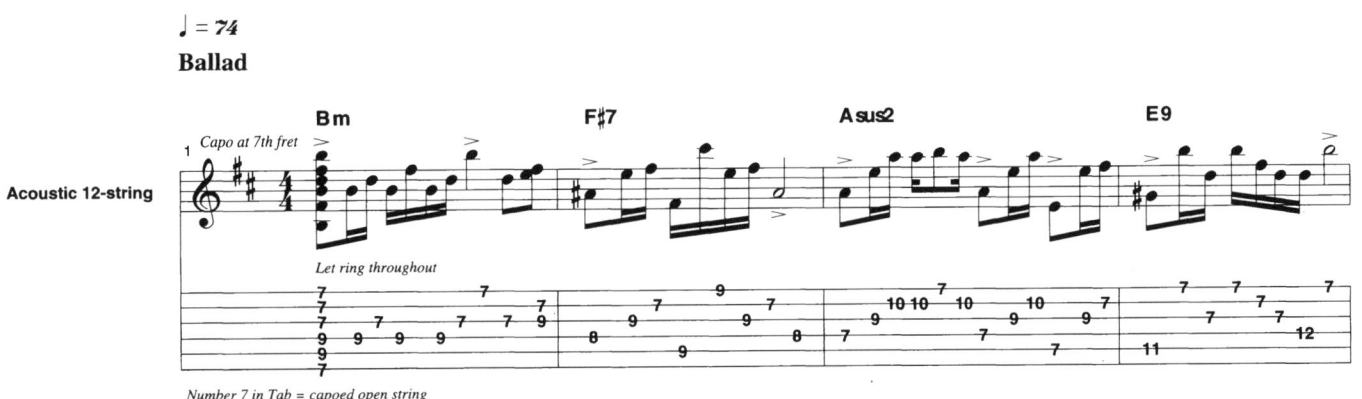

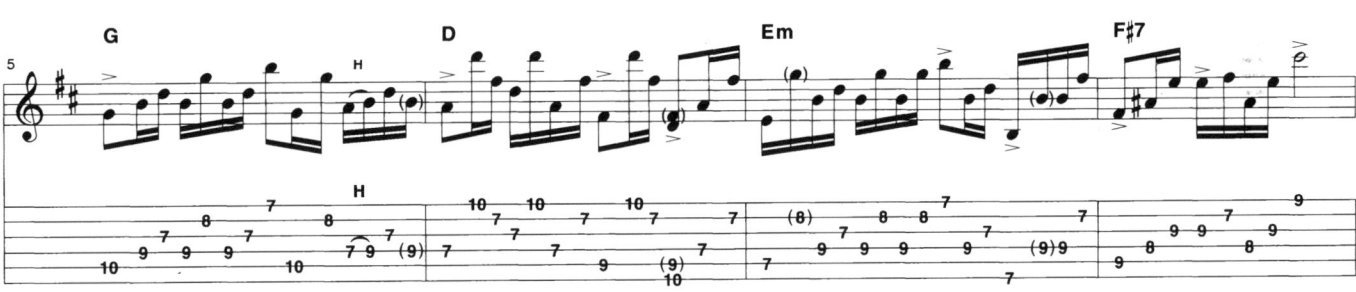

© 1977 & 1996 WB Music Corp, USA
Warner/Chappell Music Ltd, London W1Y 3FA

13
G
D
Em
F♯7add9
H
H
Let ring
Volume fade in and out

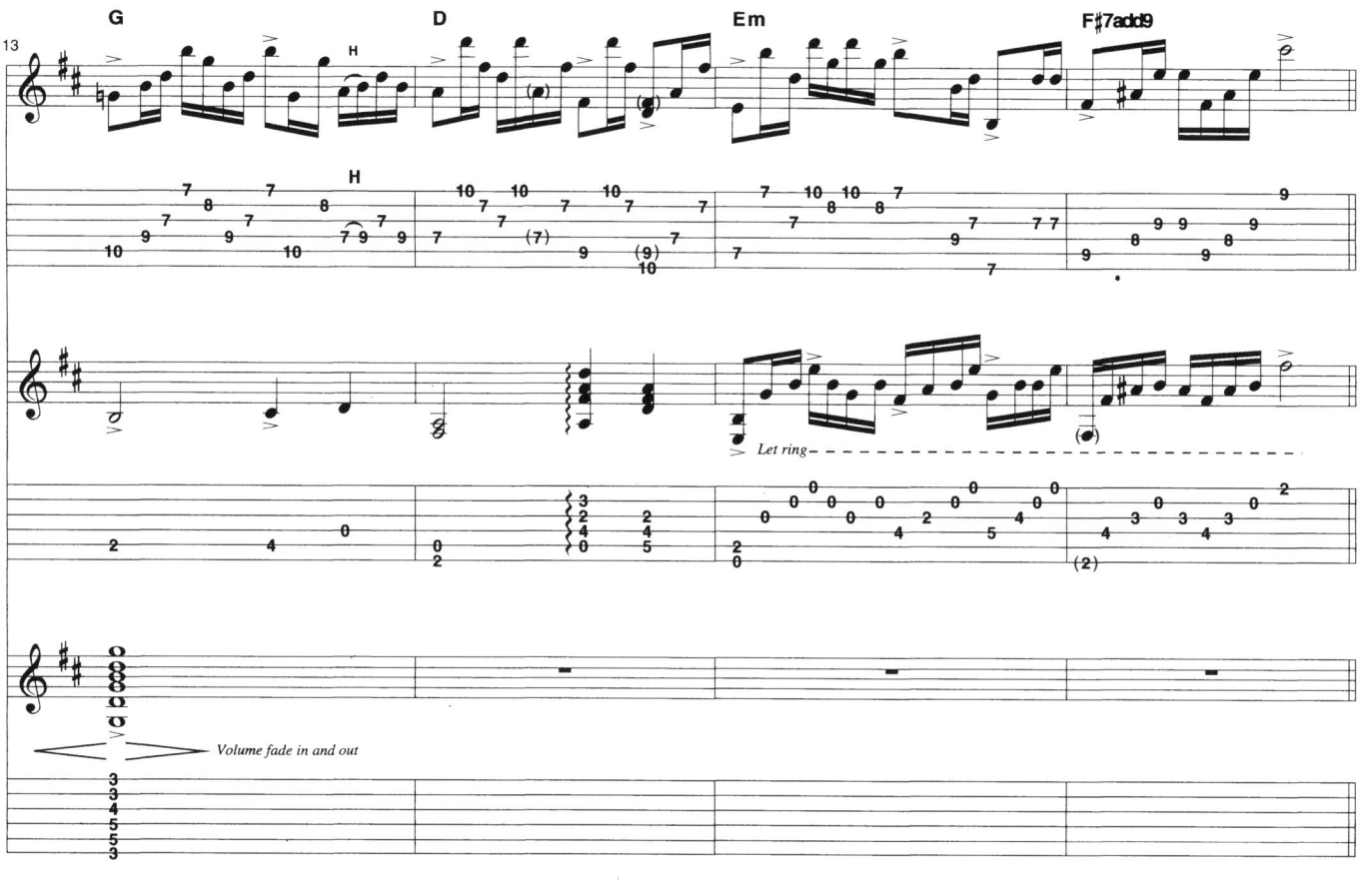

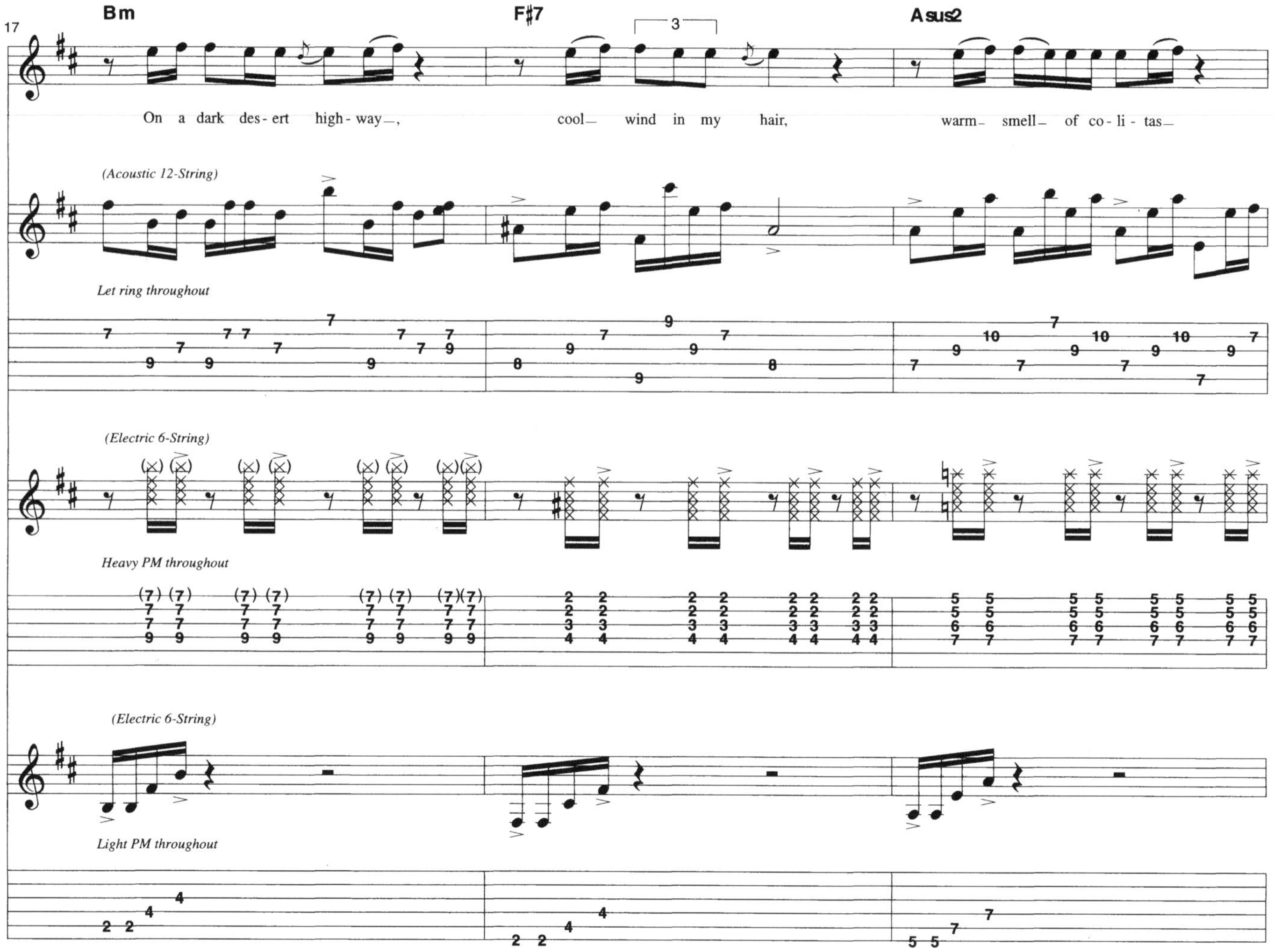

17
Bm
F♯7
Asus2
On a dark des-ert high-way,
cool wind in my hair,
warm smell of co-li-tas
(Acoustic 12-String)
Let ring throughout
(Electric 6-String)
Heavy PM throughout
(Electric 6-String)
Light PM throughout

Verse 2:

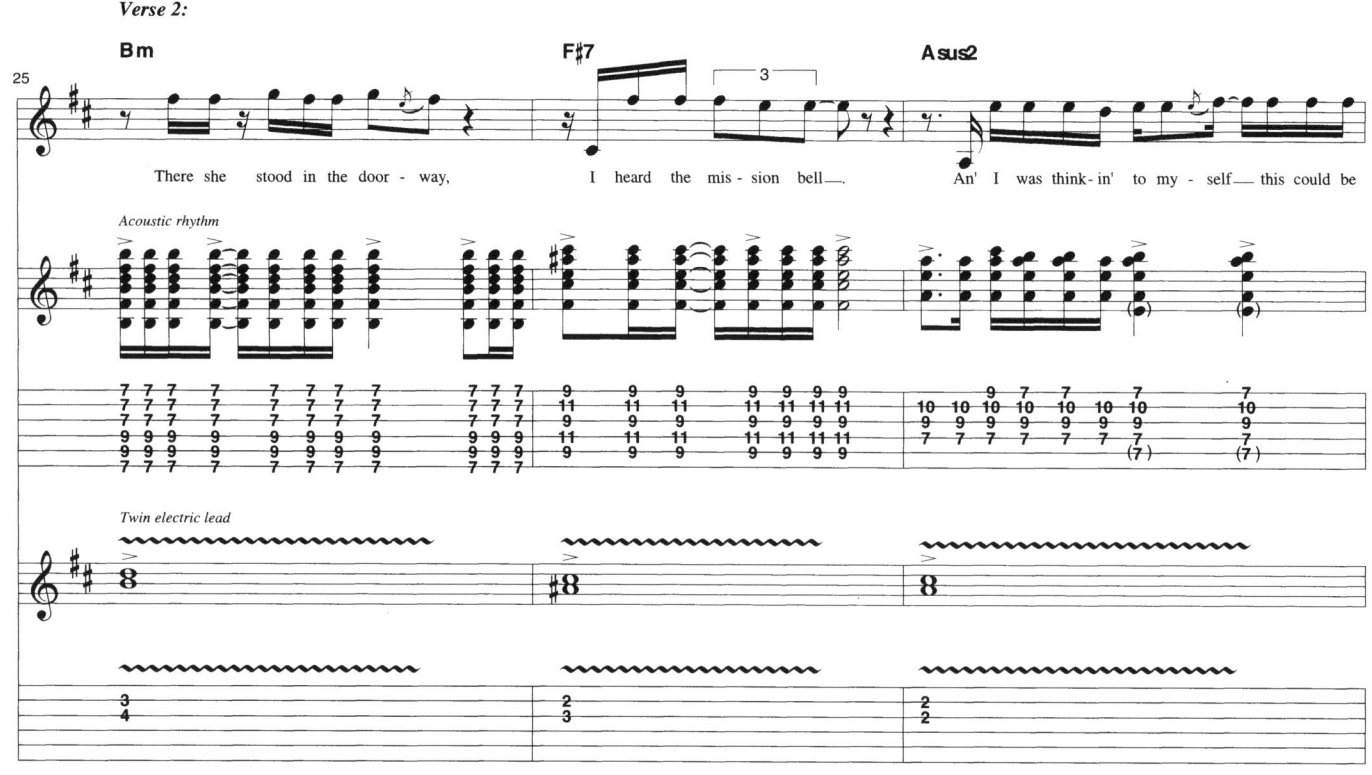

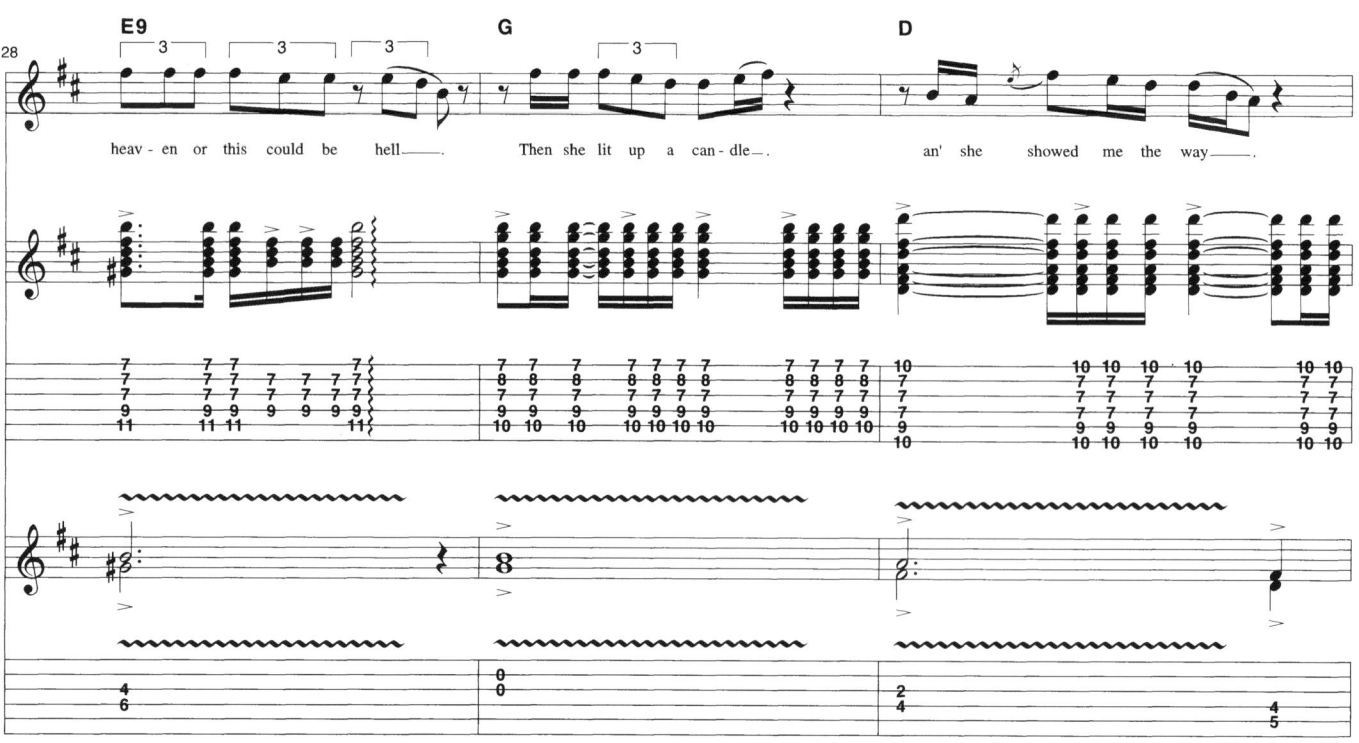

31
Em7
F#7
There were voic - es down the cor - ri - dor—, I thought I heard them— say,
1/2
1/2

Chorus:
33
G
D
"Wel - come— to the Ho - tel Cal - i - for - nia" such a
(Acoustic 12-String)
(Electric 6-String)
(Electric 6-String)
sl
sl

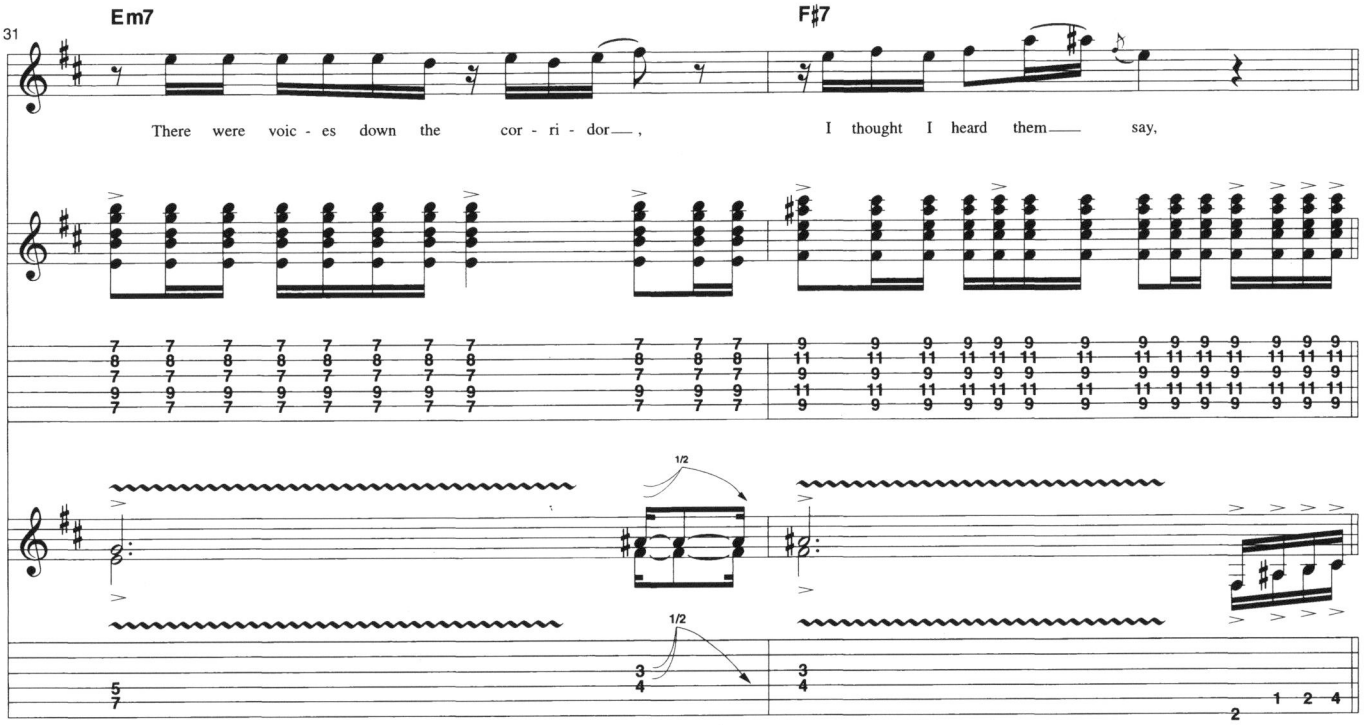

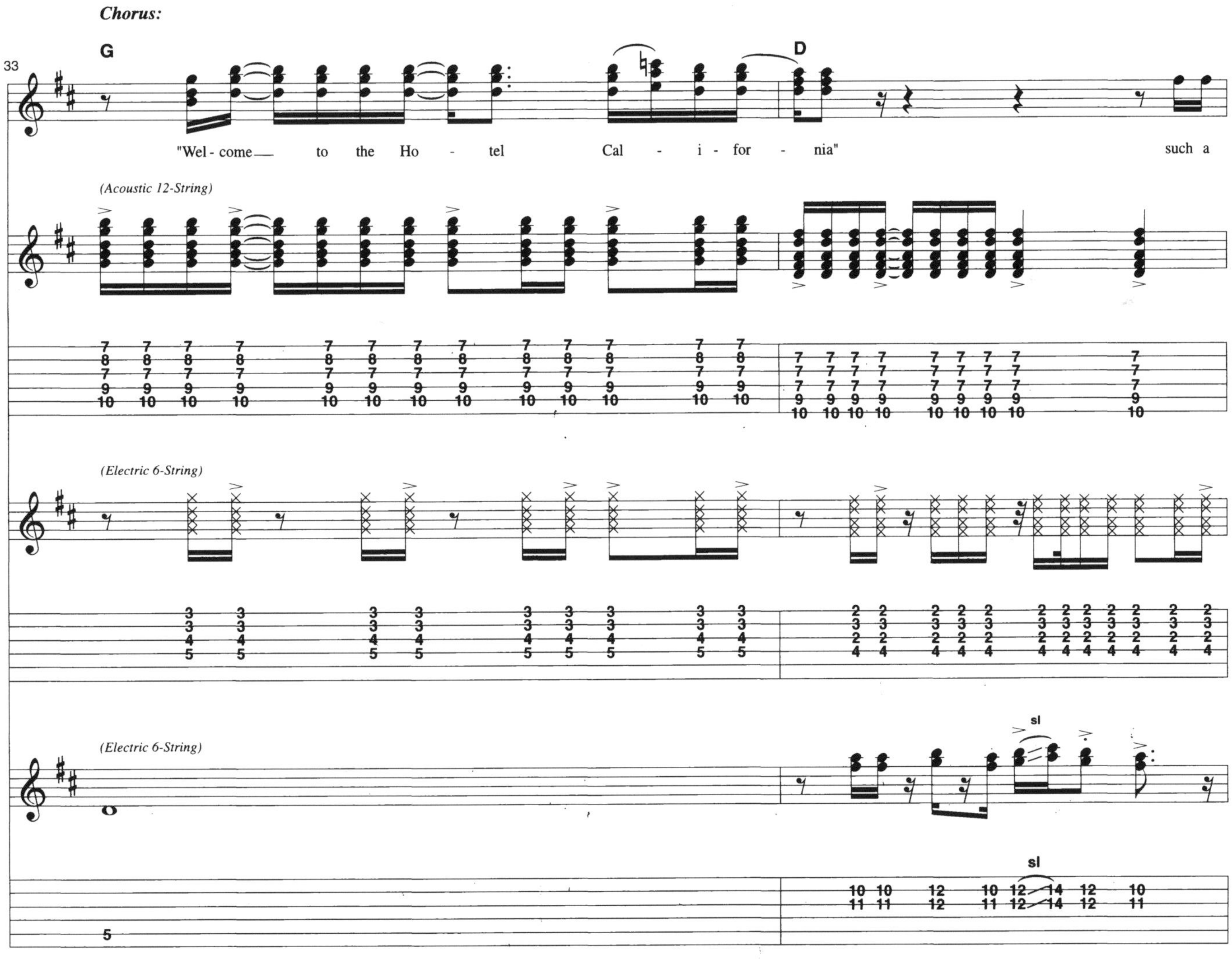

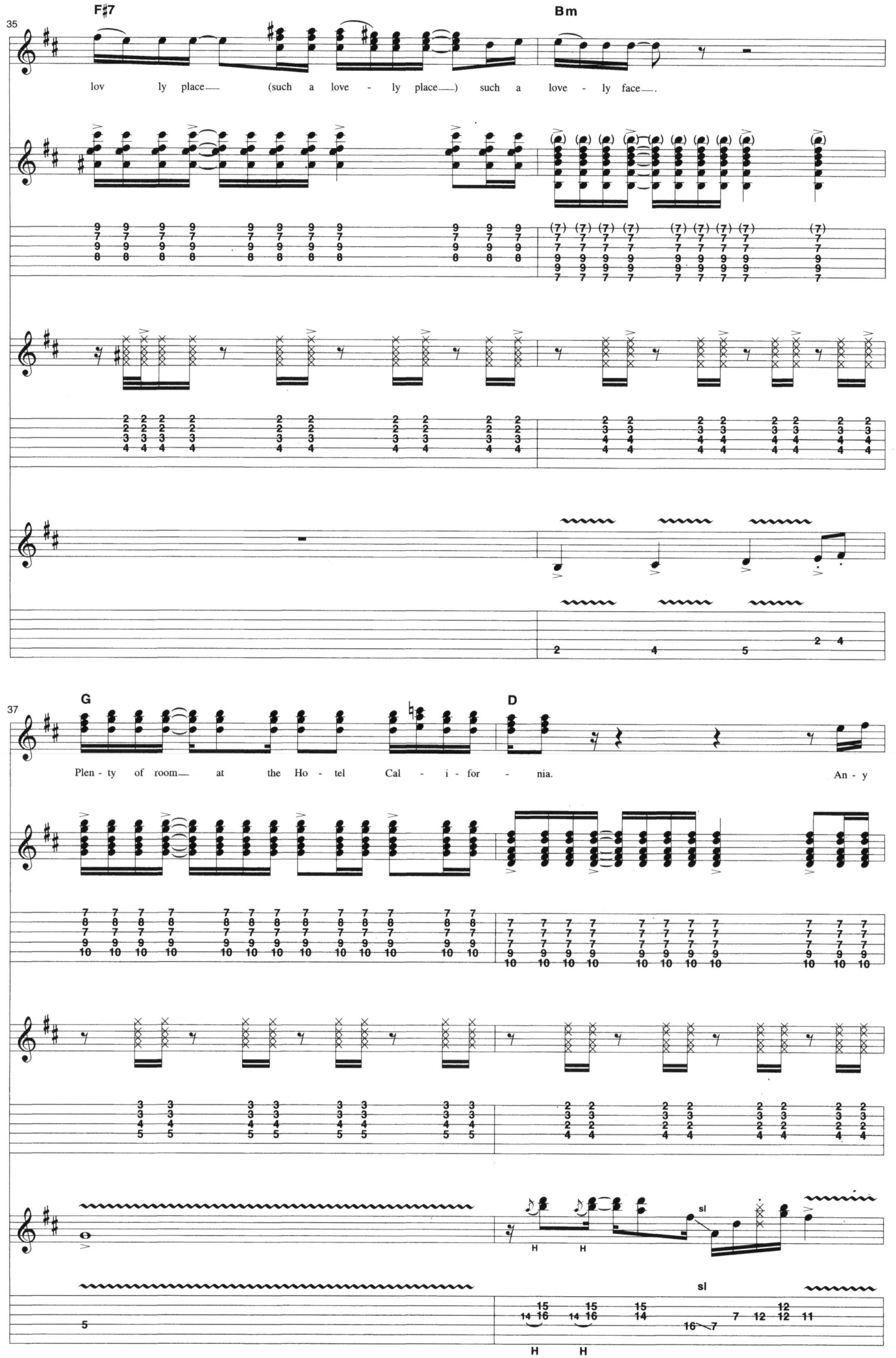

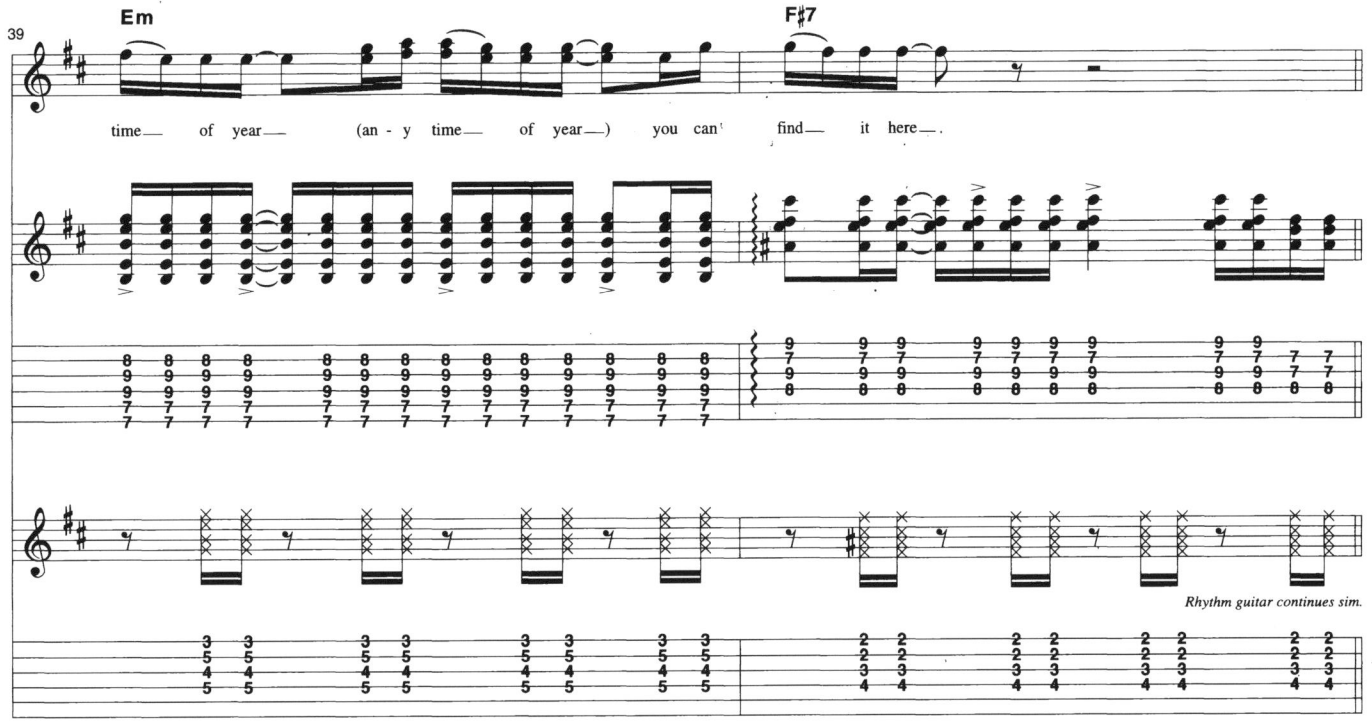

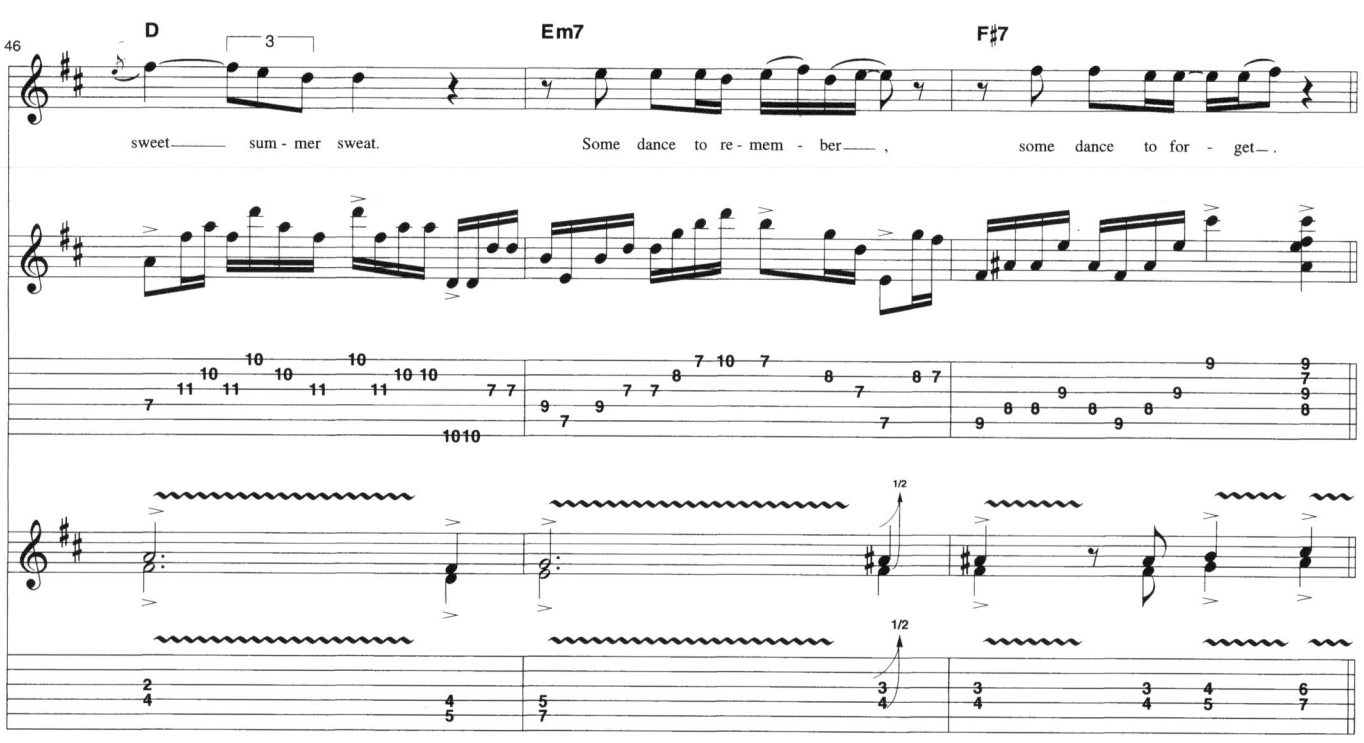

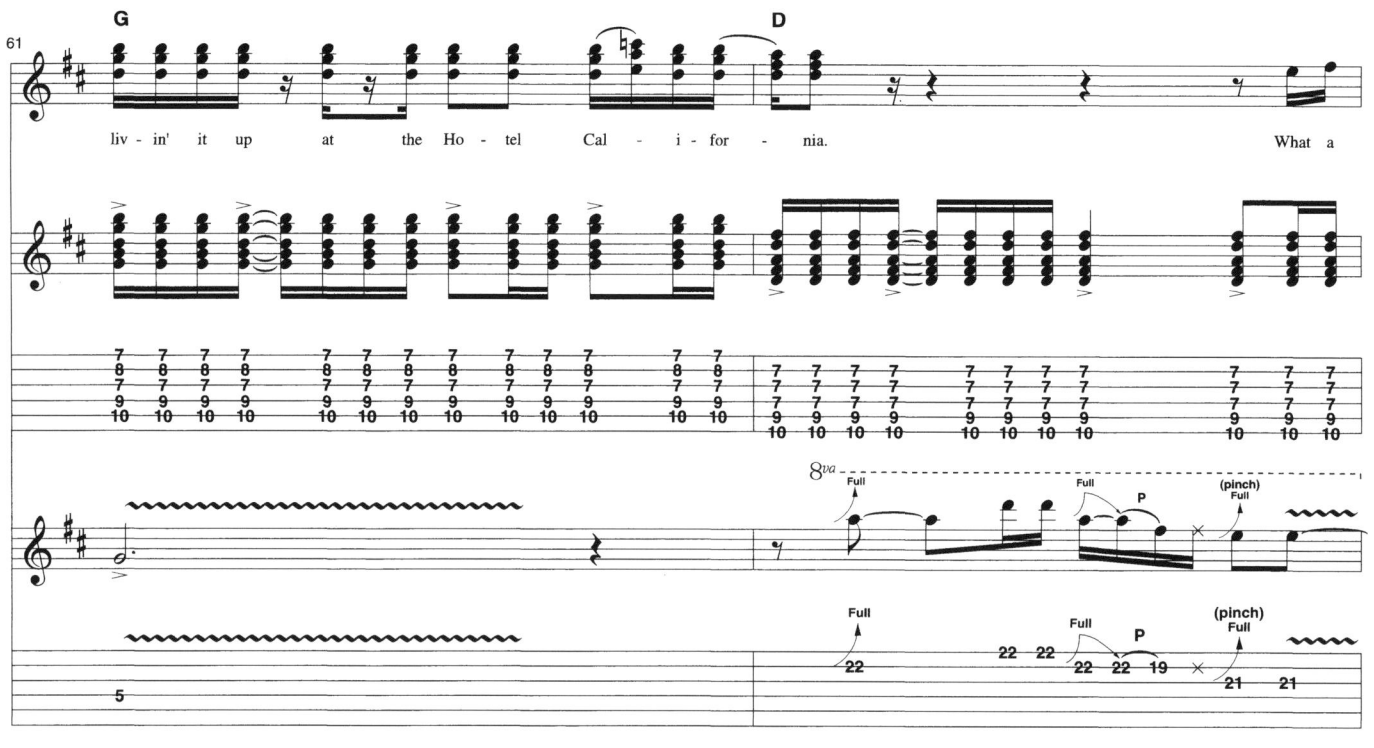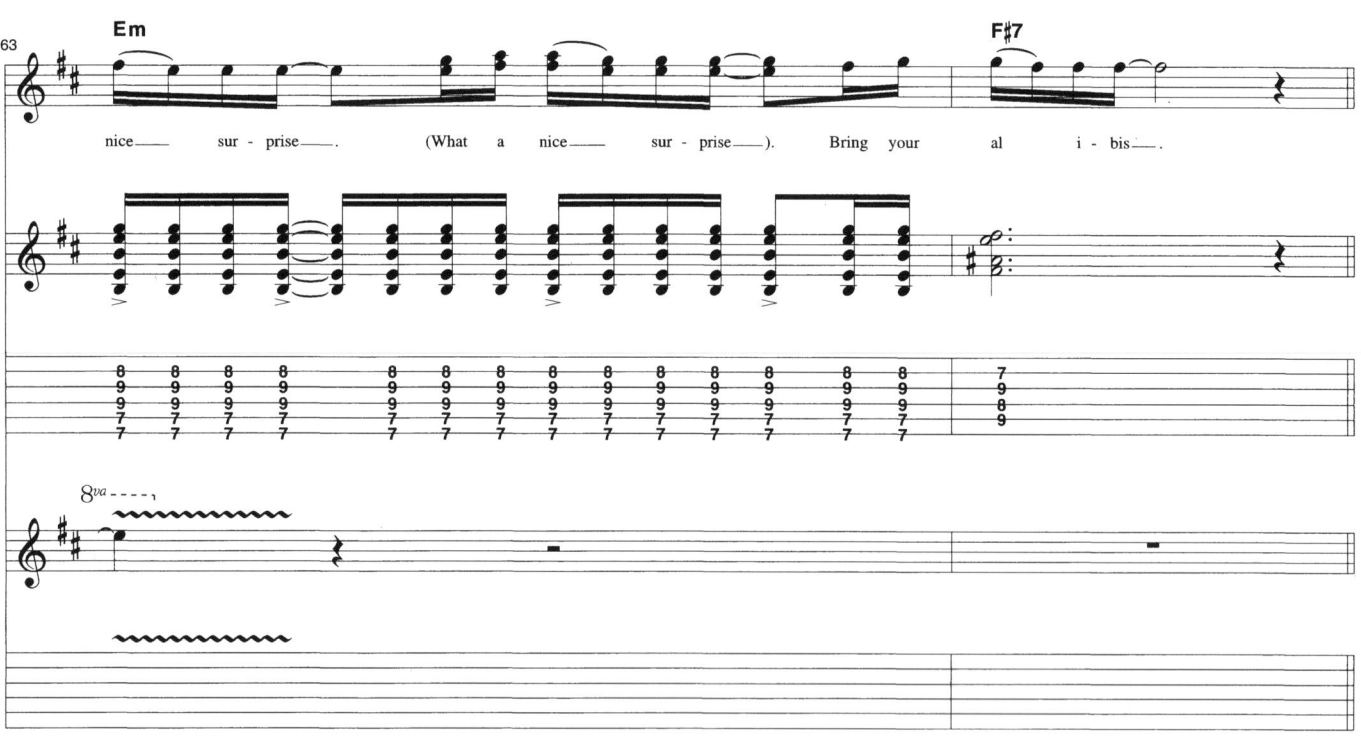

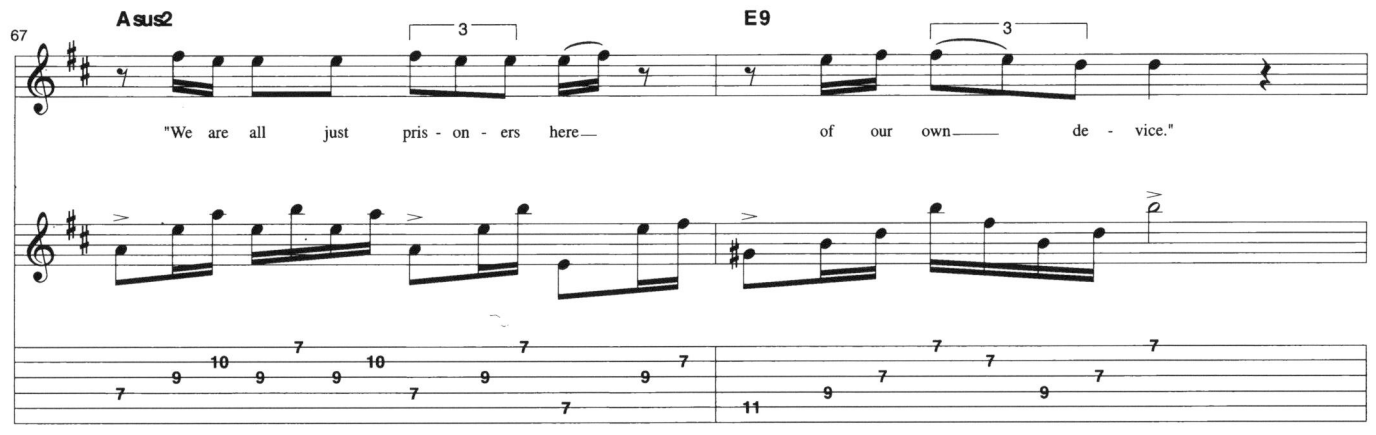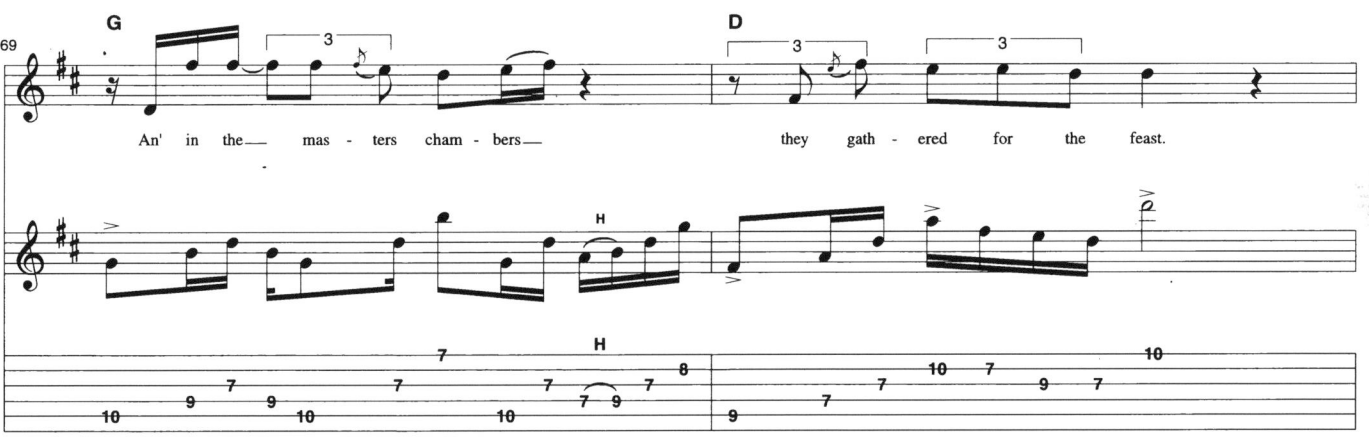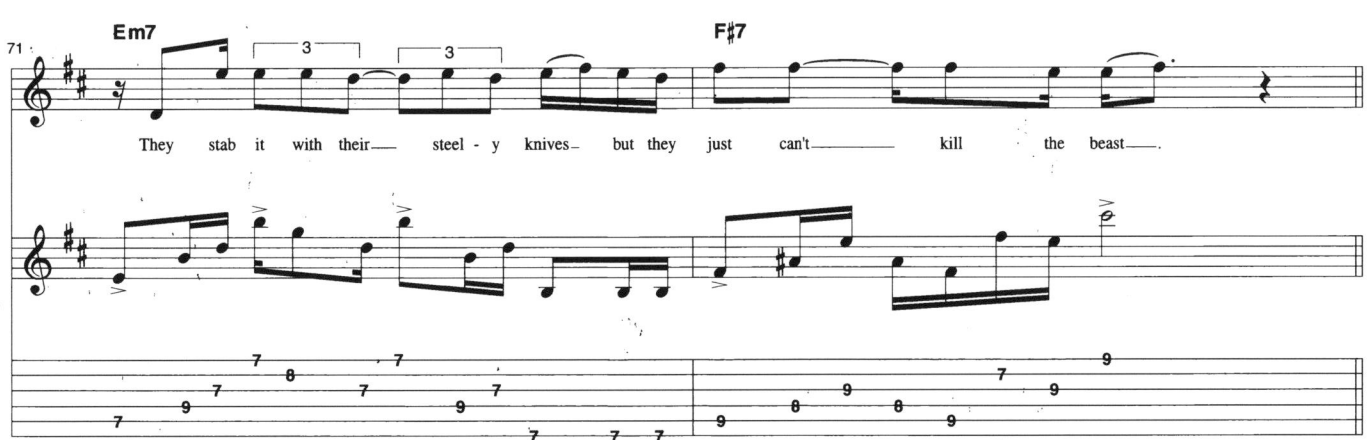

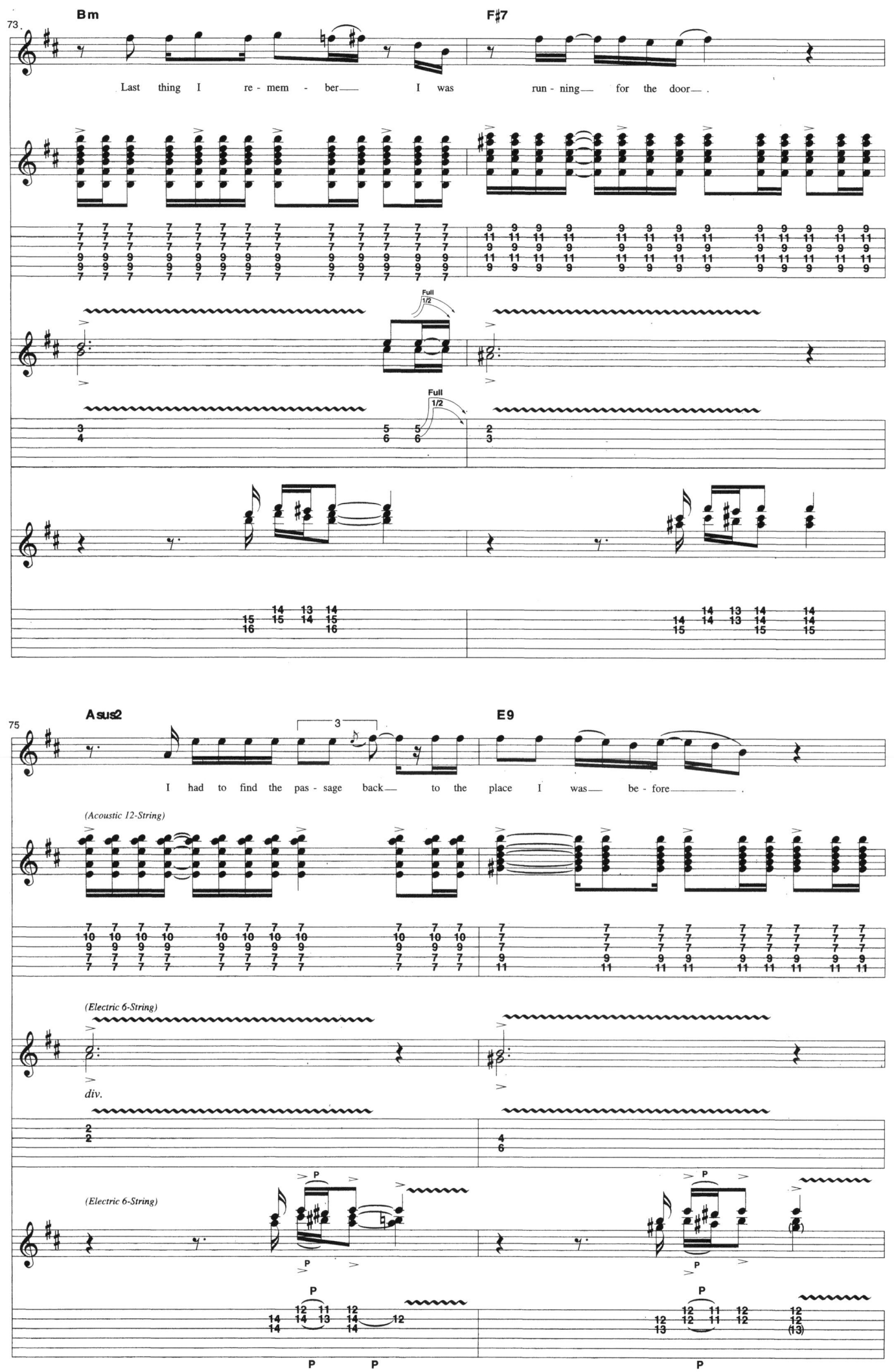

Guitar Solos:
(Electric 6-String)

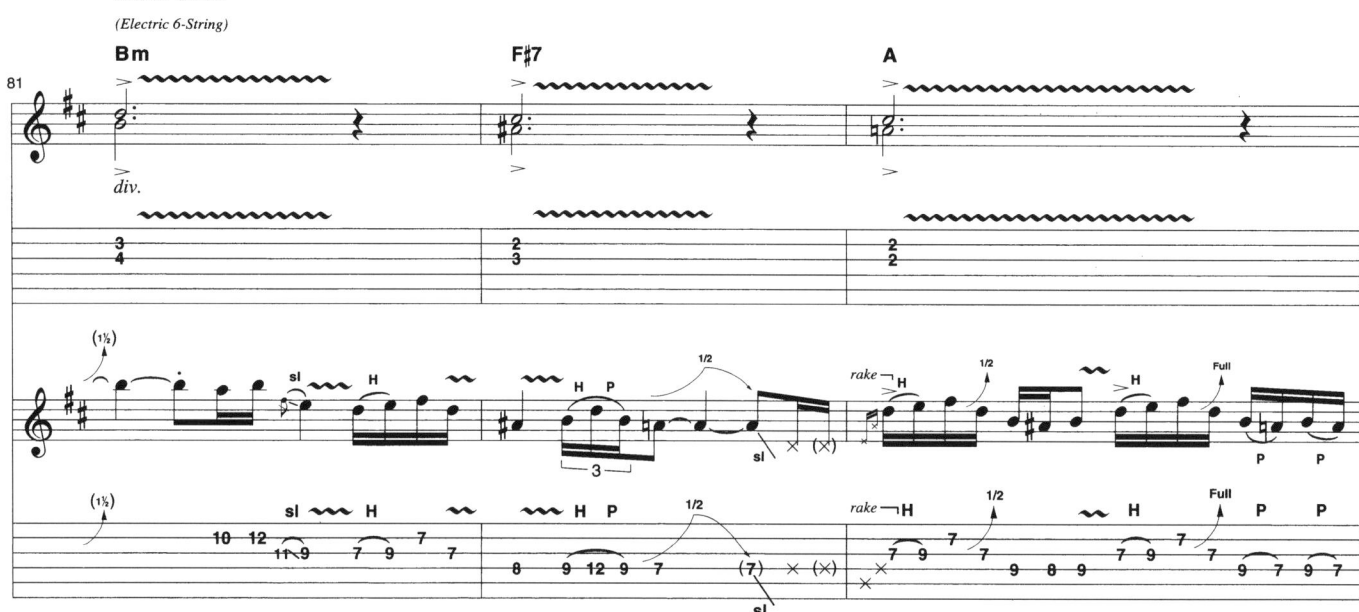
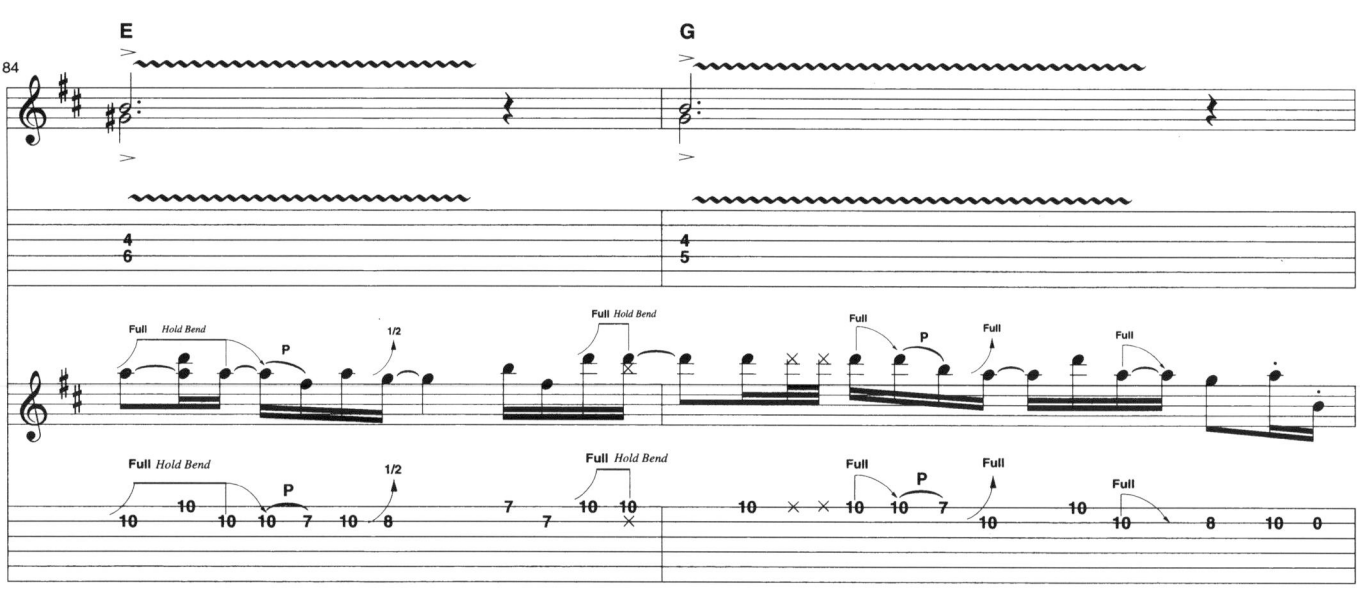

24

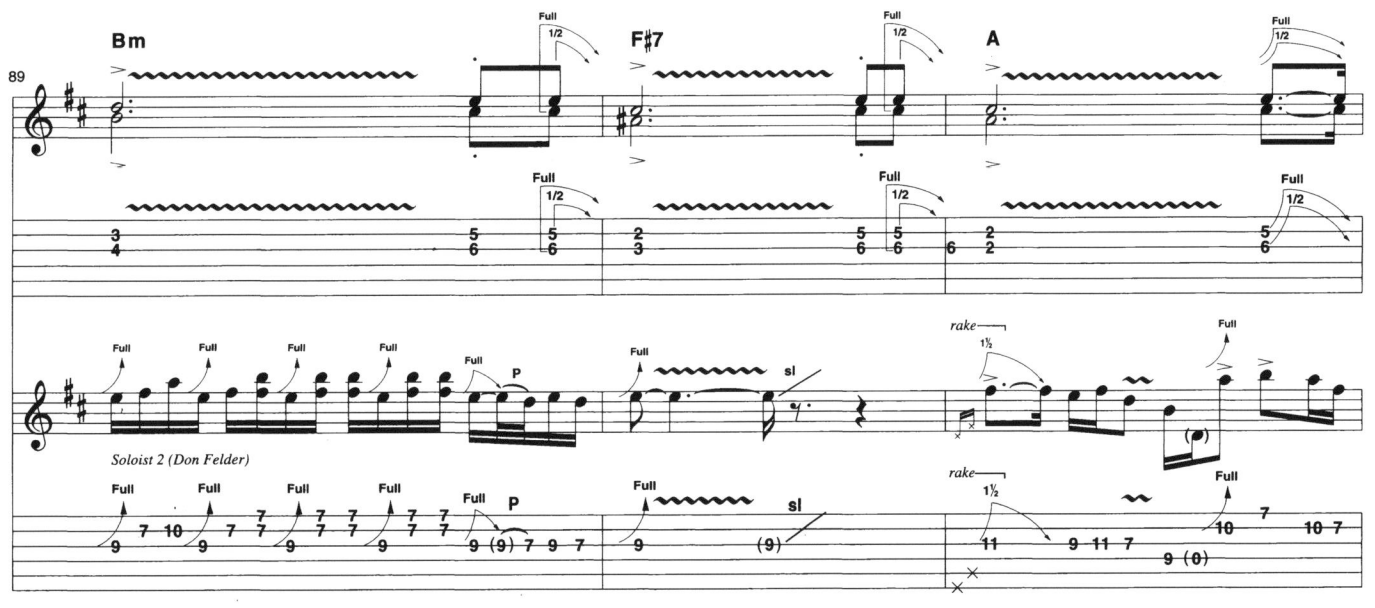
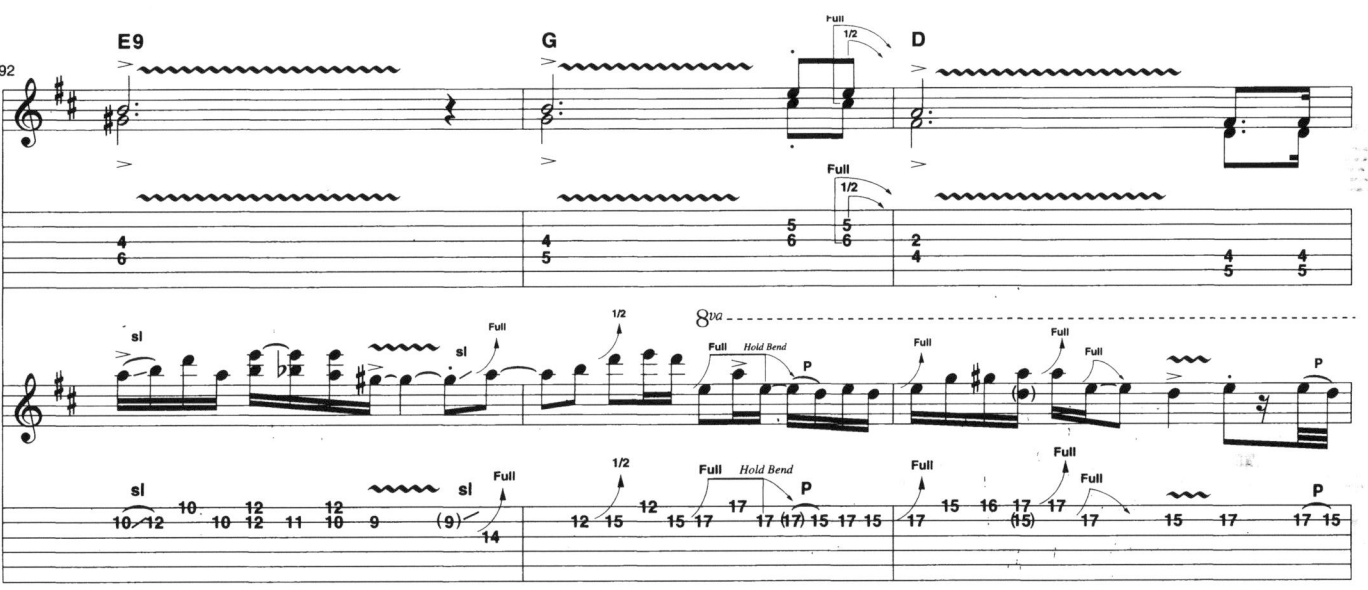
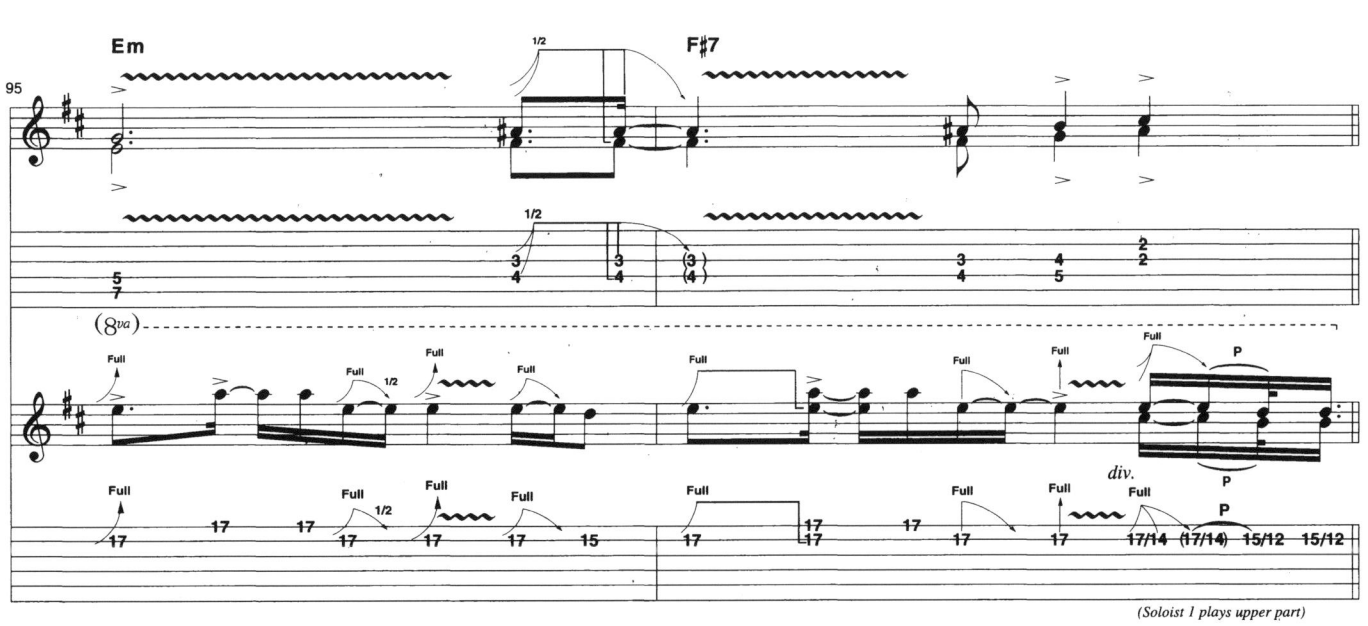

25

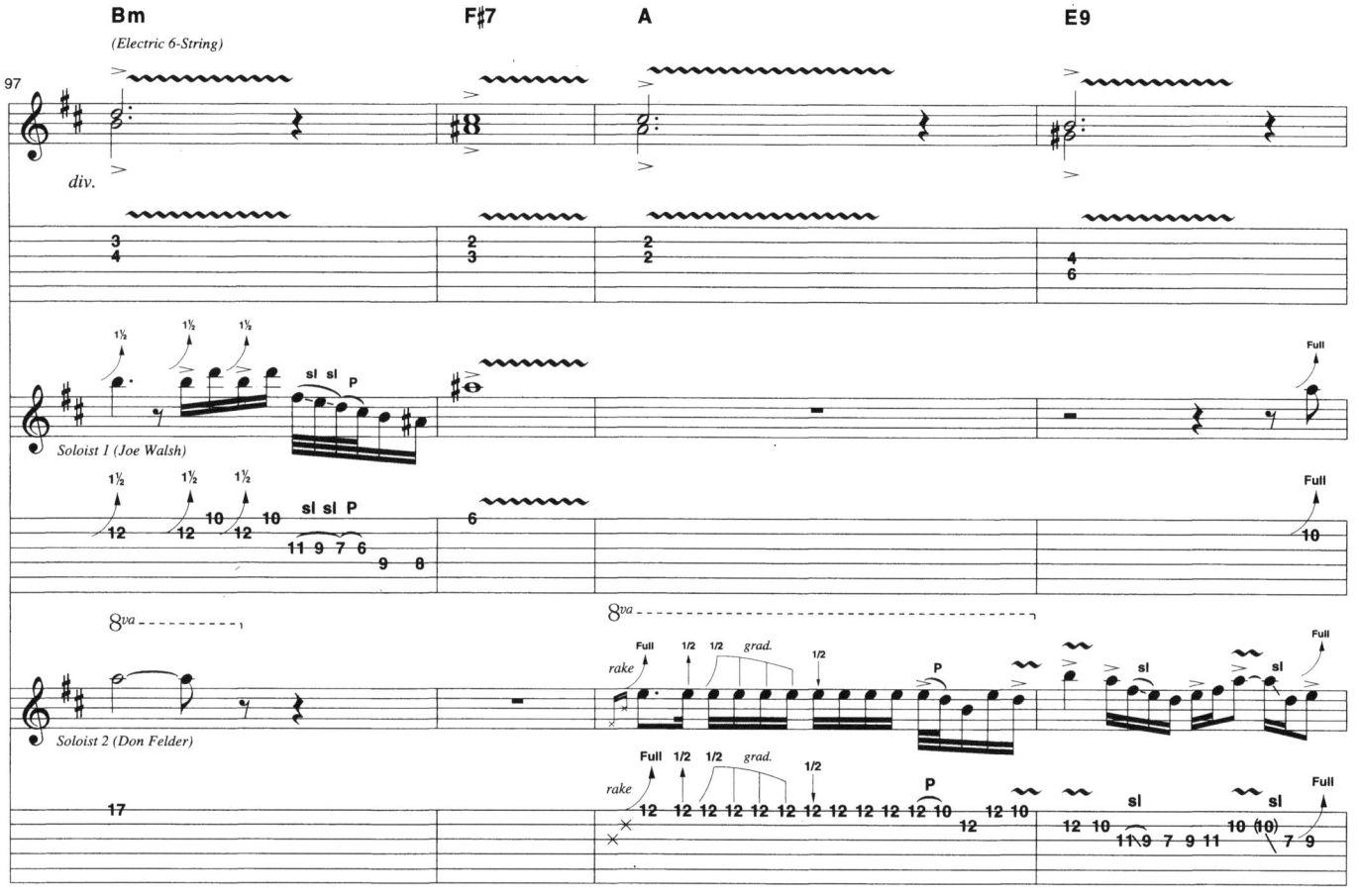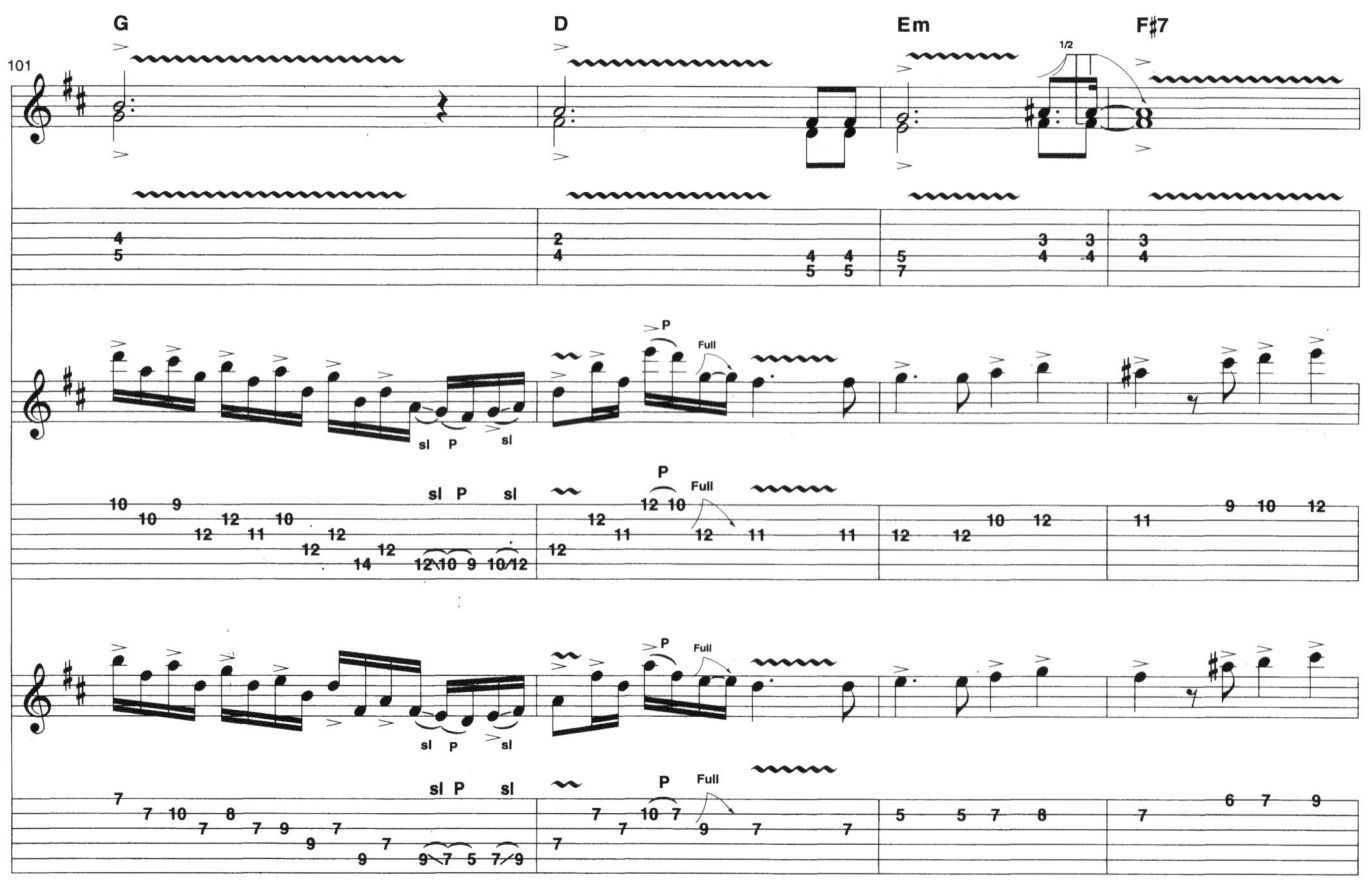

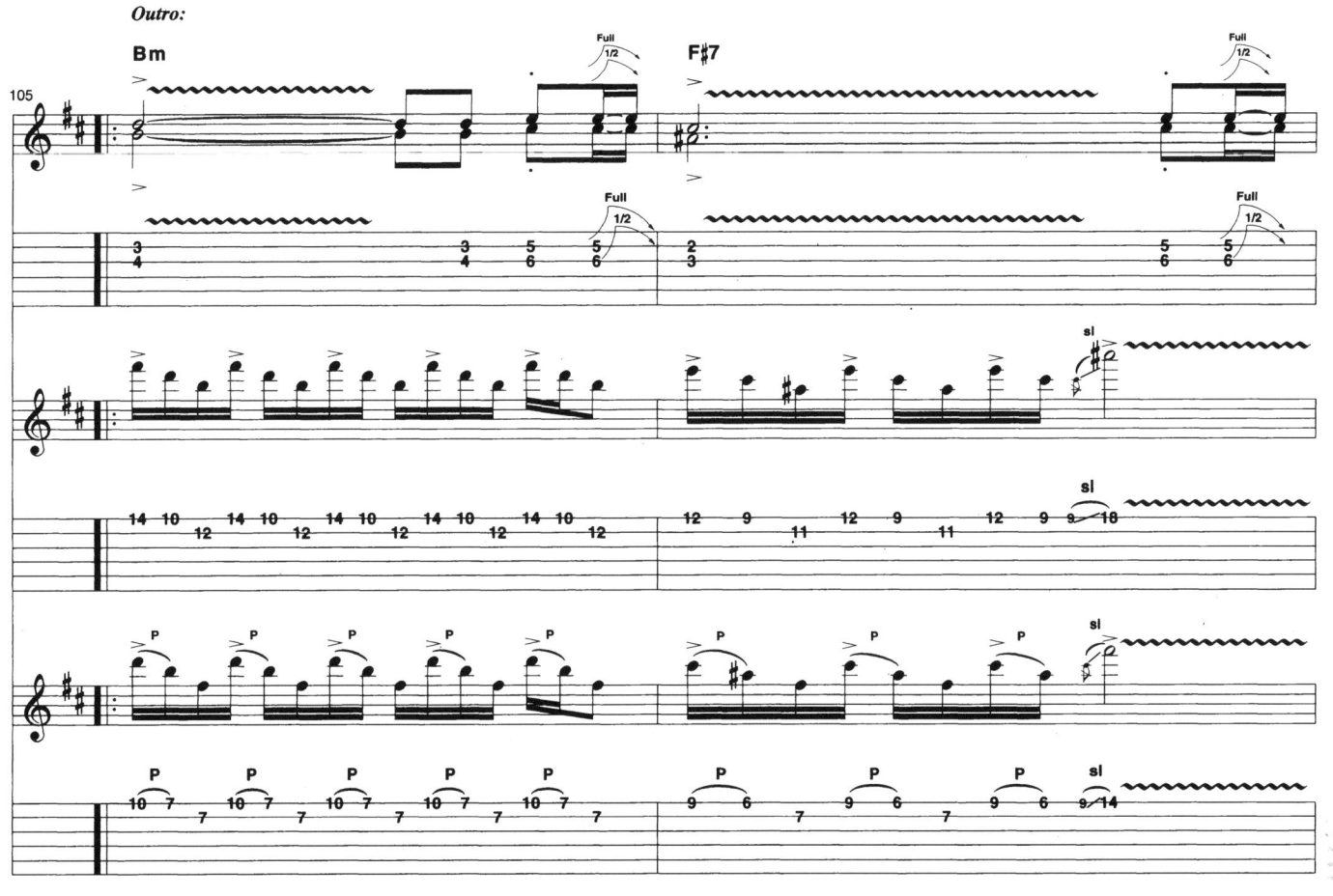
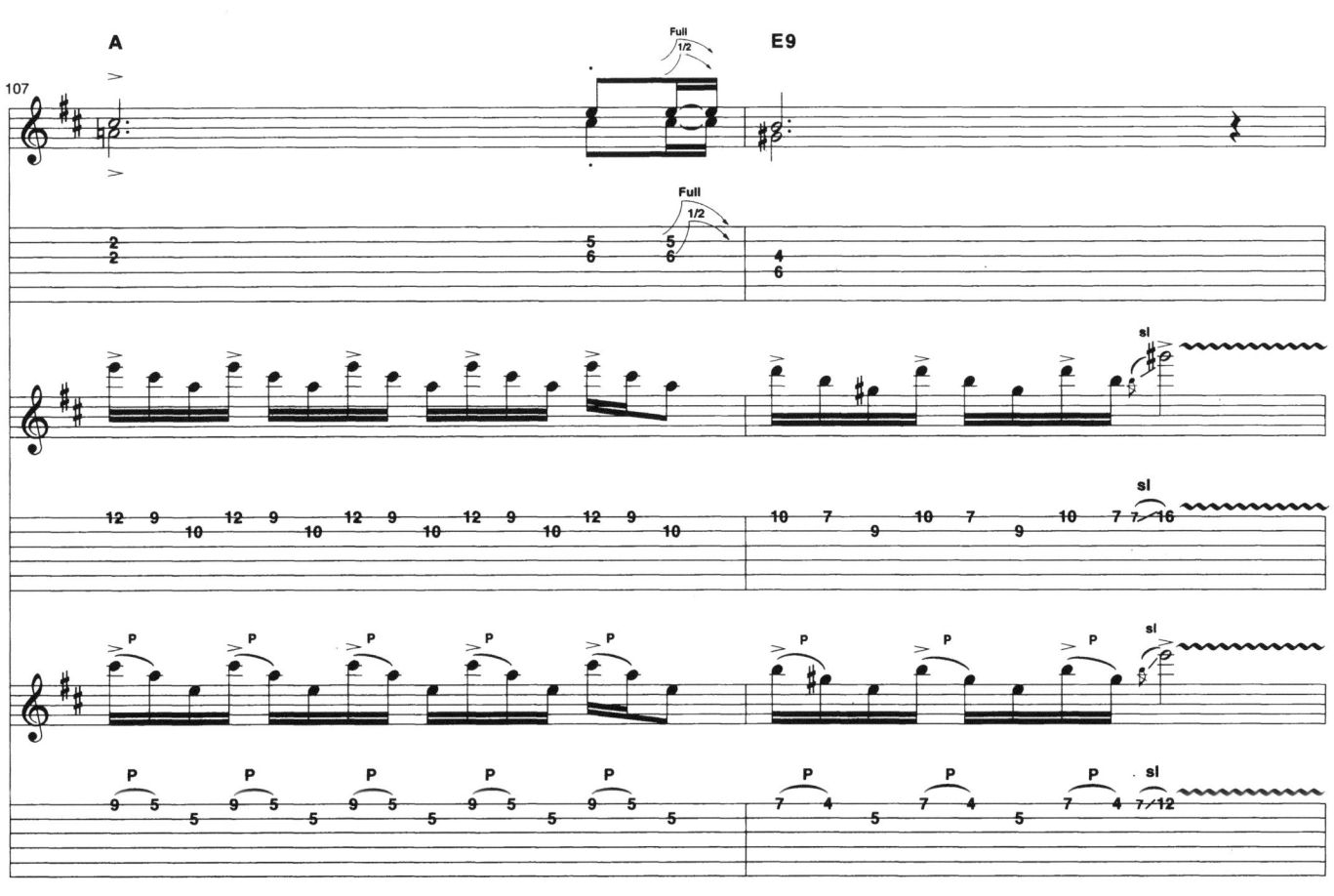

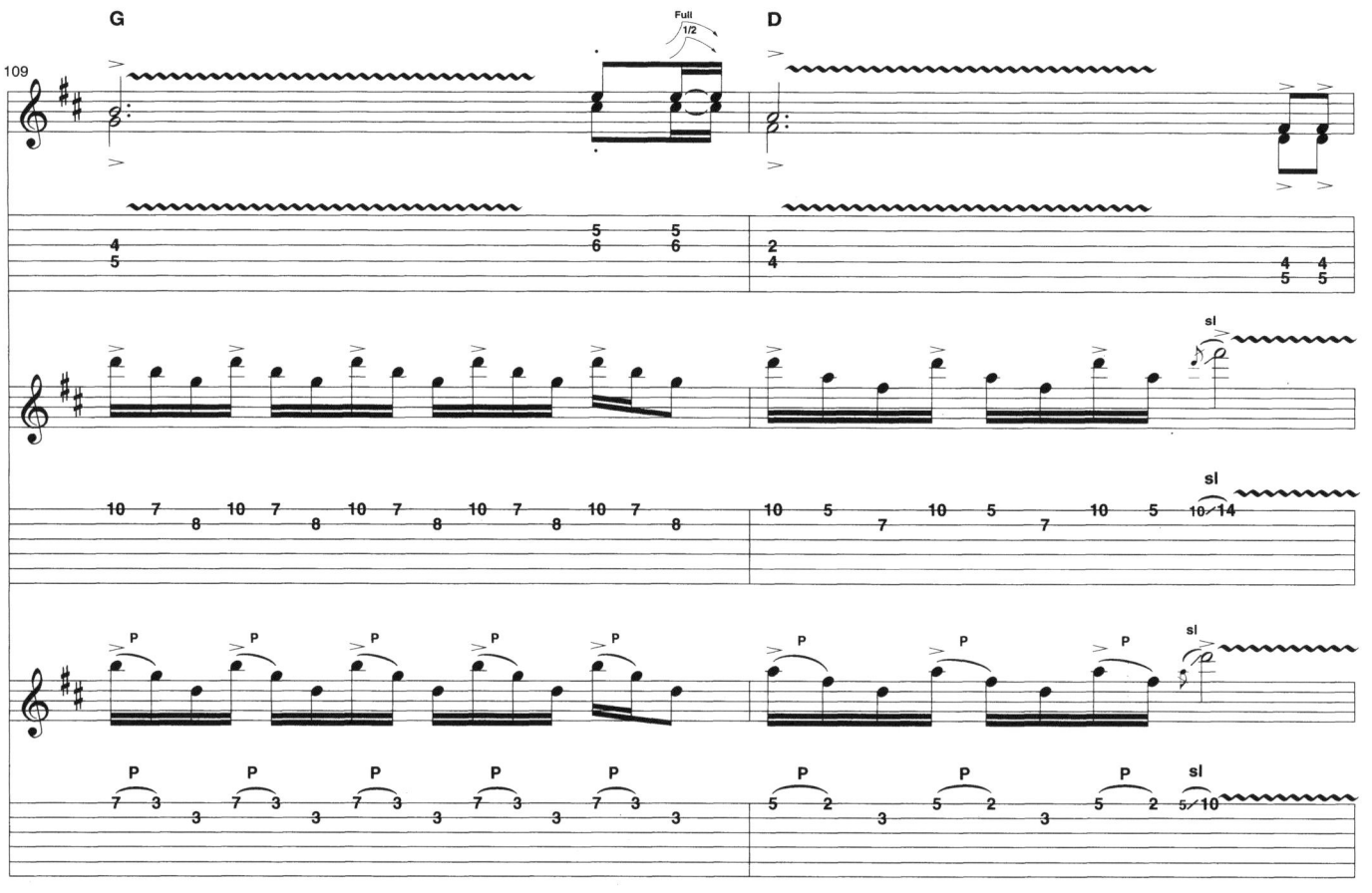

Life In The Fast Lane

Words and Music by JOE WALSH, DON HENLEY and GLENN FREY

© 1977 & 1996 Wow and Flutter Music, Cass County Music and Red Cloud Music, USA
Warner/Chappell Music Ltd, London W1Y 3FA

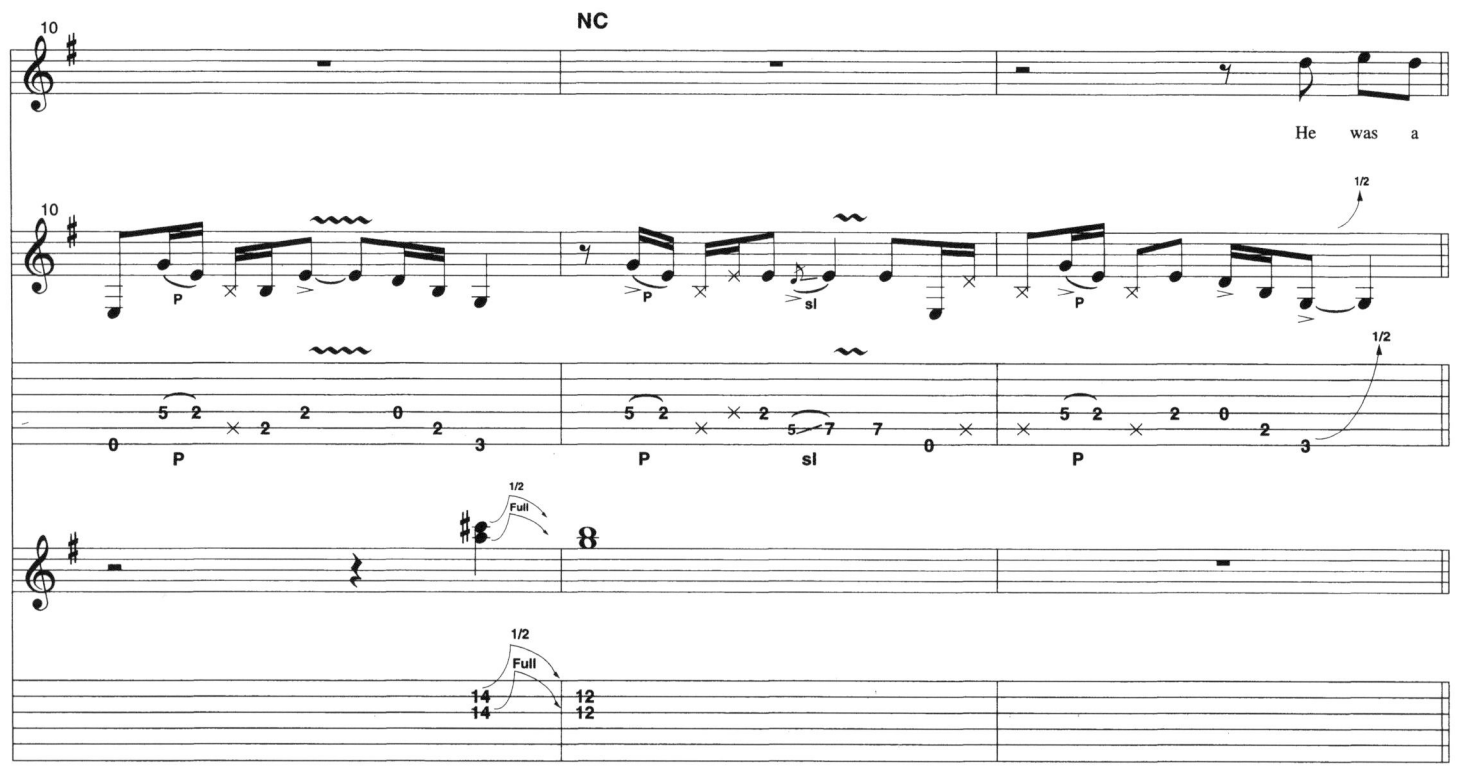

30

Verse 2:
E9 A E E9 A E
Ea - ger for ac - tion an' hot for the game. The com - ing at - trac - tion, the
E9 E5 A E
drop of a name. They knew all the right peo - ple, they took all the right pills, they threw

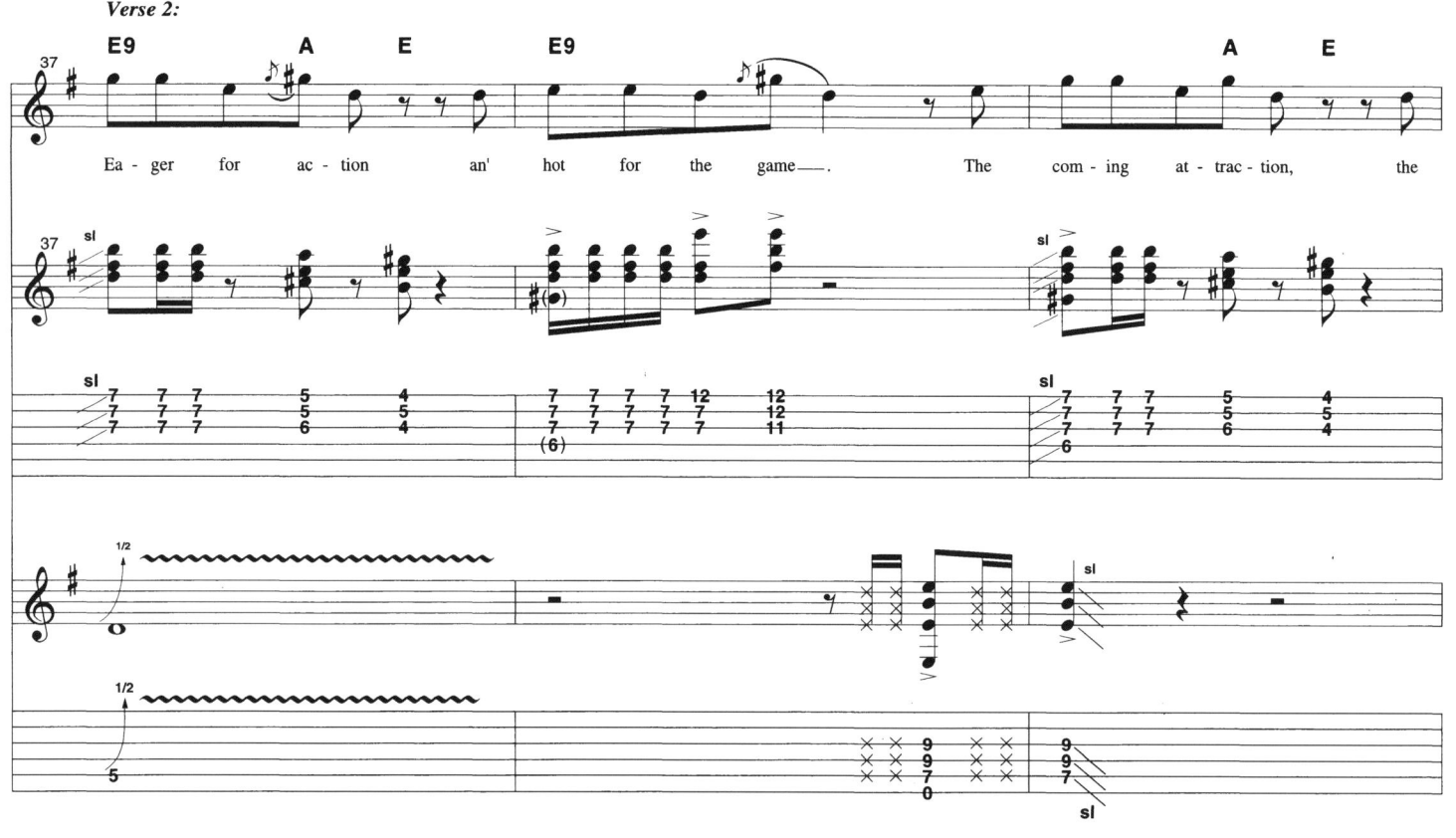

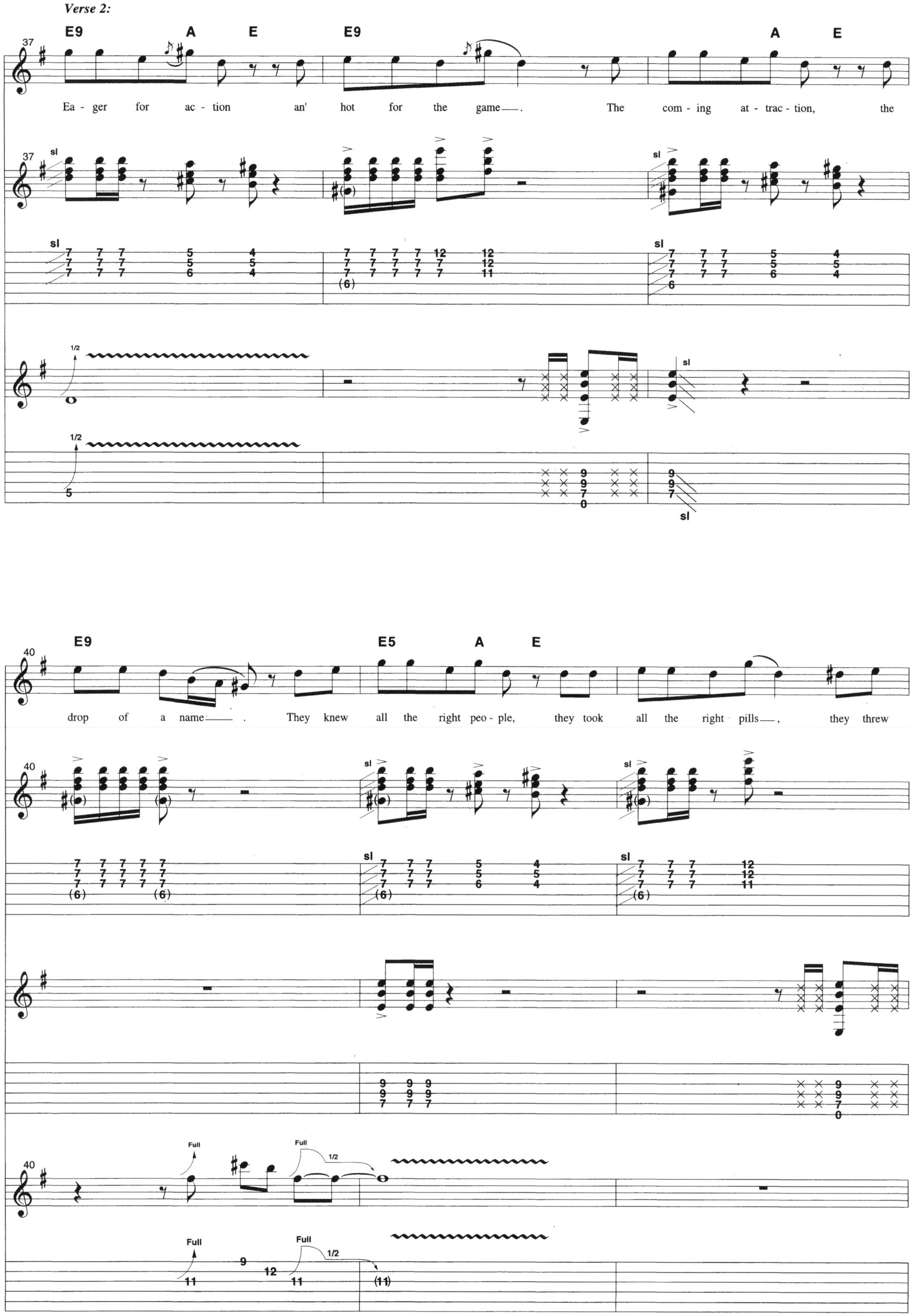

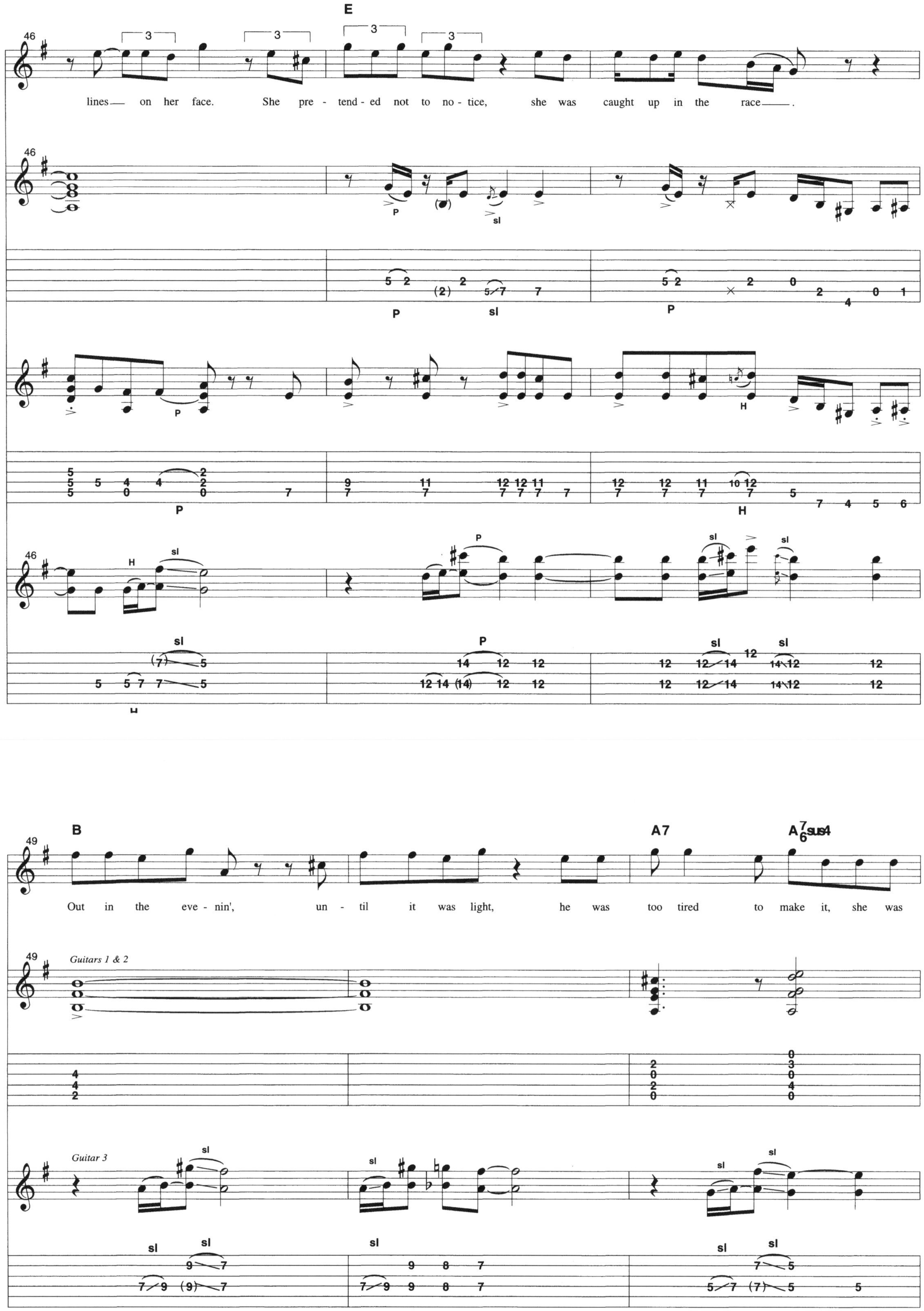
E
lines on her face. She pre - tend - ed not to no - tice, she was caught up in the race.
B
A7
Out in the eve - nin', un - til it was light, he was too tired to make it, she was
Guitars 1 & 2
Guitar 3

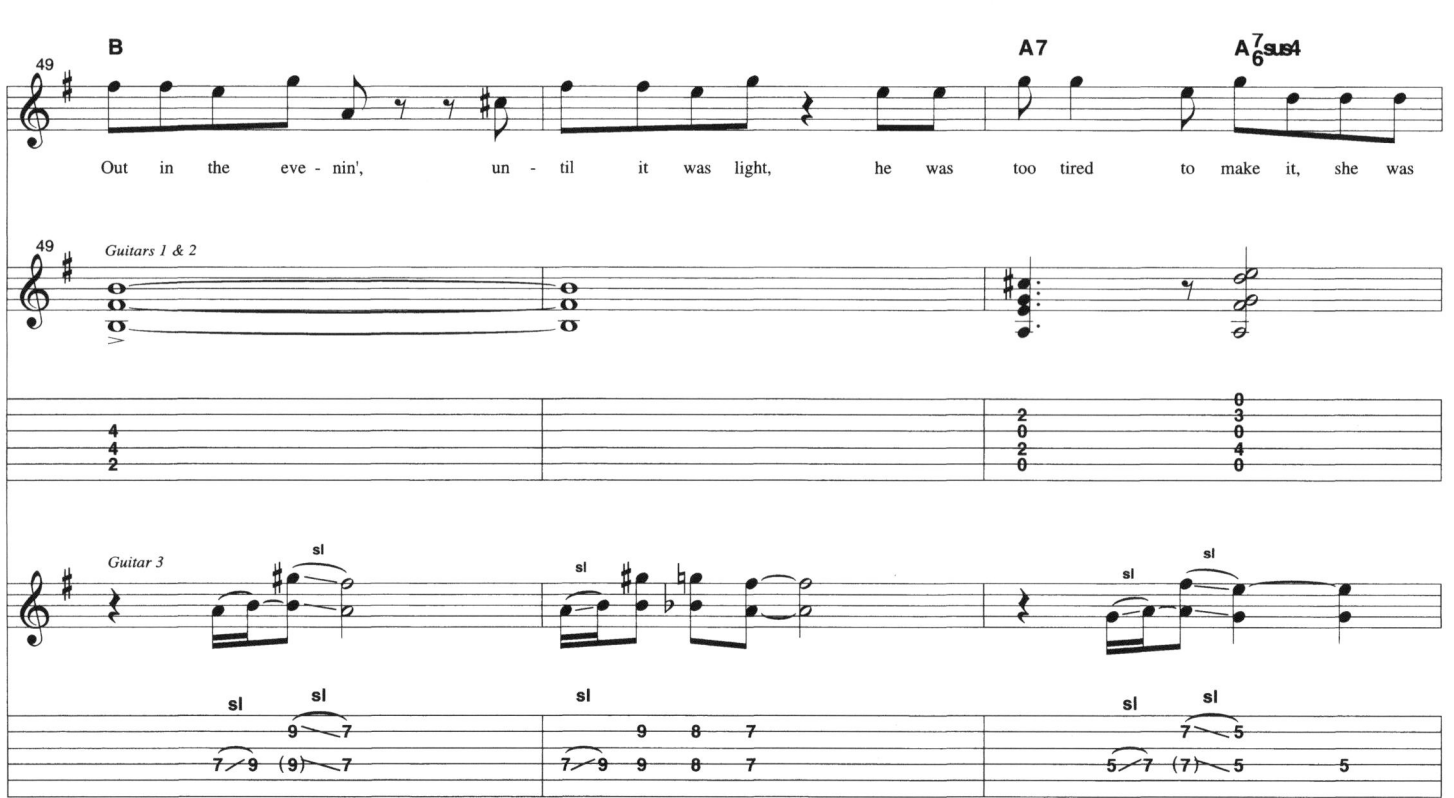

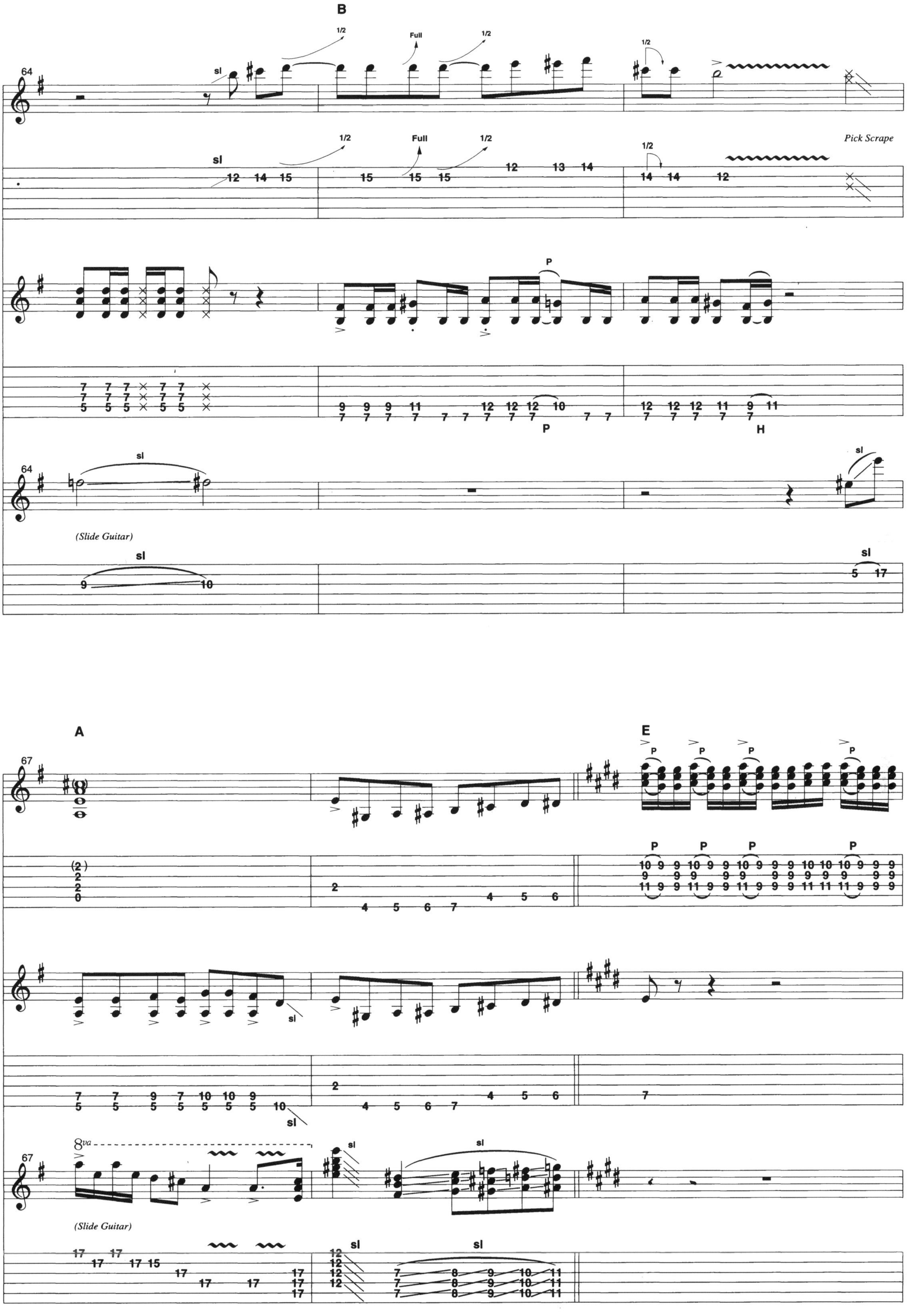
B
1/2
Full
sl
Pick Scrape
P
H
(Slide Guitar)
A
E
8va

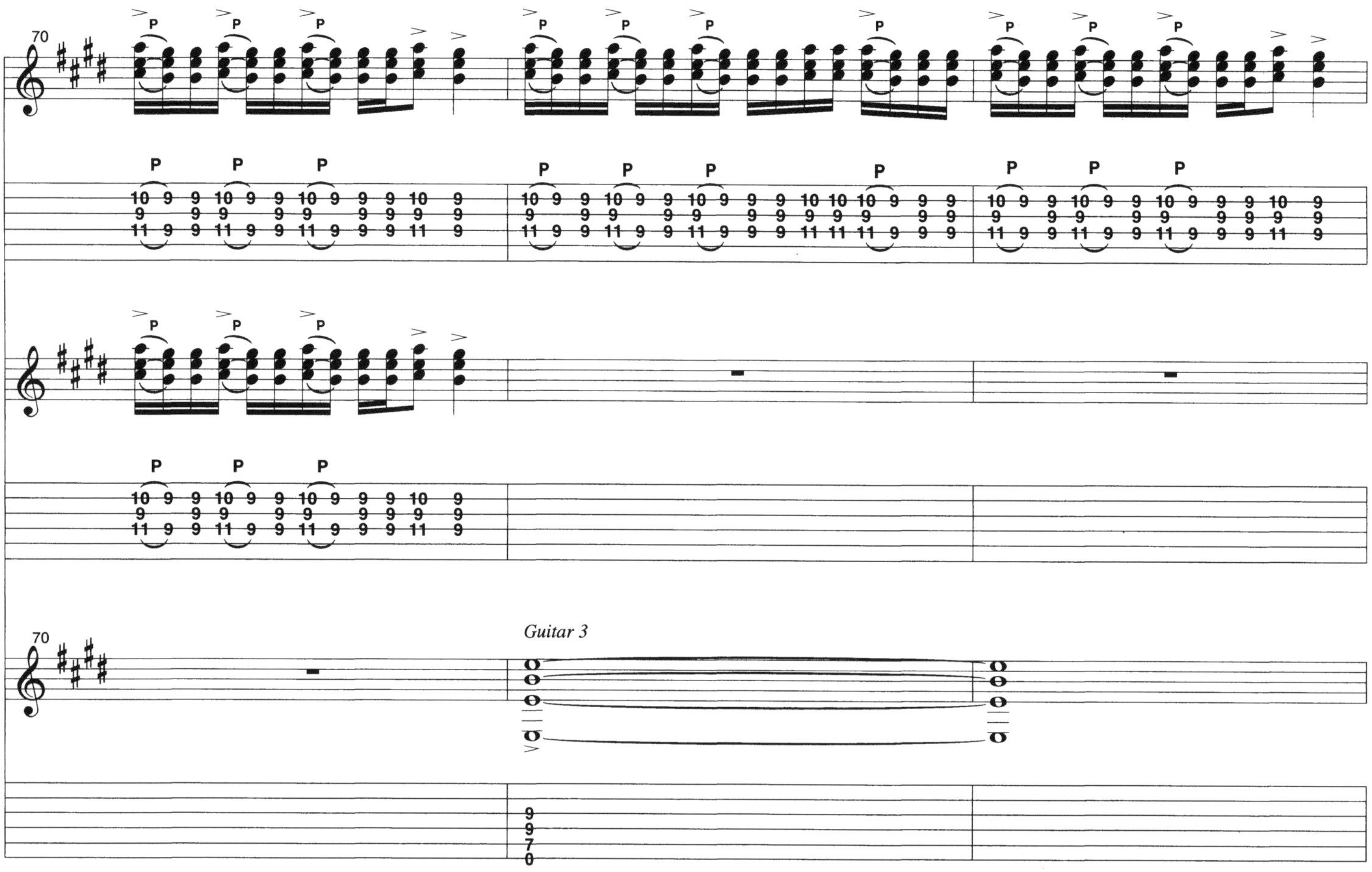
70
Guitar 3

73
Guitar 1
Guitar 3

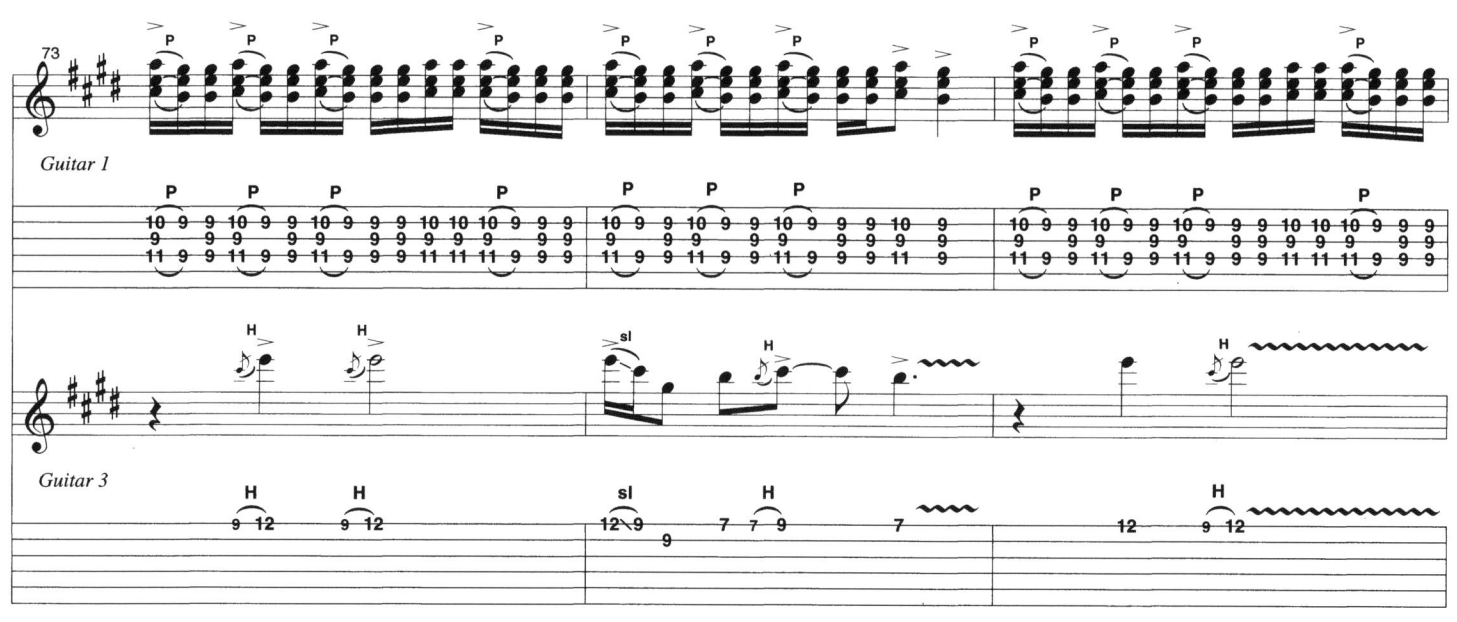

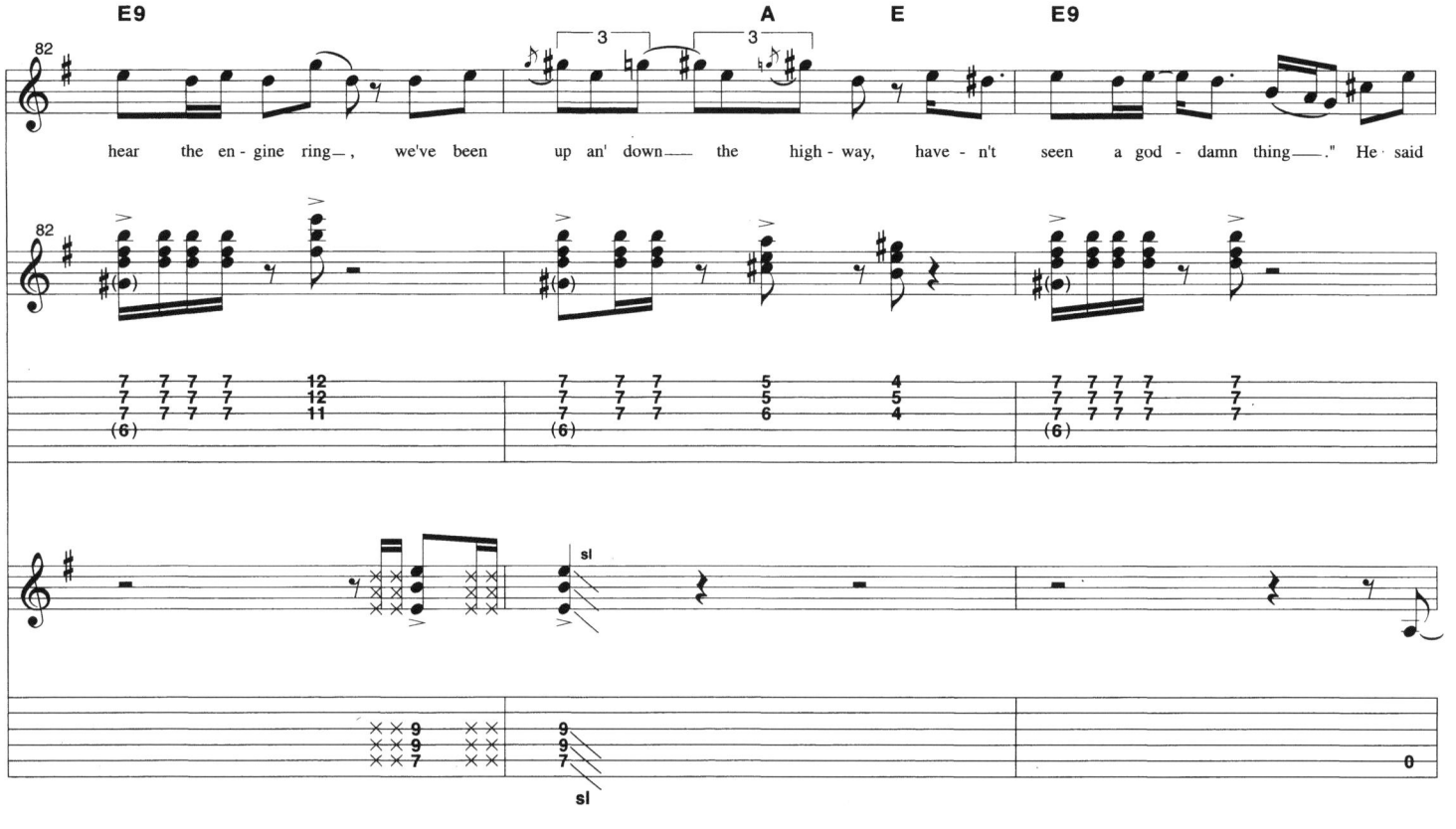

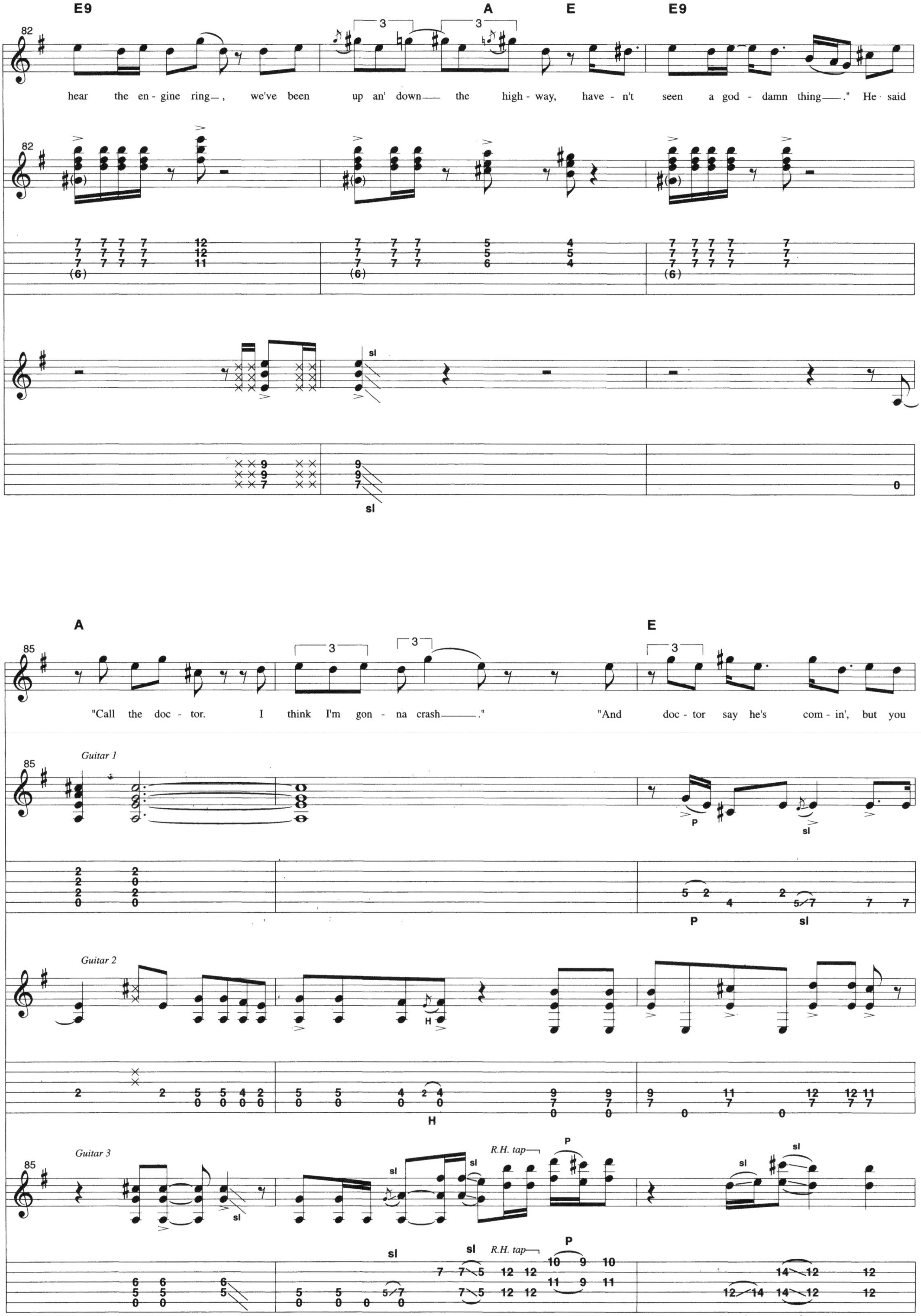
E9 A E E9
hear the en - gine ring —, we've been up an' down — the high - way, have - n't seen a god - damn thing —." He said
sl
A E
"Call the doc - tor. I think I'm gon - na crash —." "And doc - tor say he's com - in', but you
Guitar 1
Guitar 2
Guitar 3
R.H. tap

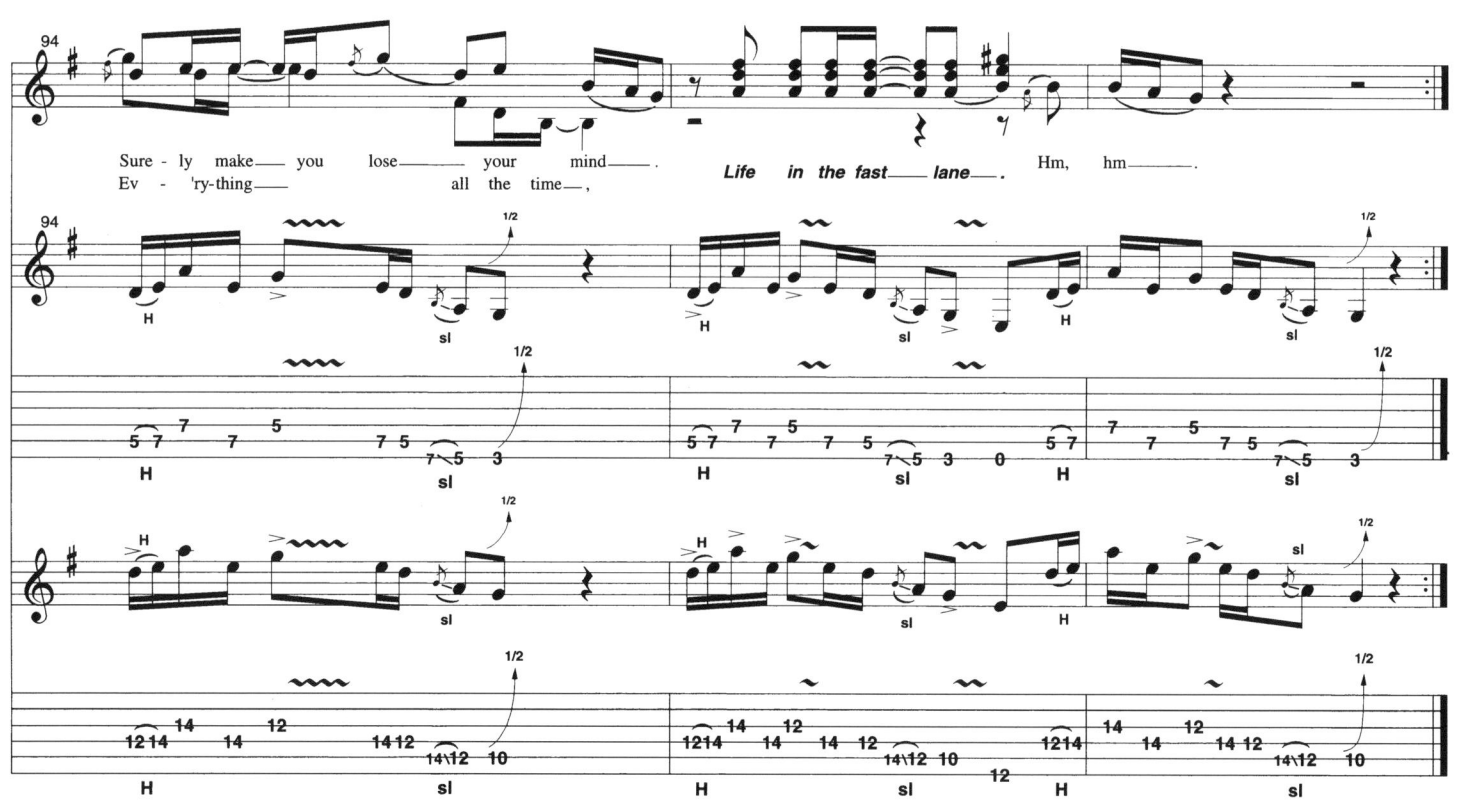

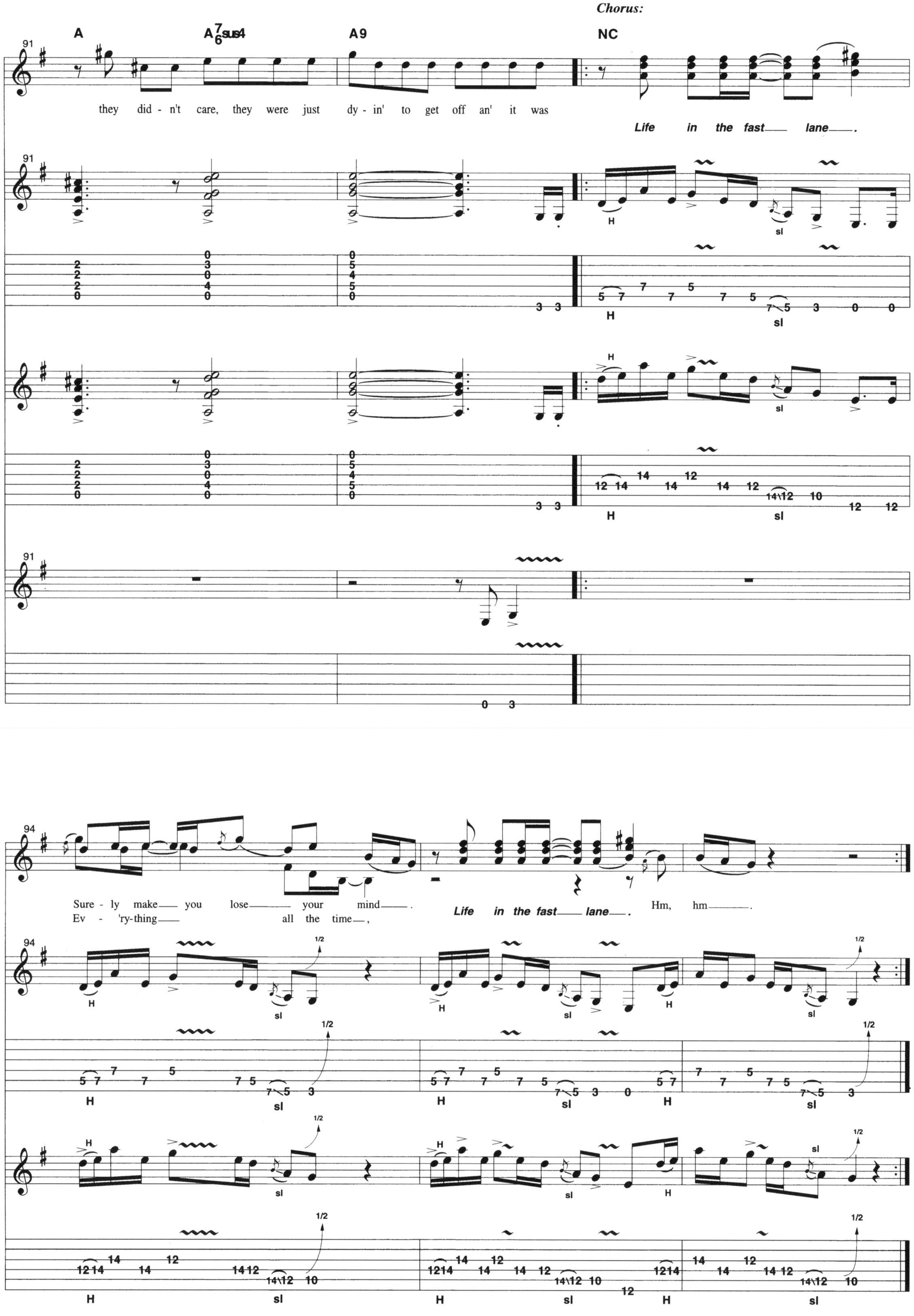
Chorus:
A
A7/6sus4
A9
NC
they did-n't care, they were just dy-in' to get off an' it was
Life in the fast lane.
Sure-ly make you lose your mind.
Ev-'ry-thing all the time,
Life in the fast lane.
Hm, hm.

A/E
Guitar 1 (Rhythm figure 1)
Guitar 2
Pick Scrape

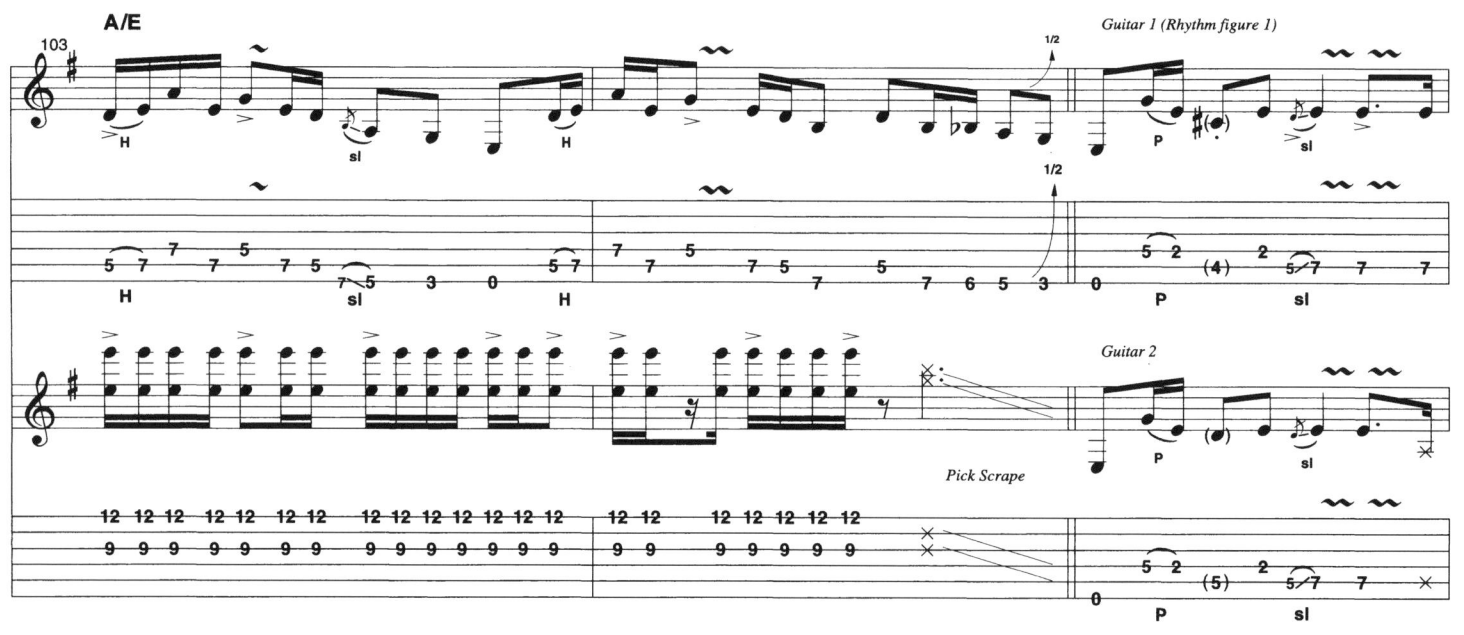

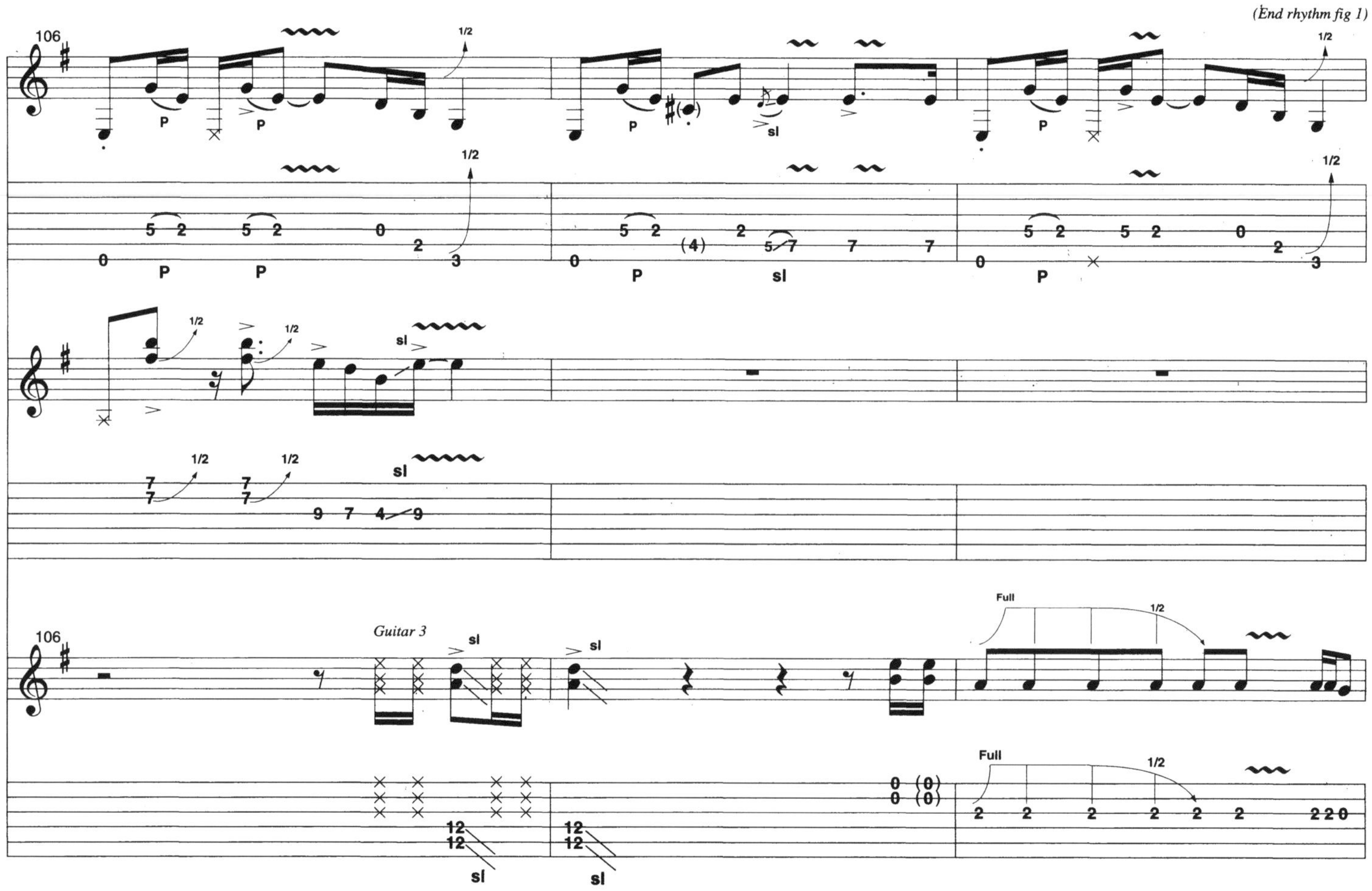
(End rhythm fig 1)
Guitar 3
Full

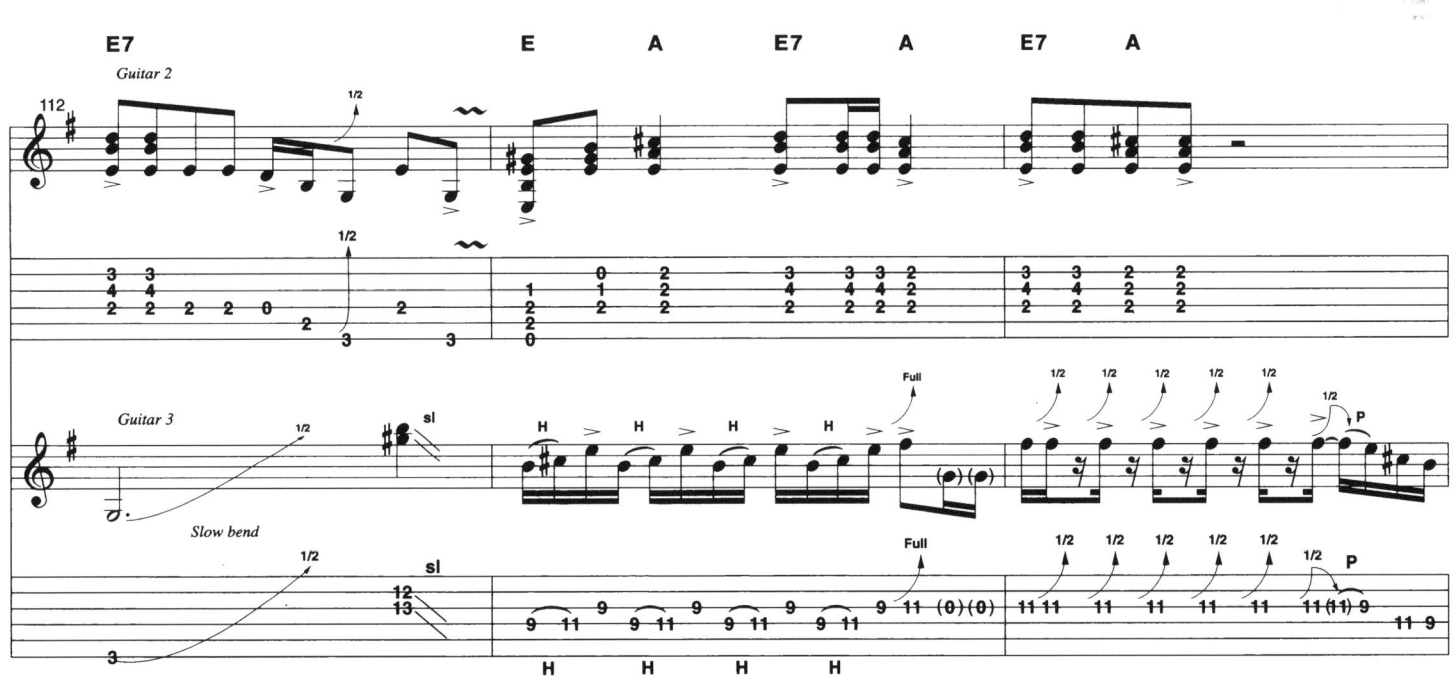

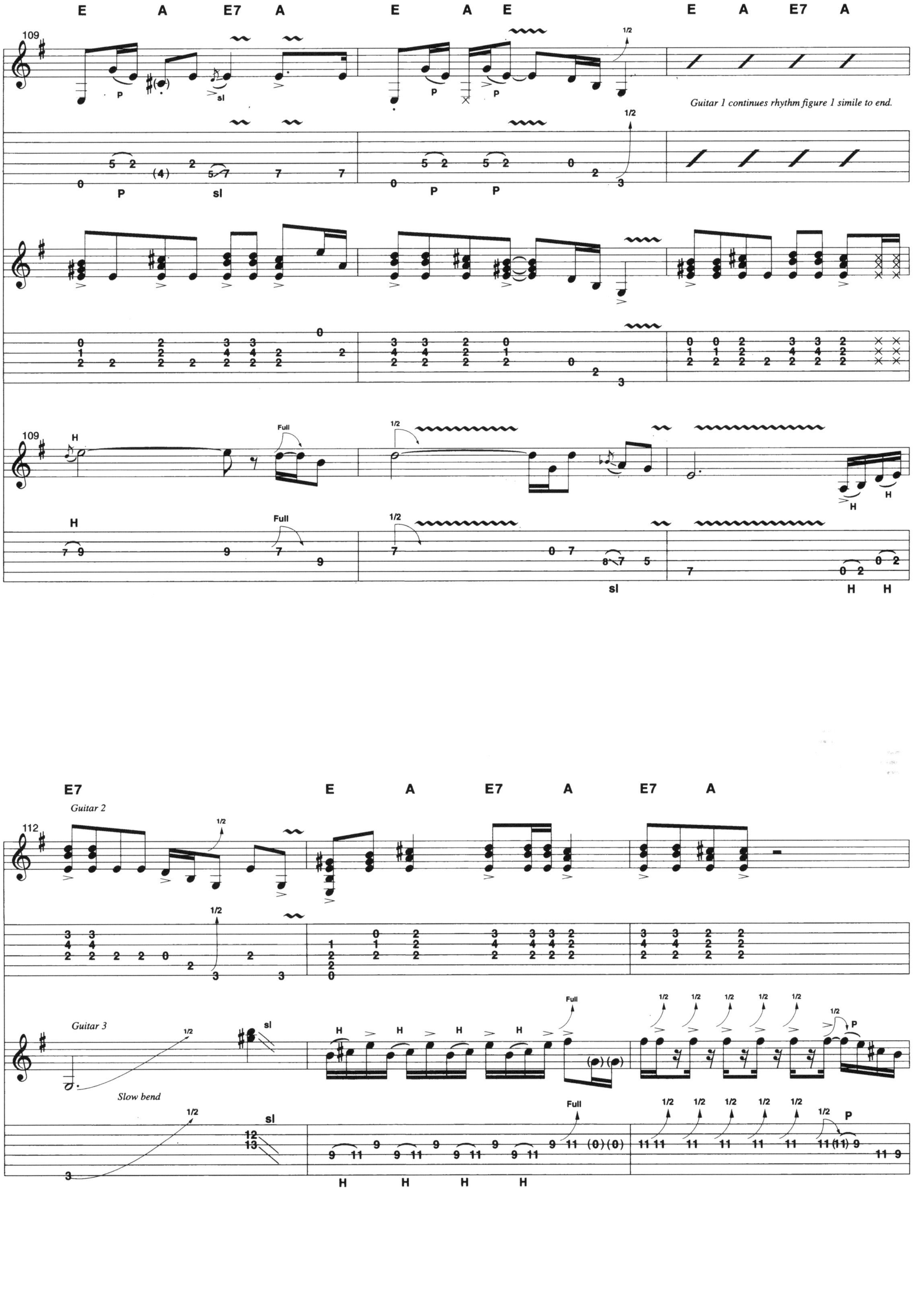
E A E7 A E A E E A E7 A
Guitar 1 continues rhythm figure 1 simile to end.
E7 E A E7 A E7 A
Guitar 2
Guitar 3
Slow bend

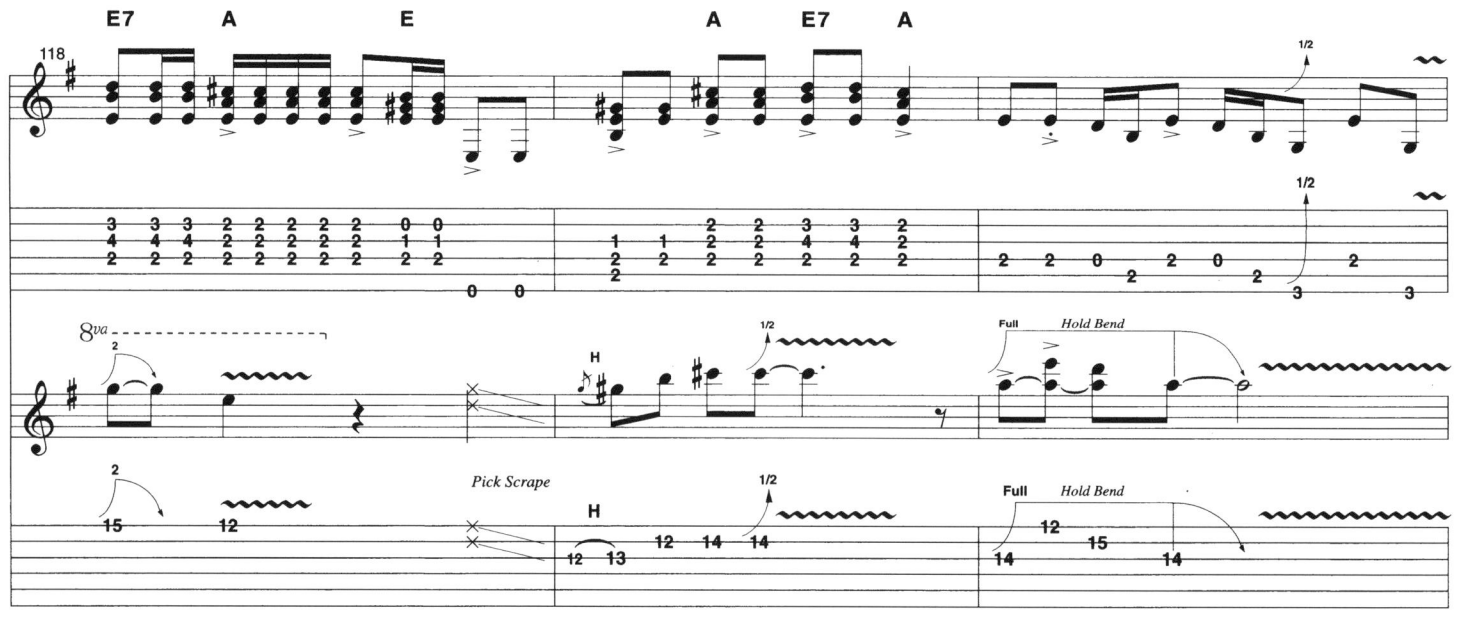
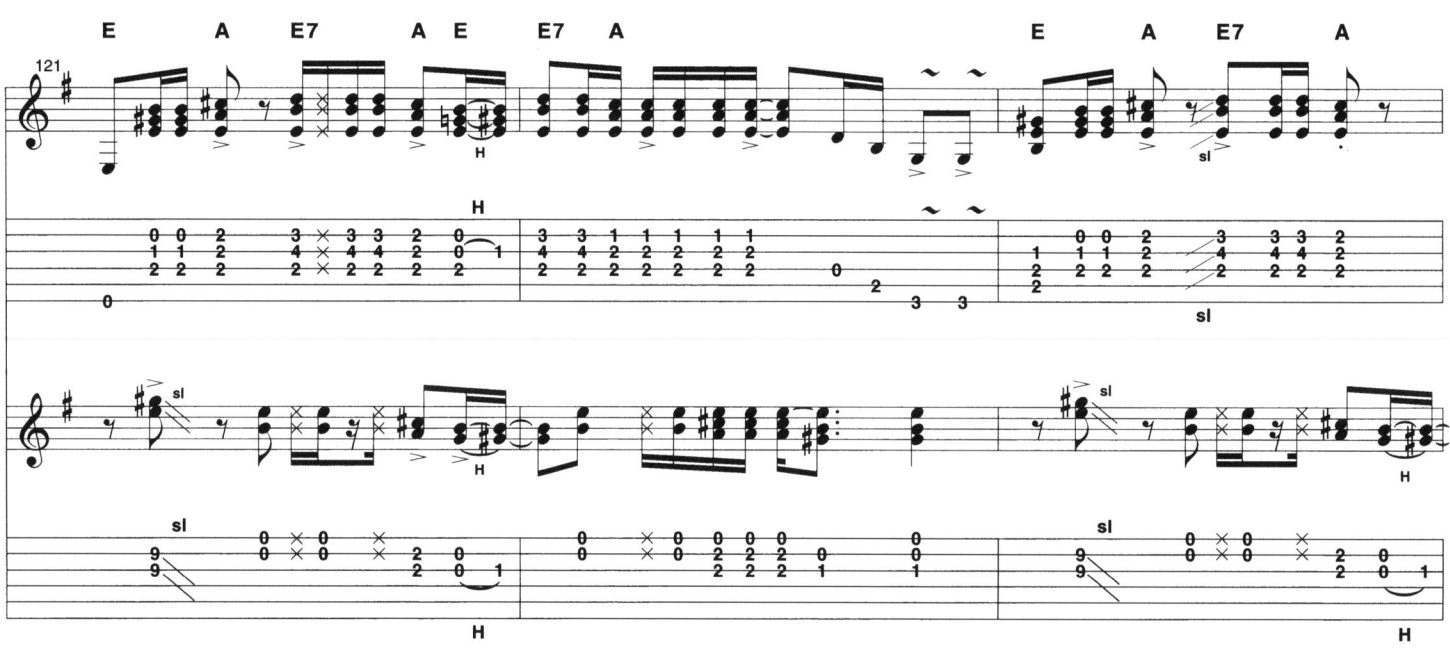
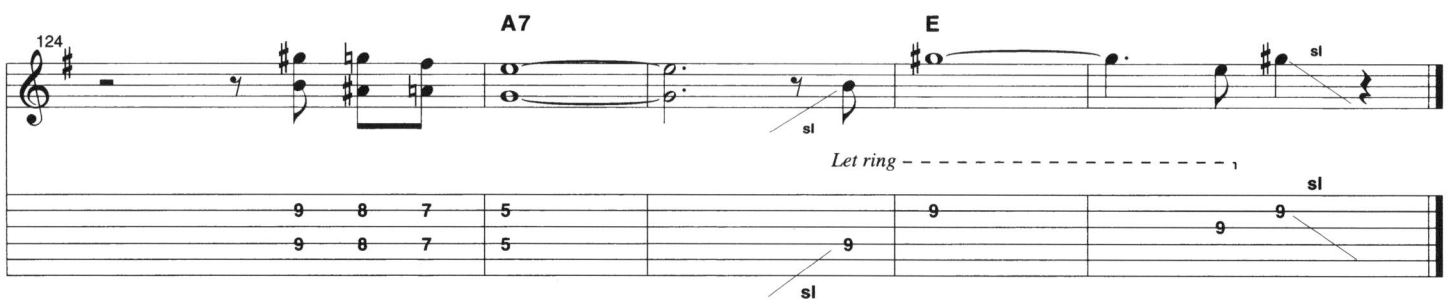

One Of These Nights

Words and Music by GLENN FREY and DON HENLEY

© 1975 & 1996 Benchmark Music and Kicking Bear Music, USA
Warner/Chappell Music Ltd, London W1Y 3FA

1
2
Bm7
One of these
Verse 1:
Em7
Em/D
Cmaj7
nights,
one of these cra zy old nights
(Rhythm Guitar - clean sound)
(Rhythm Guitar - clean sound)

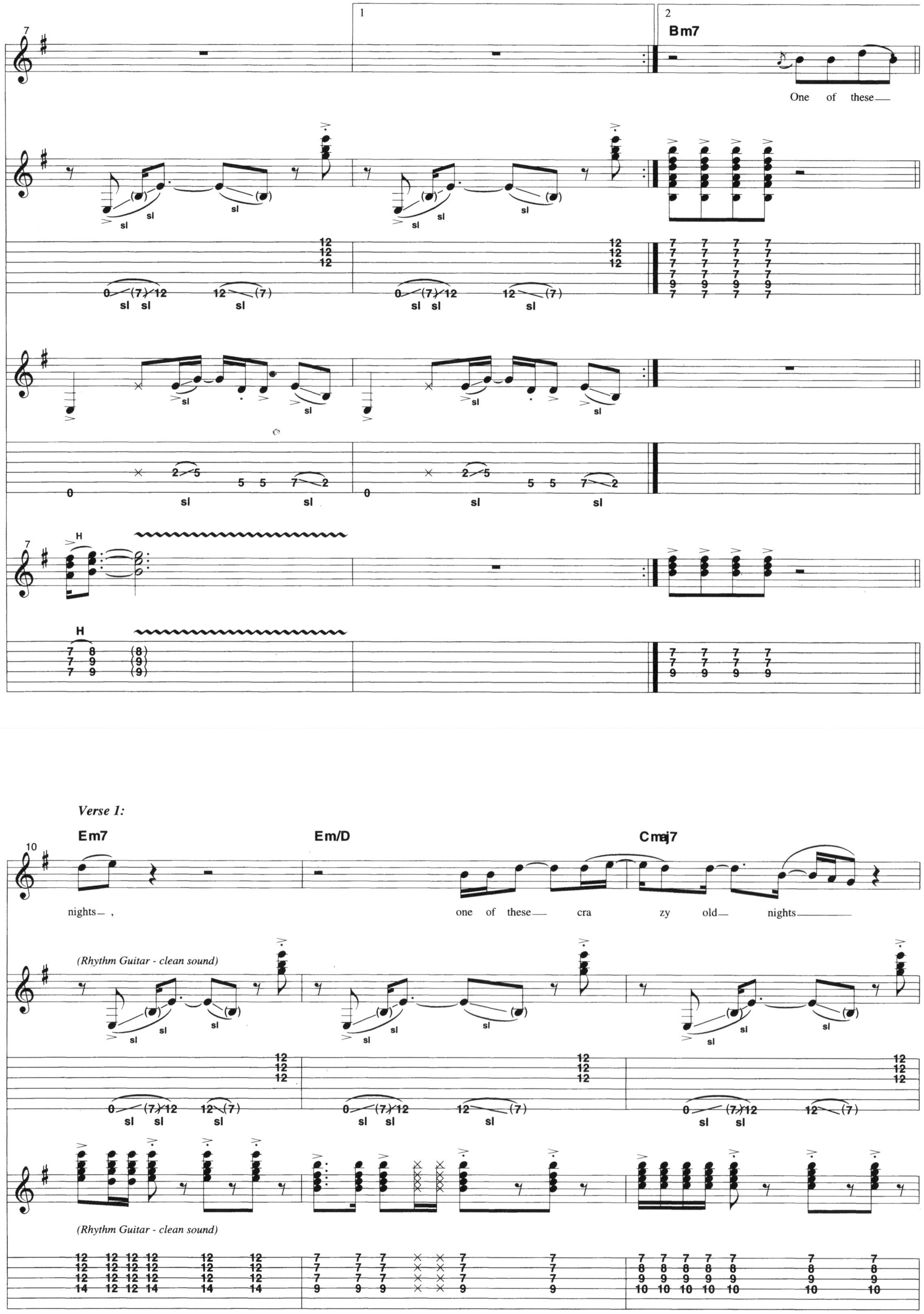

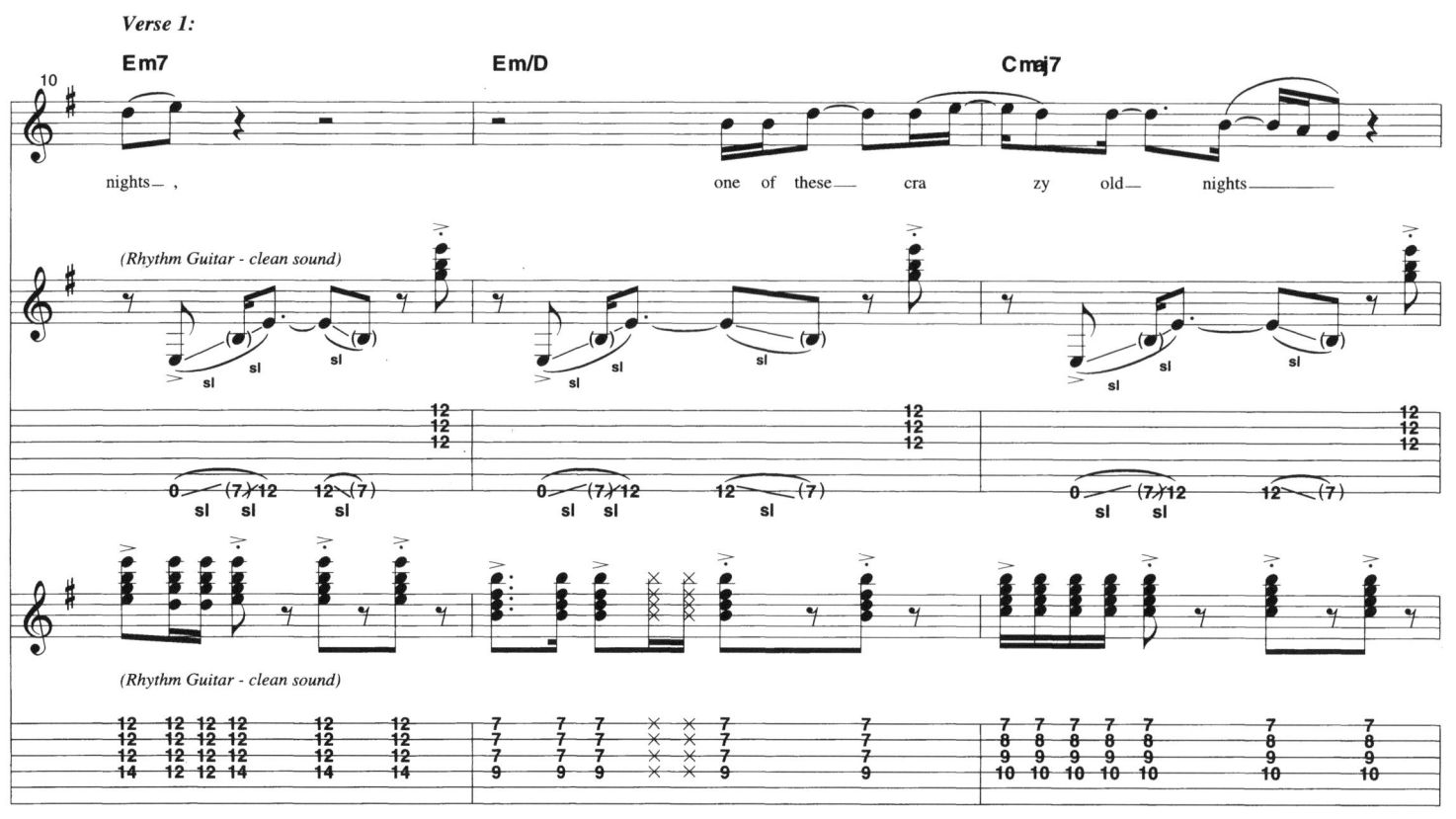

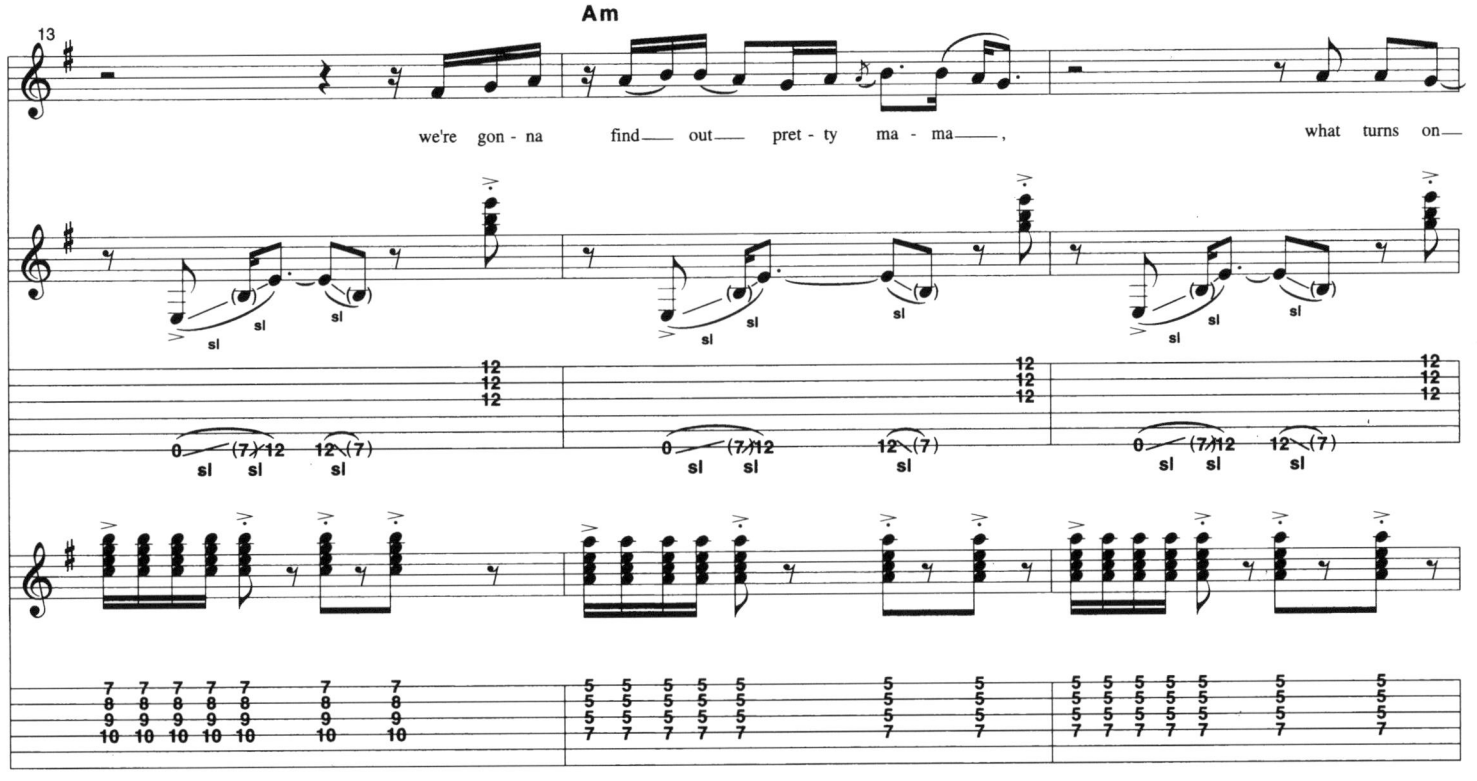

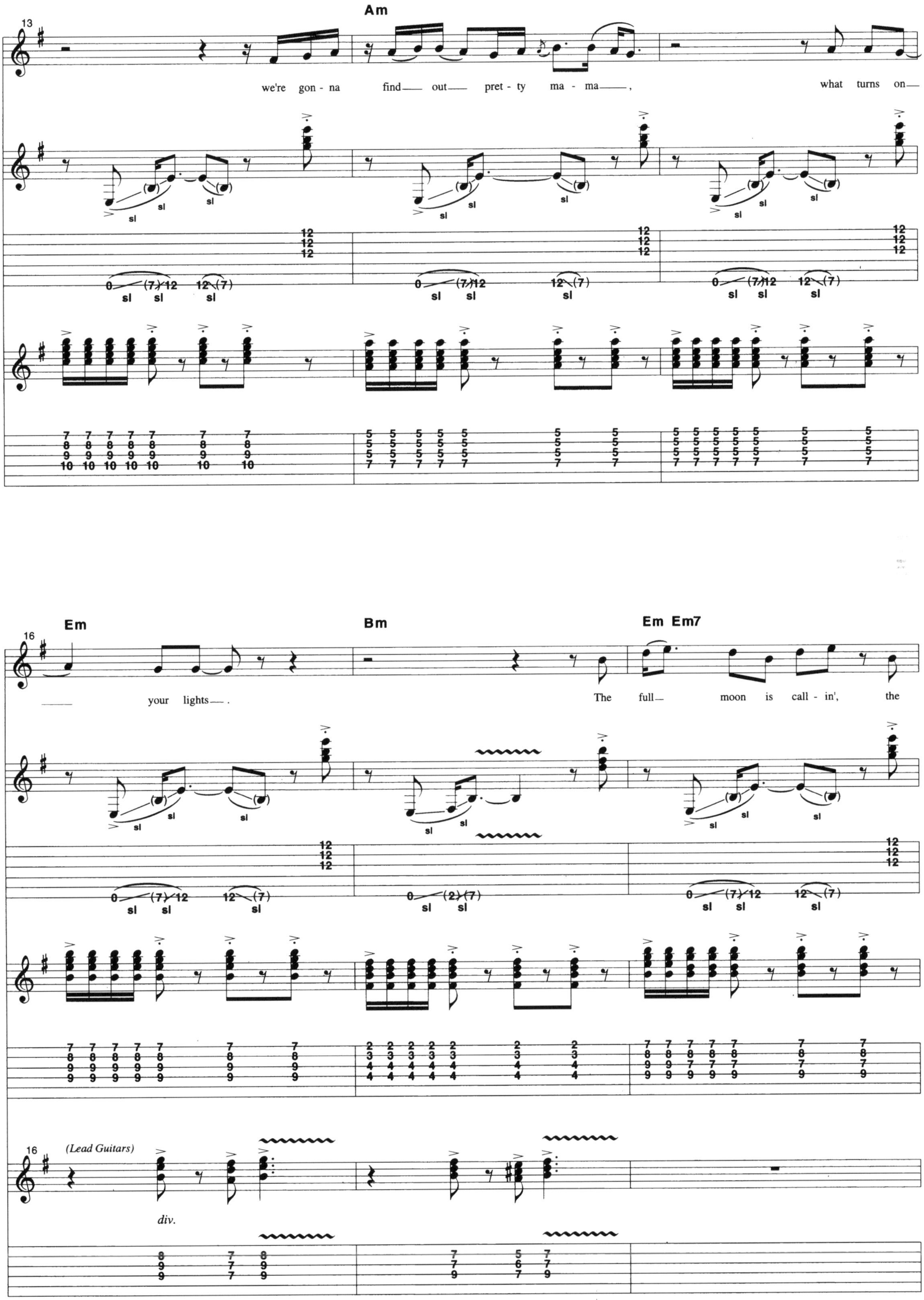
13
Am
we're gon - na find — out — pret - ty ma - ma —,
what turns on —
16
Em
Bm
Em Em7
— your lights —.
The full — moon is call - in', the
16
(Lead Guitars)
div.

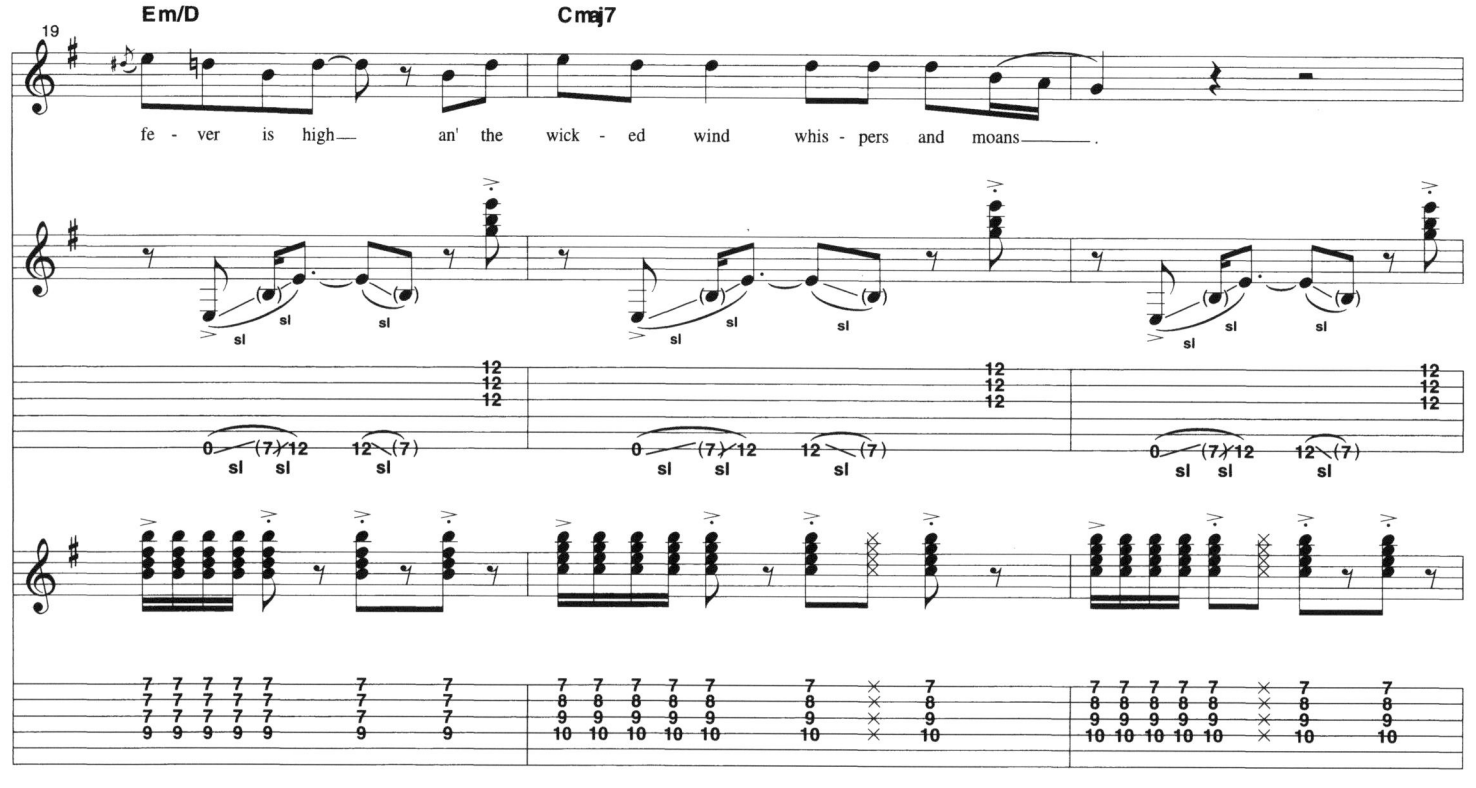

Chorus:
Cmaj7
Gmaj7
Oo, some - one to be kind to— in be - tween the dark and the light—
rake
let ring
let ring
Cmaj7
—, oo, come - in' right be - hind you,
rake
let ring
let ring
(Lead Guitars) div.

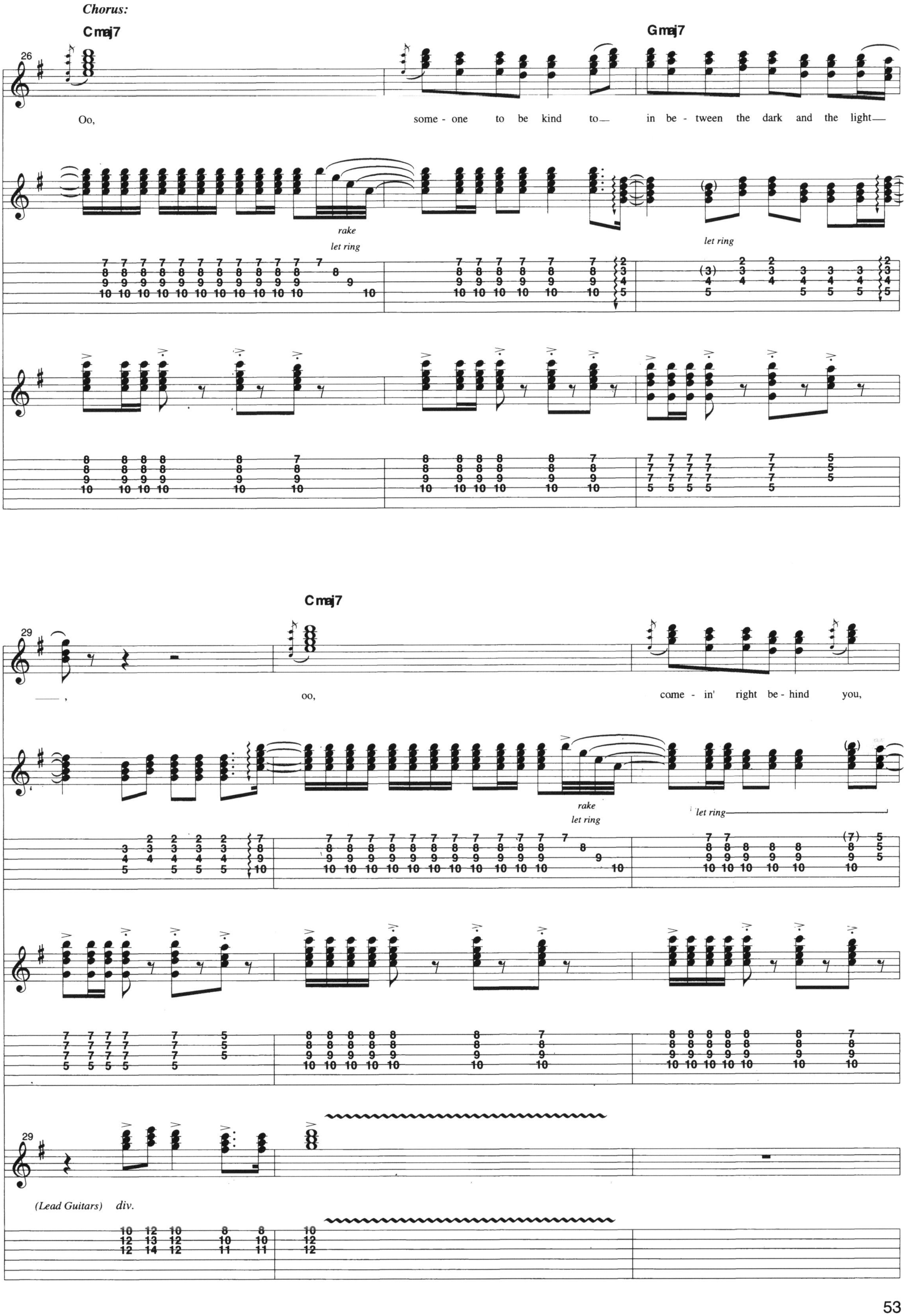

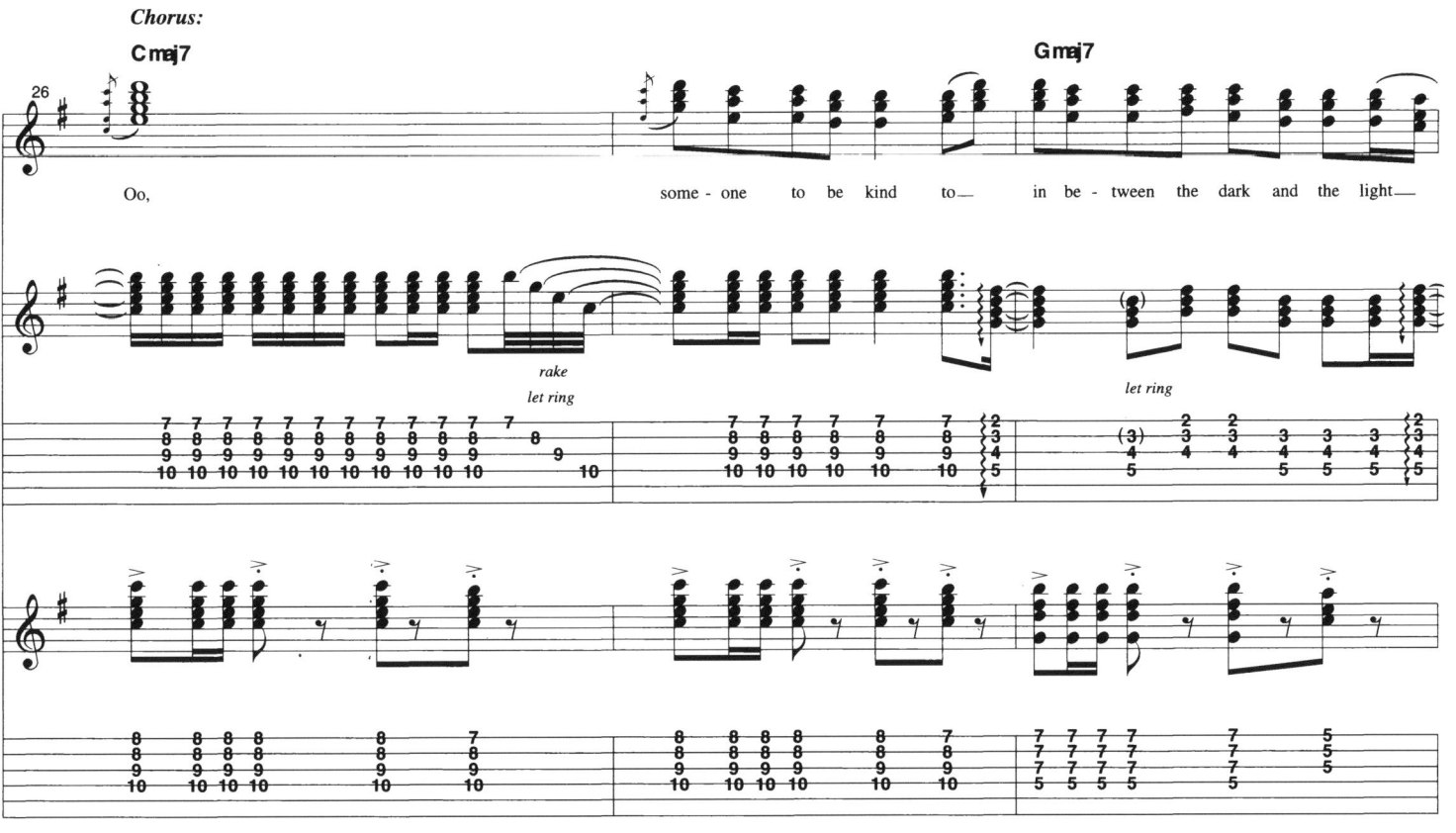

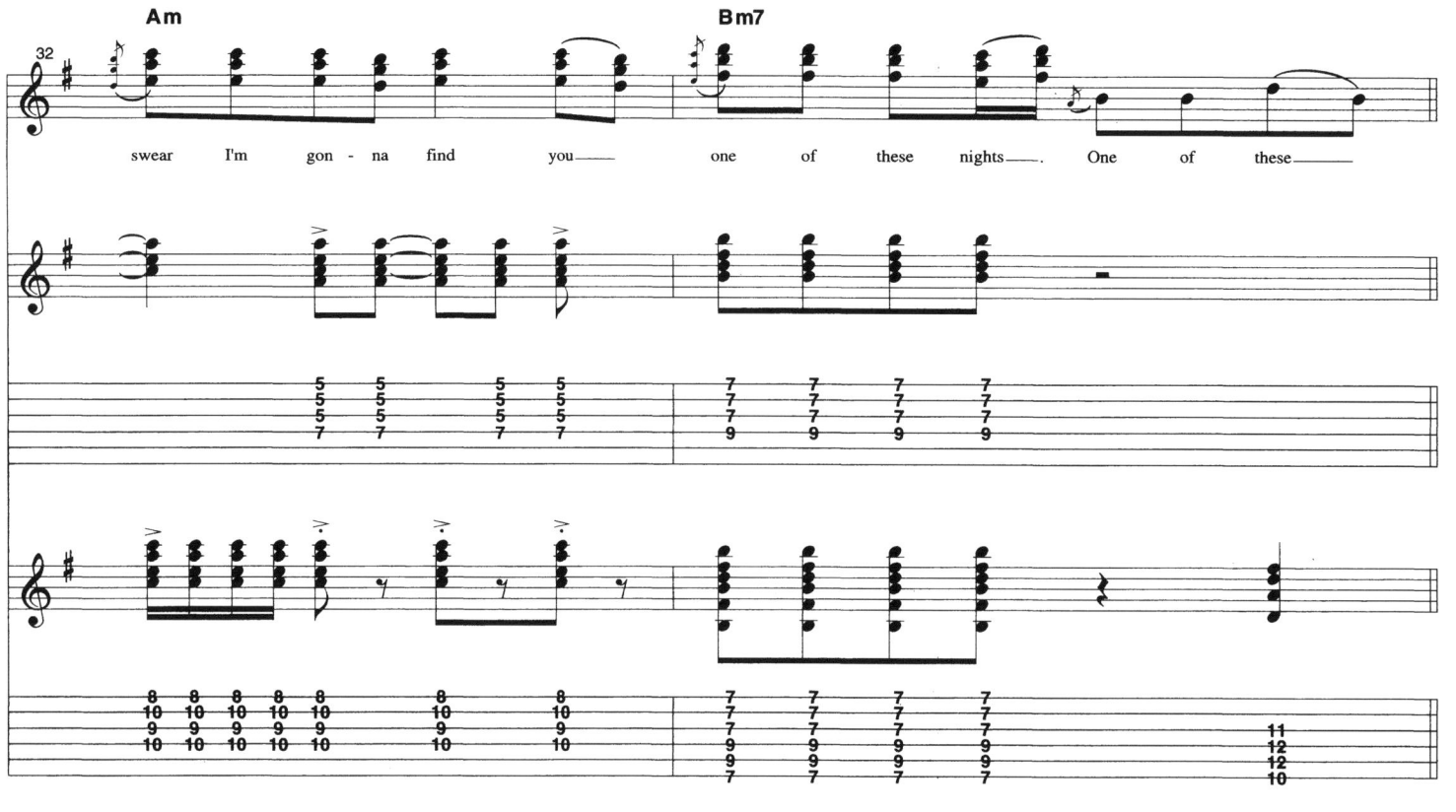

Verse 2: (All guitars as Verse 1)

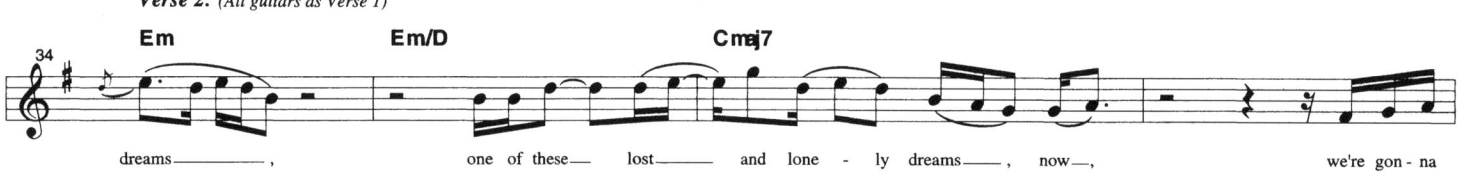

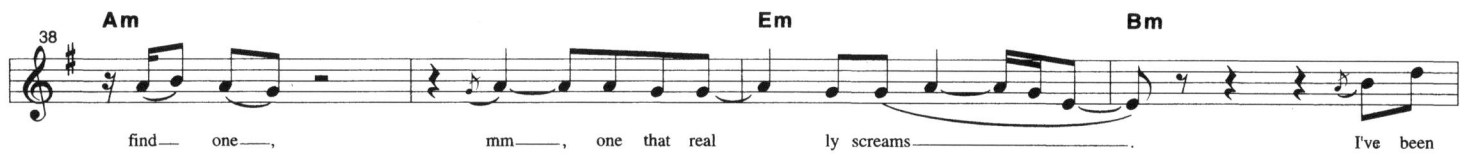

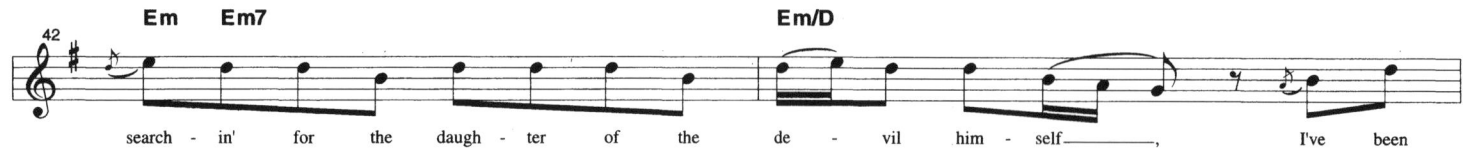

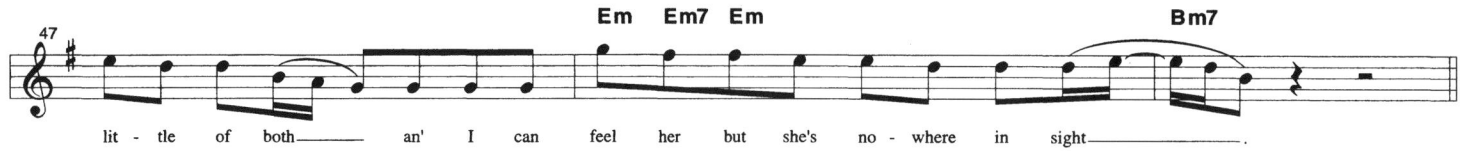

Chorus:
Cmaj7
Gmaj7
Oo, lon - li - ness will blind you— in be - tween the wrong and the right——
let ring
Cmaj7
oh——————! oo, com - in' right be - hind you—,
let ring
sl
H P
(Lead Guitars) div.

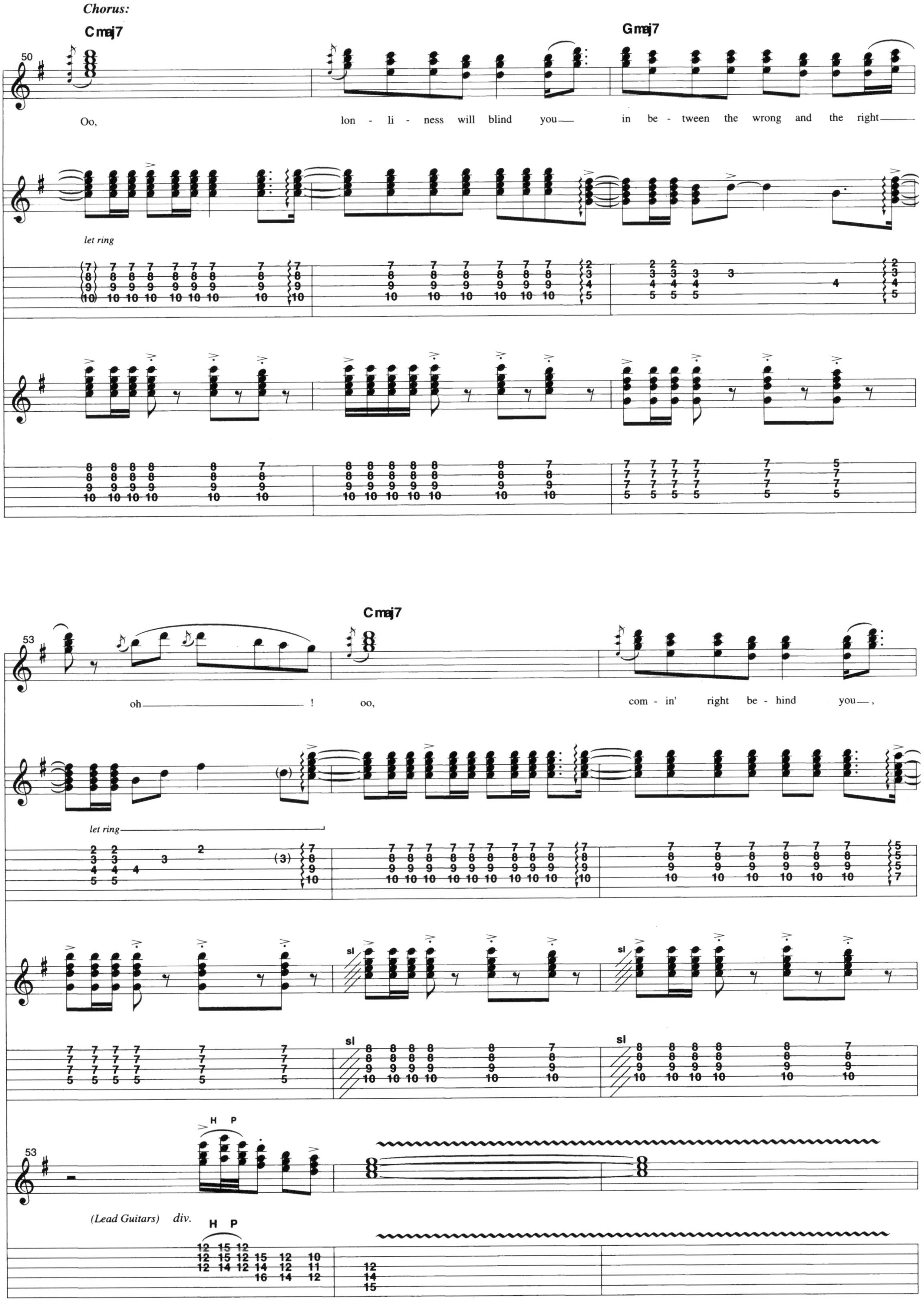

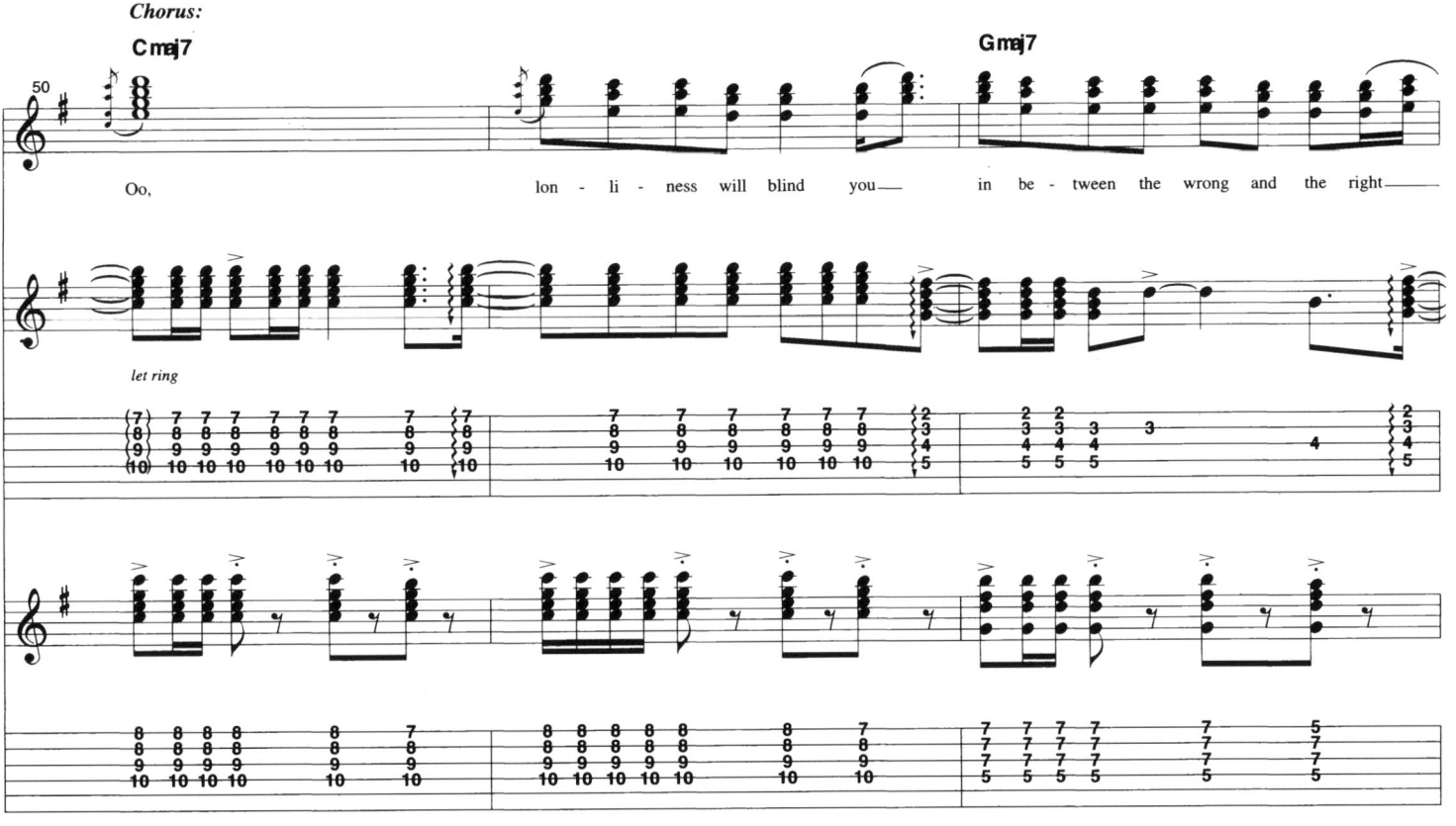

Am7
Bm7
swear I'm gon - na find you one of these nights.
Guitar Solo
Em7
Em/D
Cmaj7
Am
Em
Bm

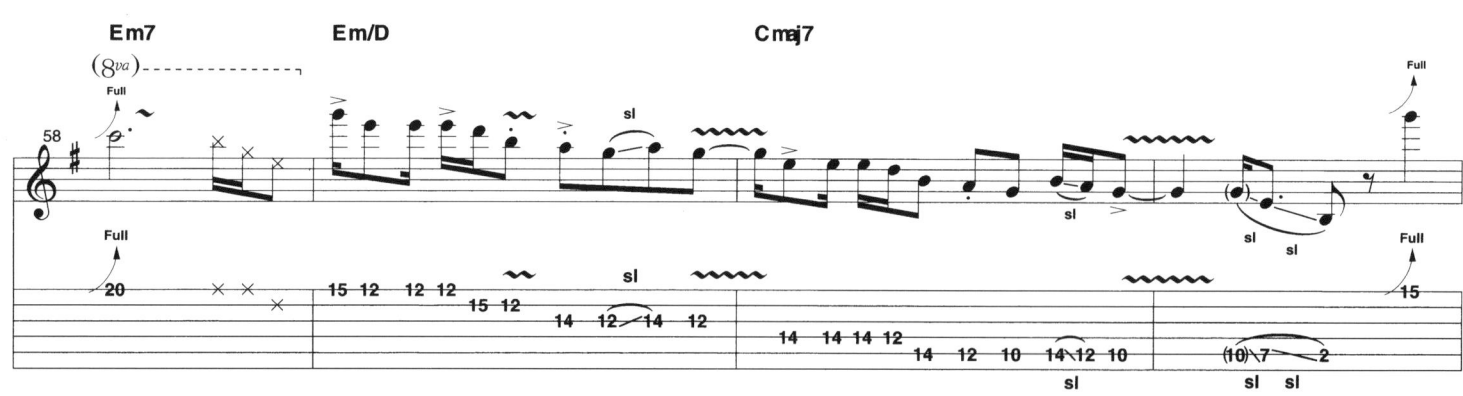

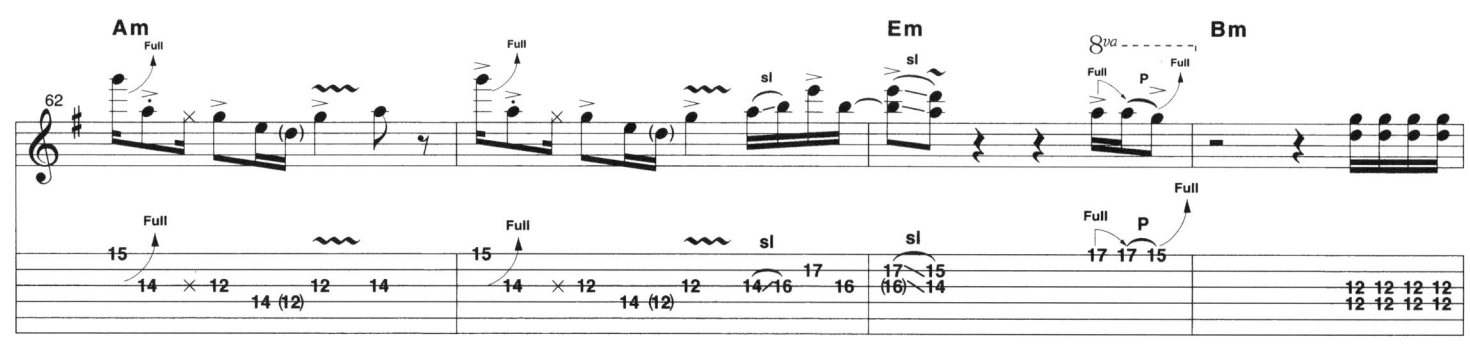

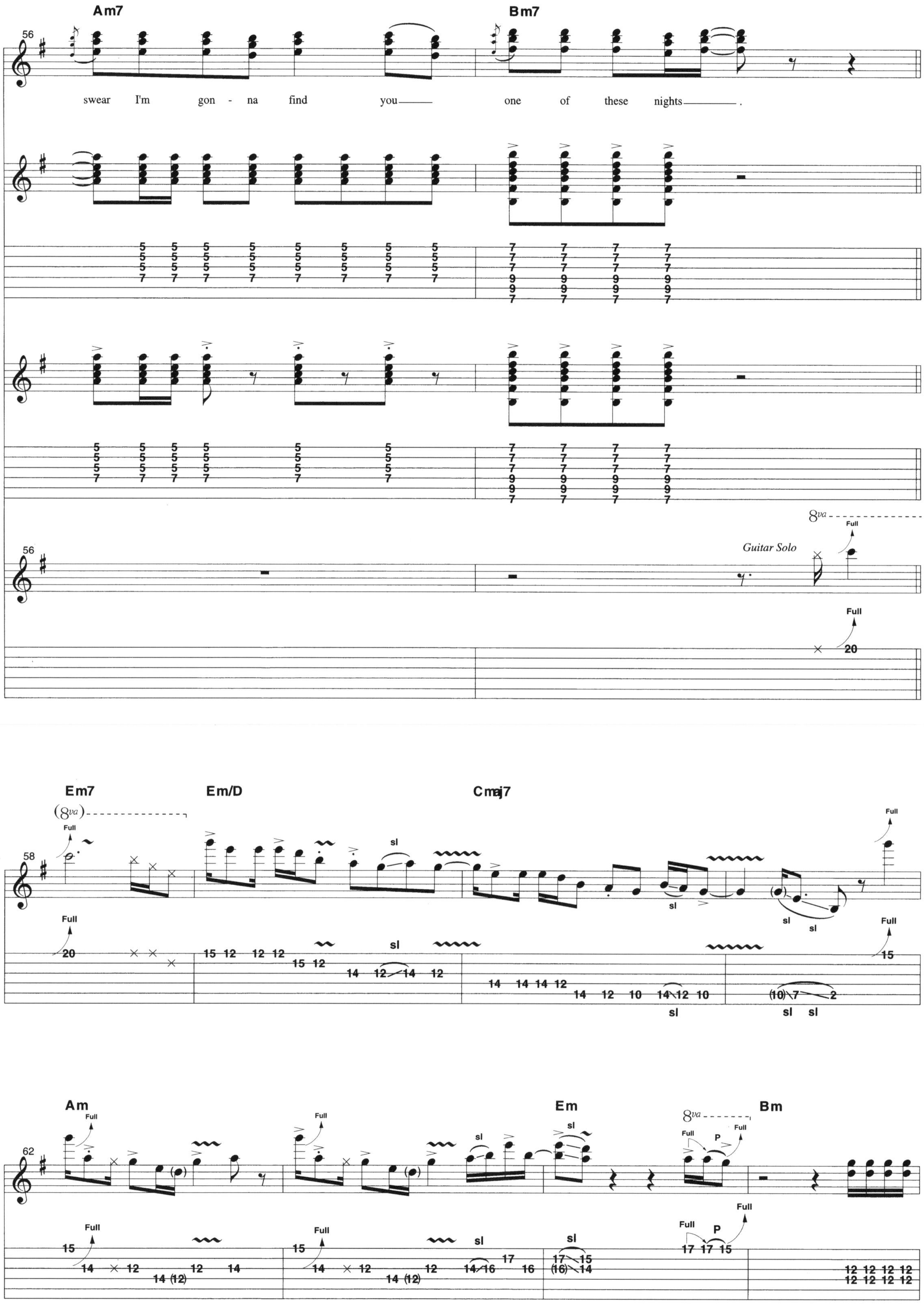

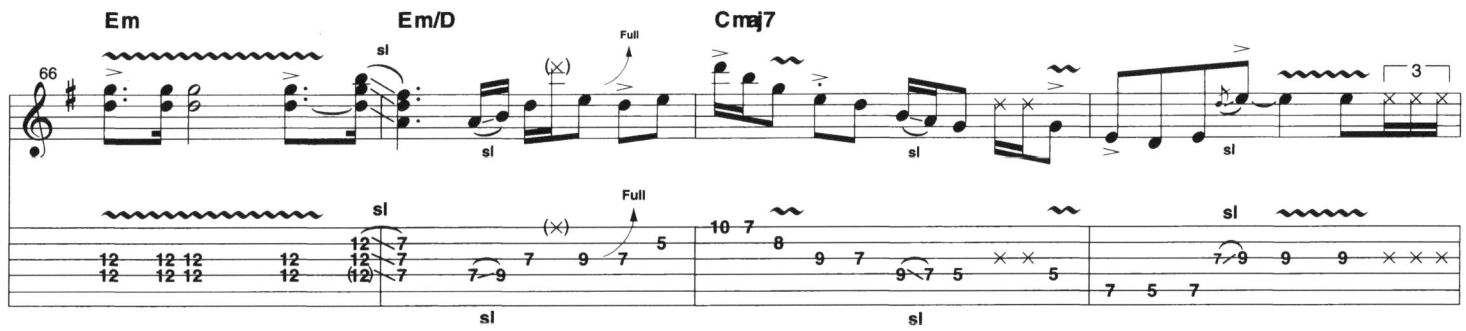
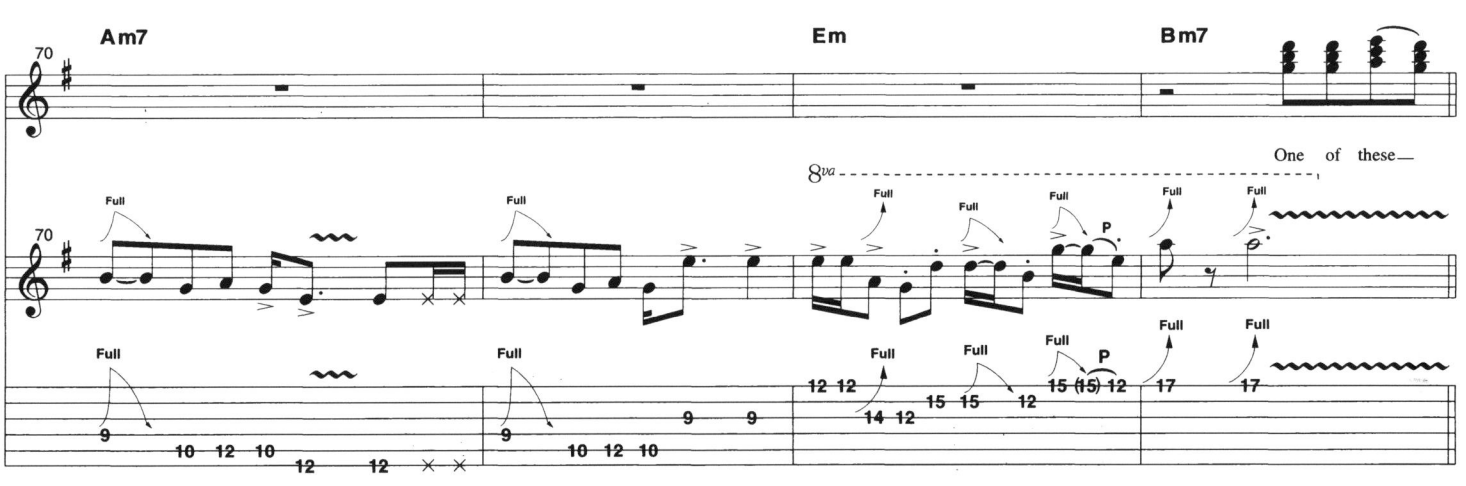
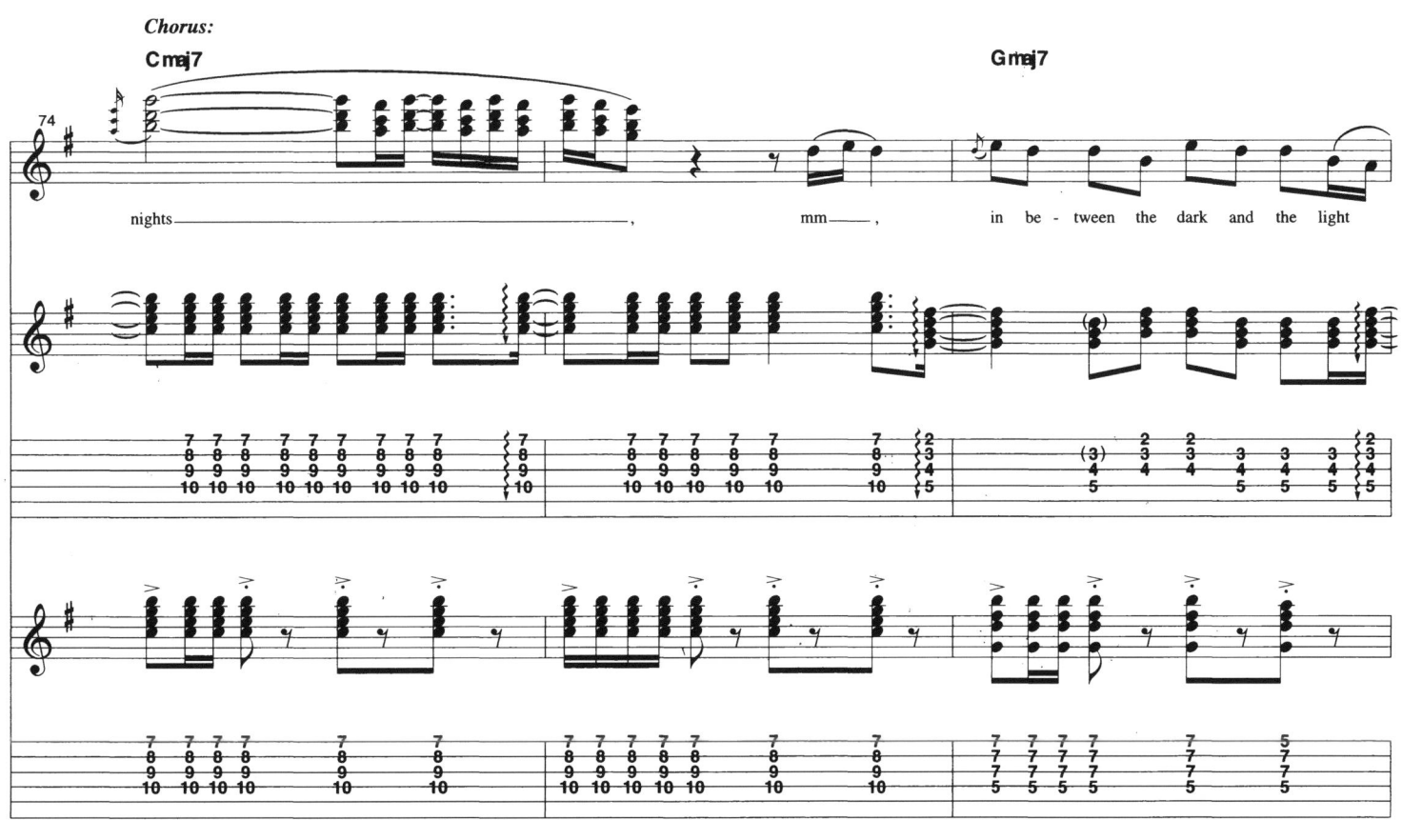

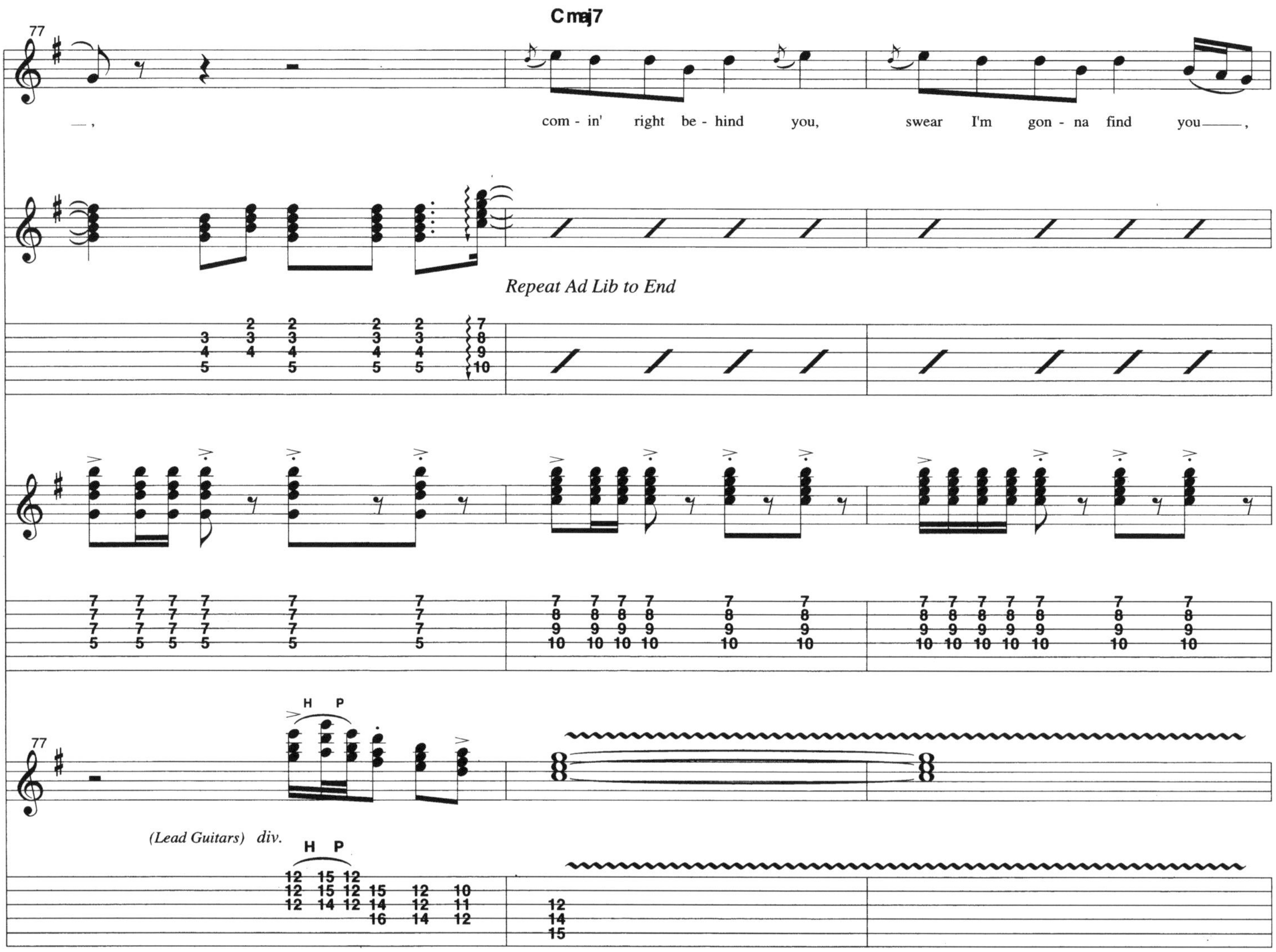
Cmaj7
—, com - in' right be - hind you, swear I'm gon - na find you—,
Repeat Ad Lib to End
H P
(Lead Guitars) div.
H P

Gmaj7
Cmaj7
get you ba - by, one of these nights—. One of these— nights

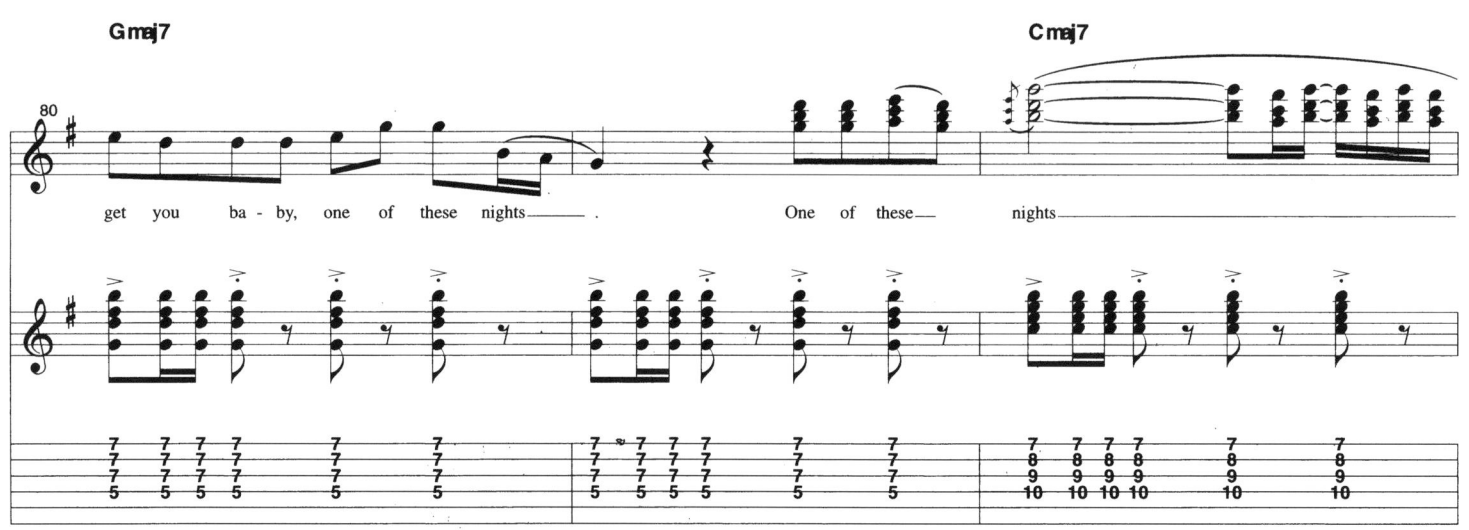

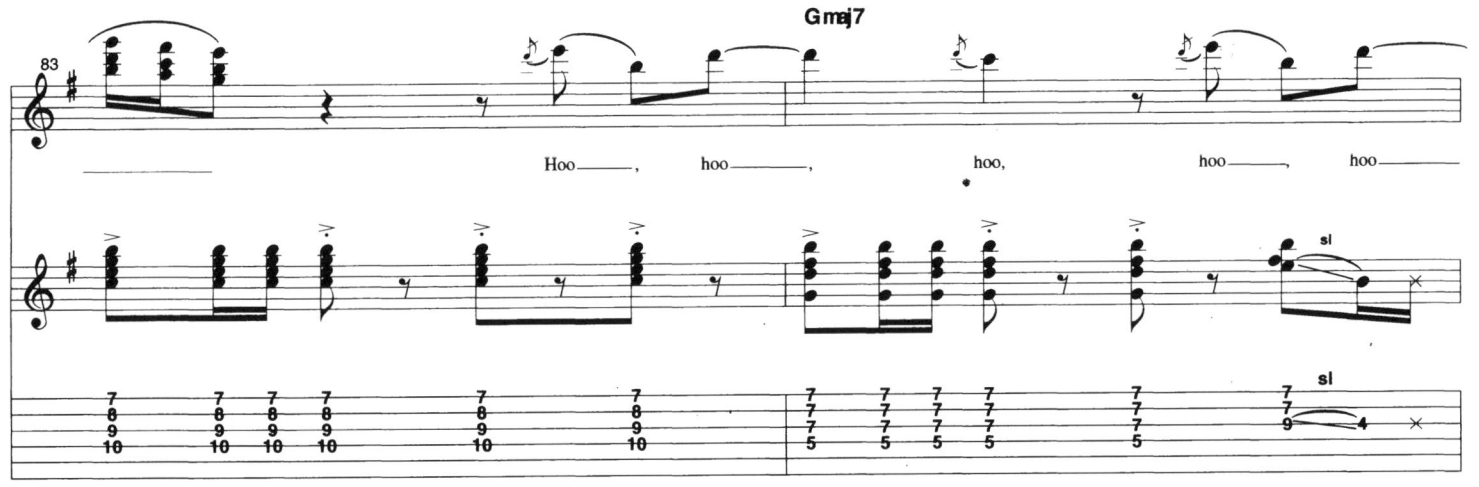
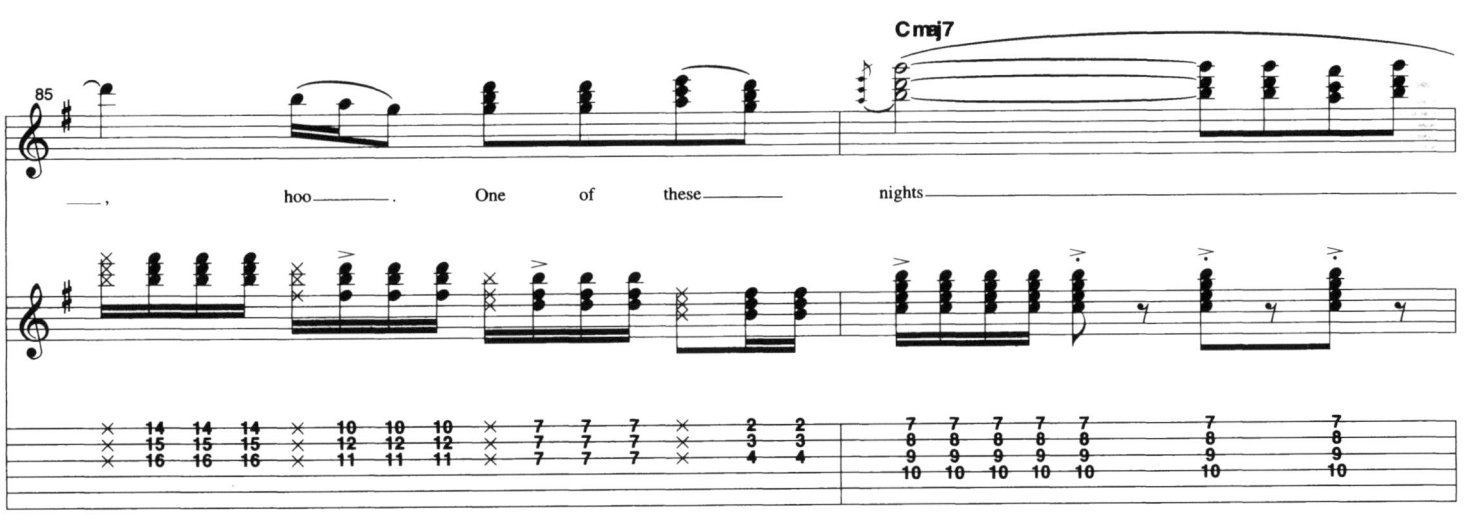
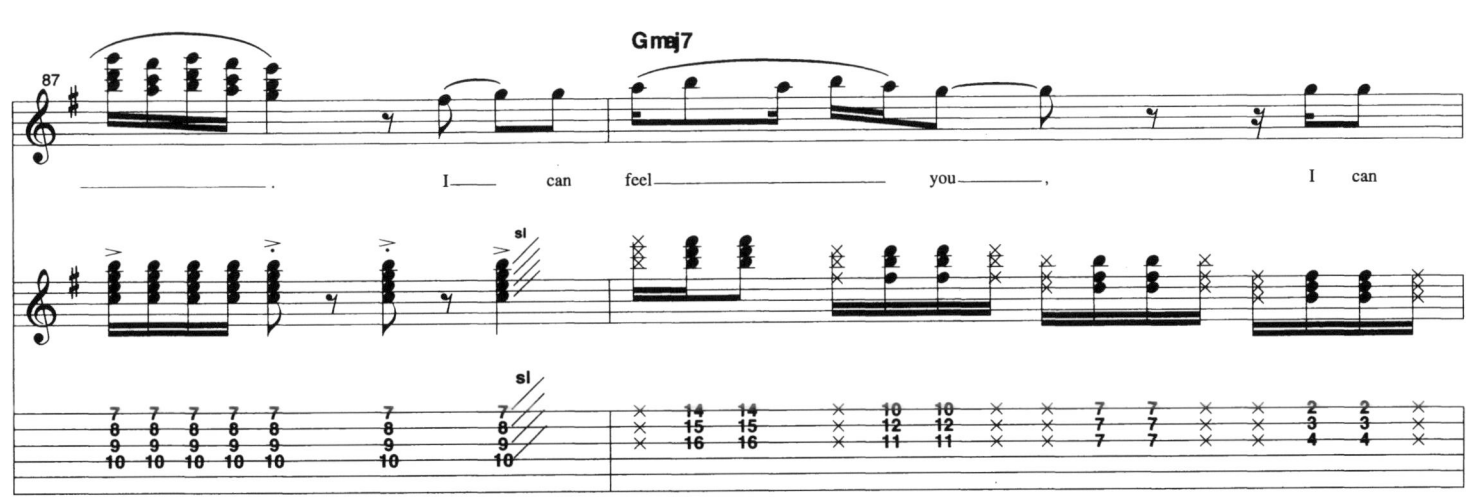

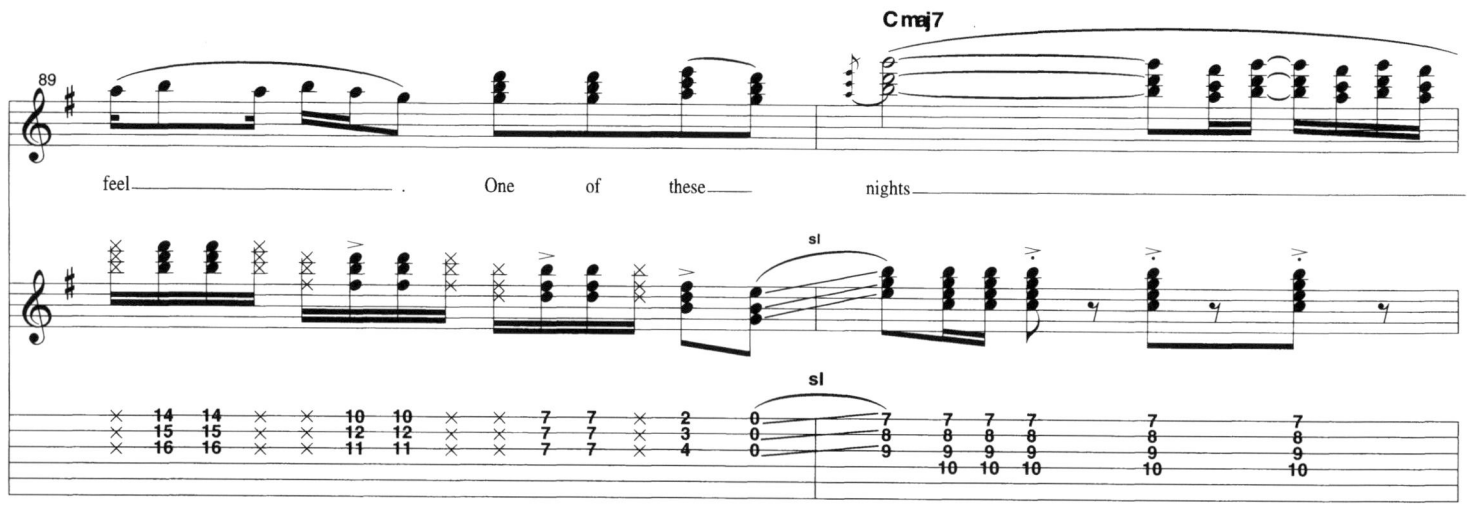

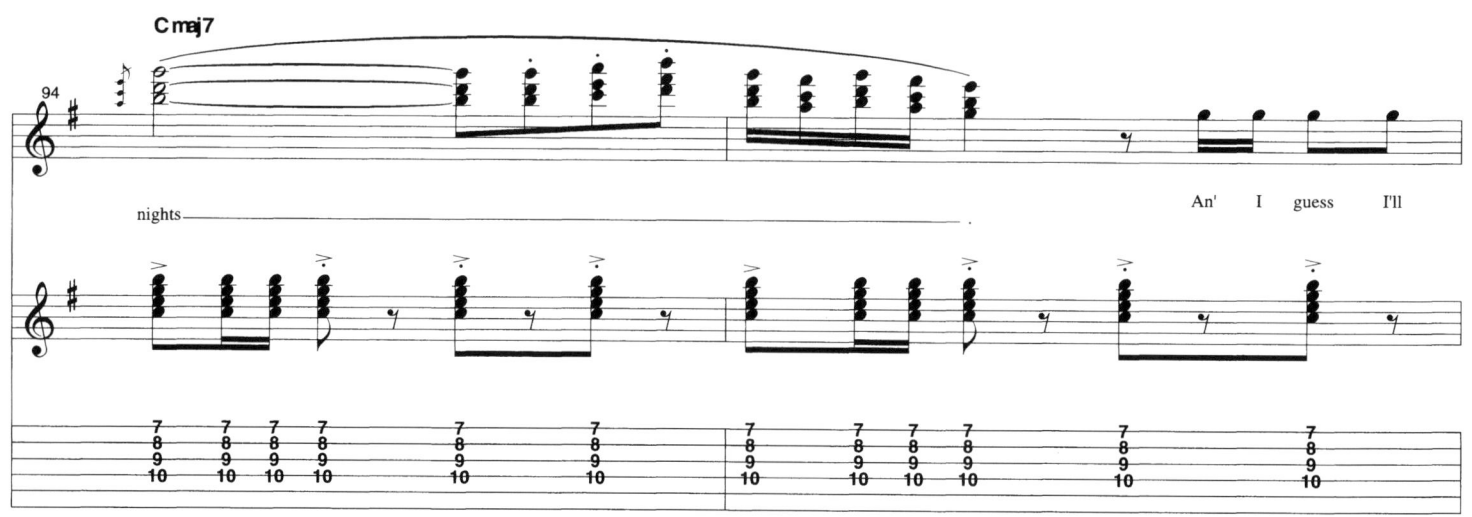

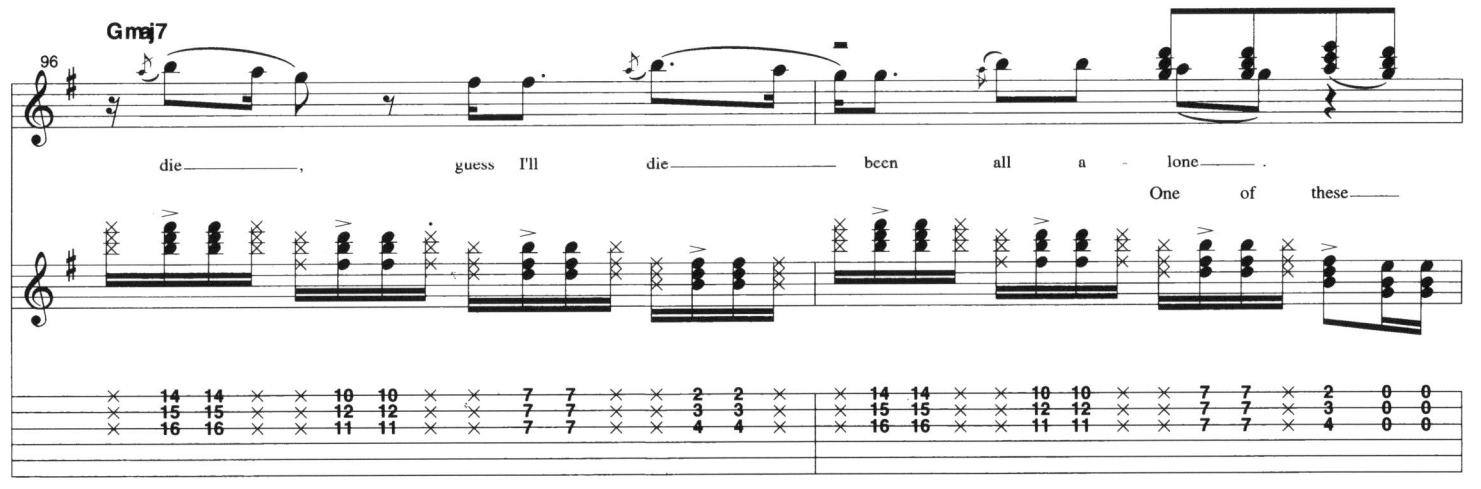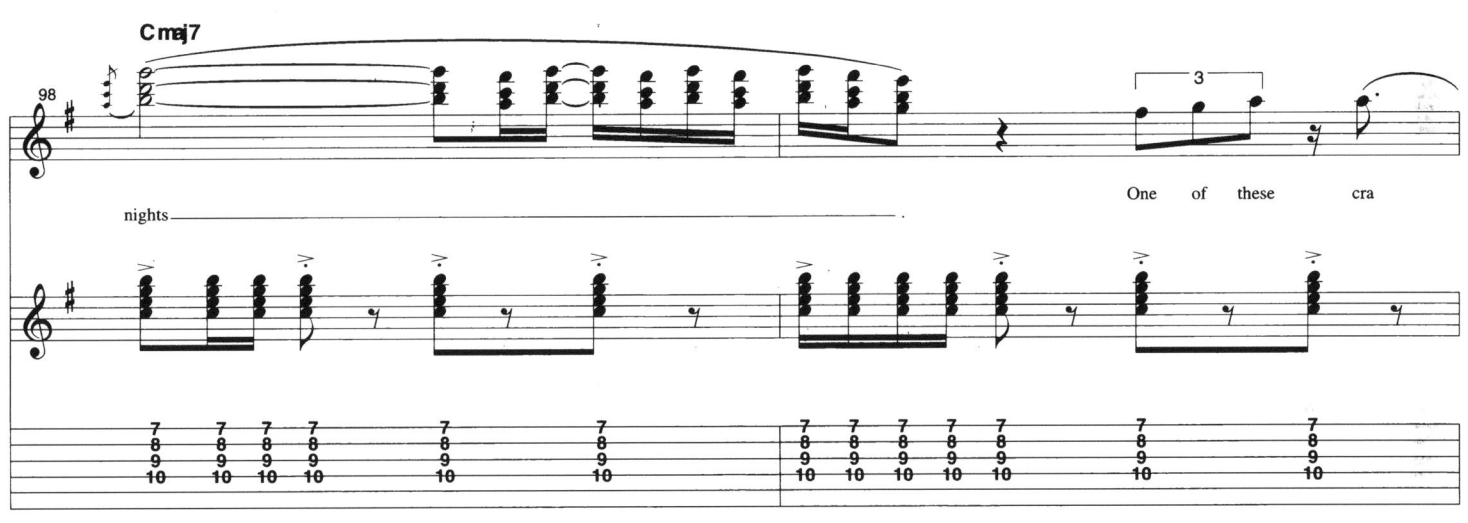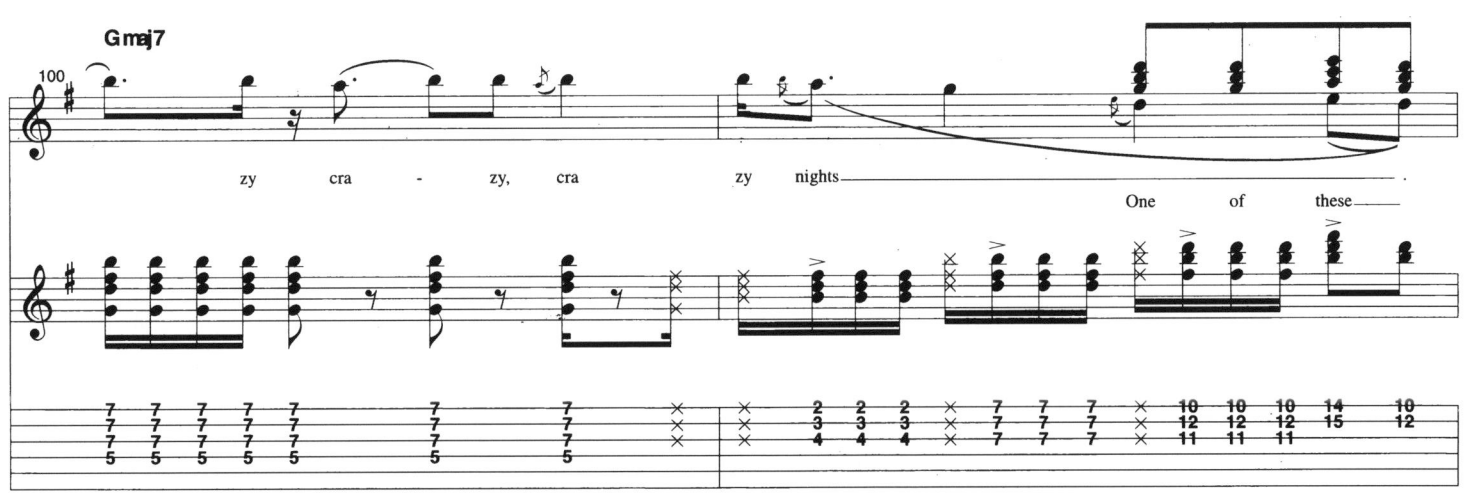

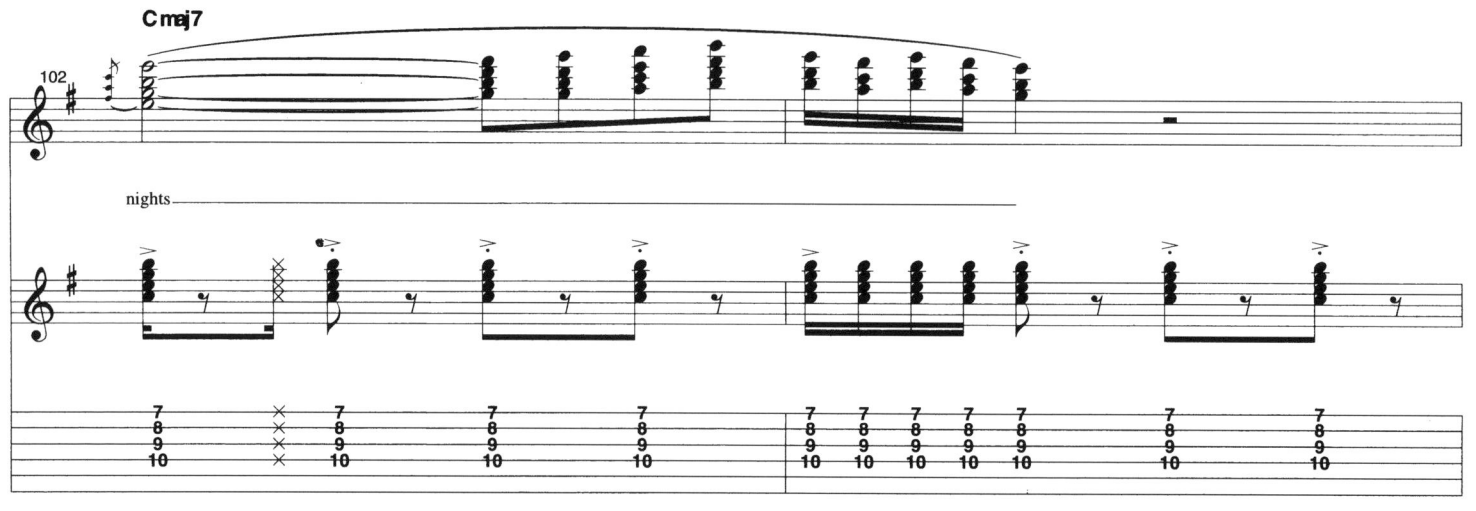
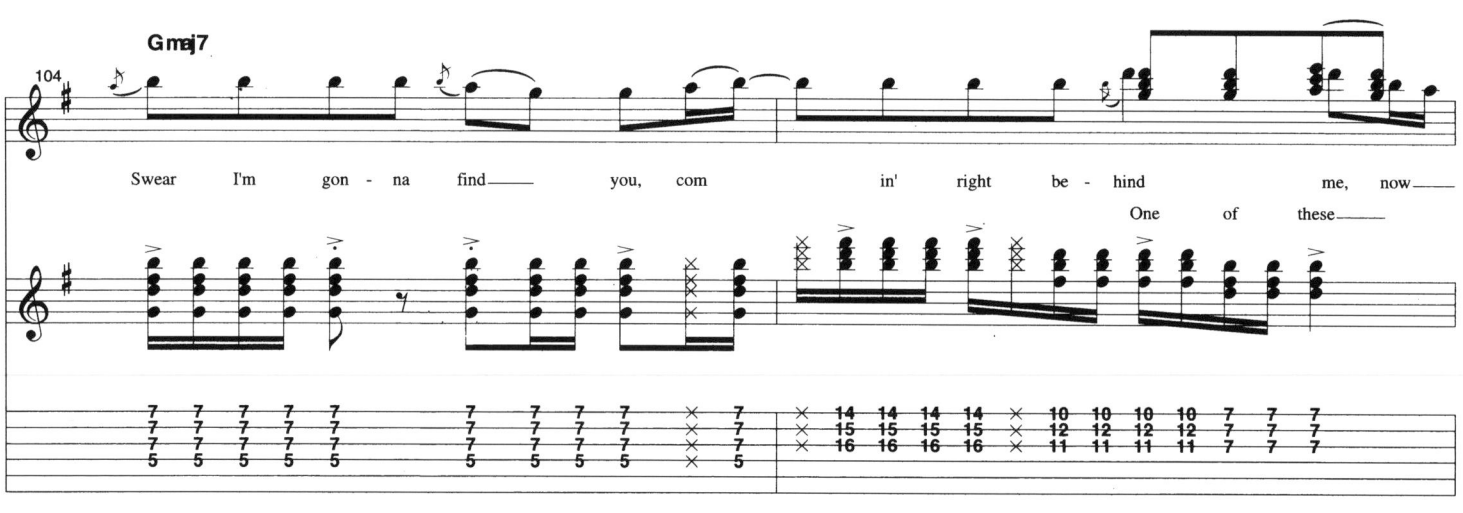
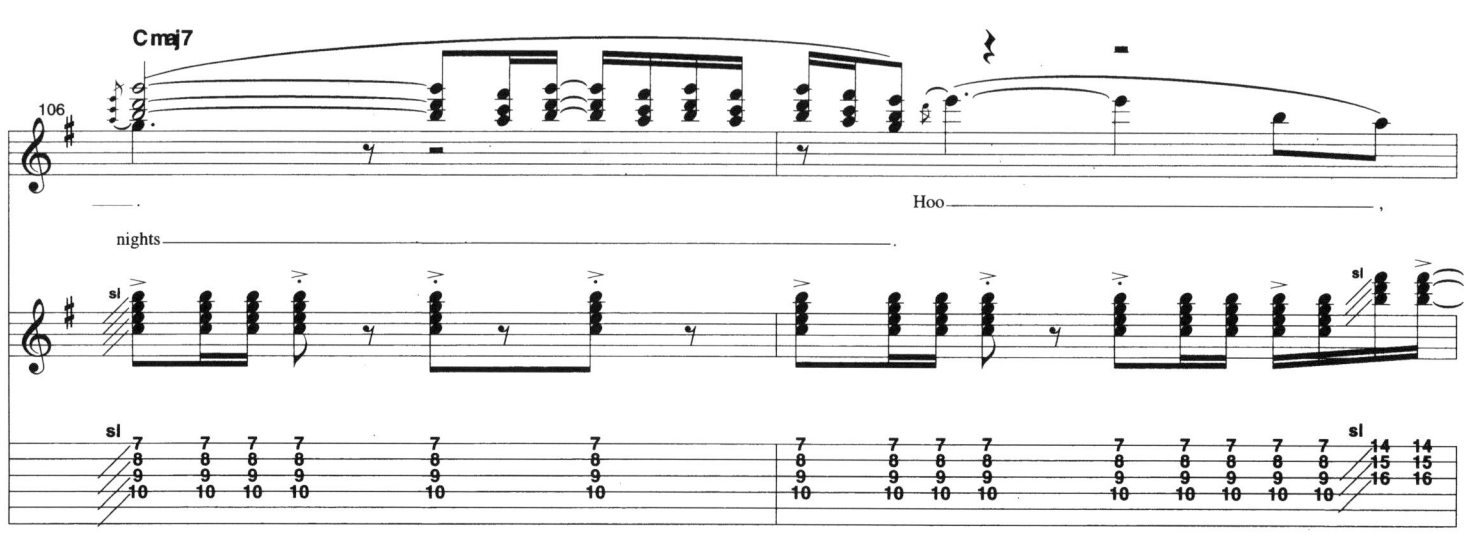

62

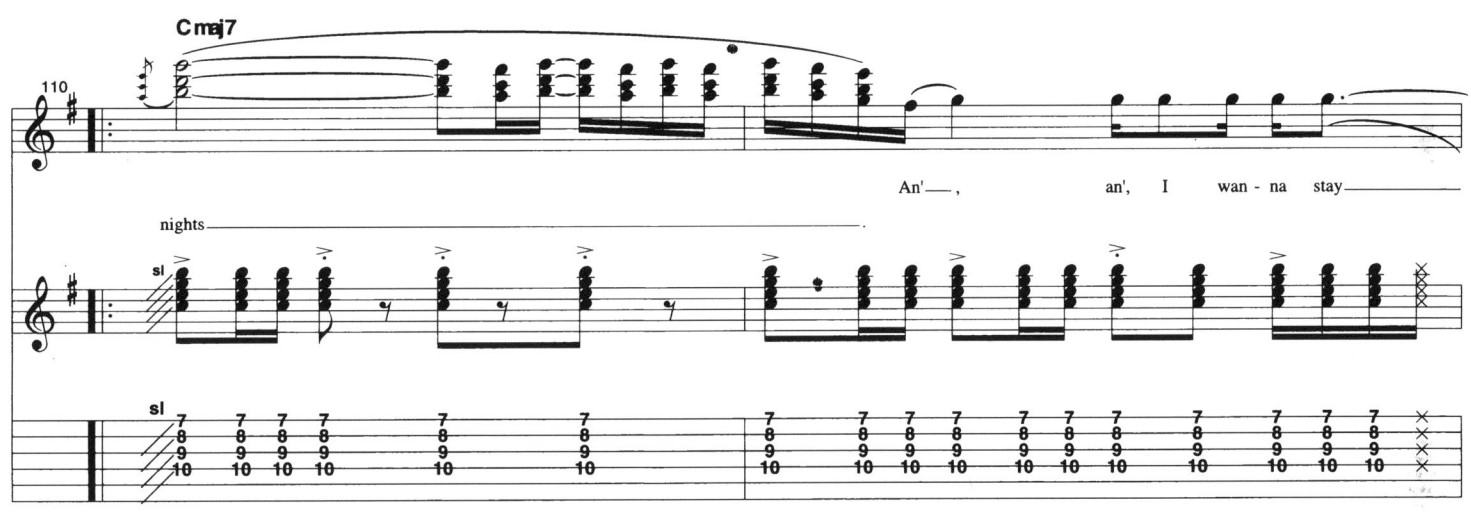
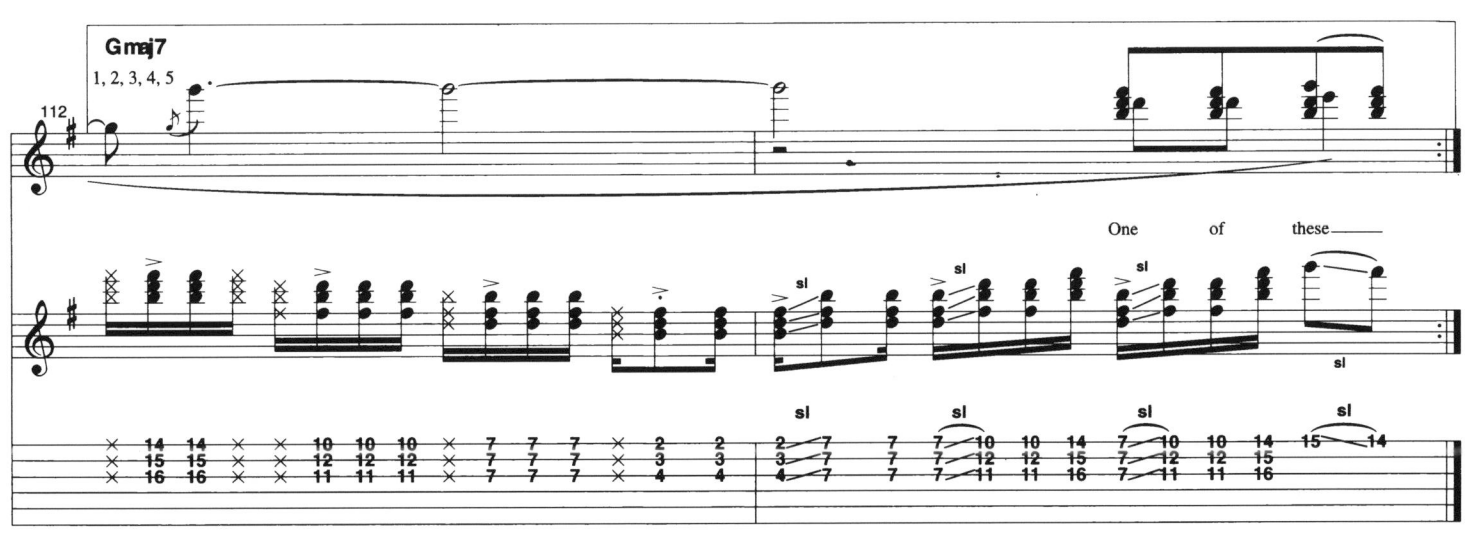

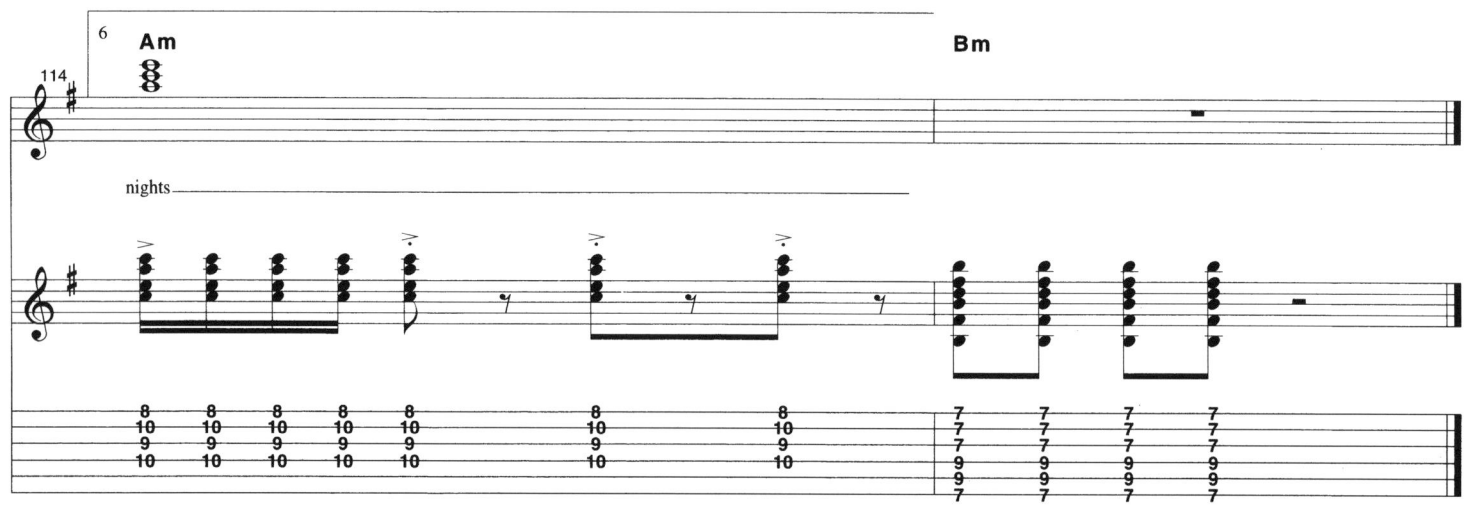

Tequila Sunrise

Words and Music by DON HENLEY and GLENN FREY

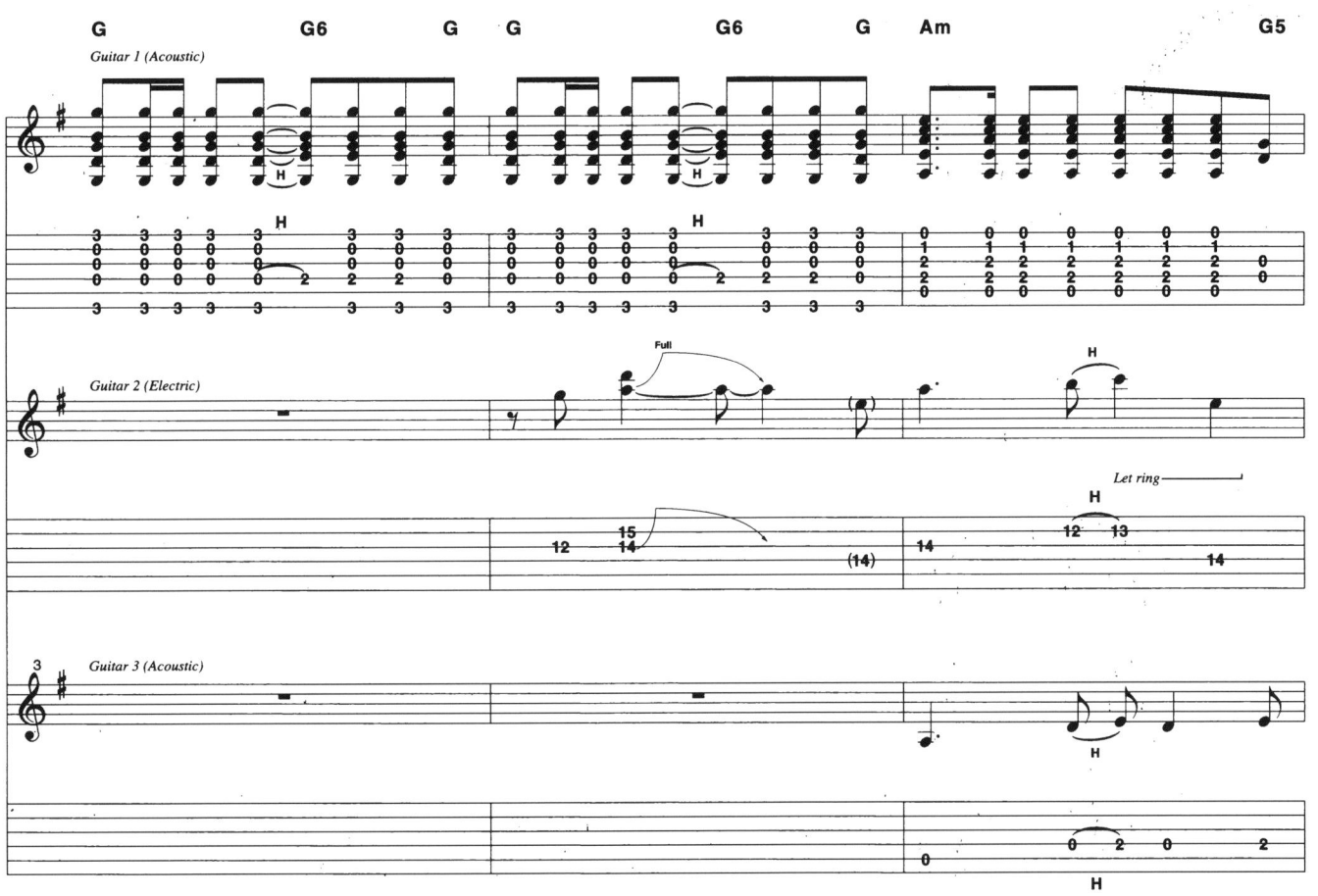

© 1973 & 1996 Country Cass Music, Red Cloud Music and WB Music Corp, USA
Warner/Chappell Music Ltd, London W1Y 3FA

Verse 1:

D7 G G6 G G G6 G
said good bye
(End rhythm figure 1)
continue sim
Let ring
Let ring
Let ring
(End rhythm figure 1b)

G D7
He was just a hir - ed hand, work - ing on the
Guitar 2 (Electric)
Let ring
Full
Full
Guitar 3 (Acoustic)

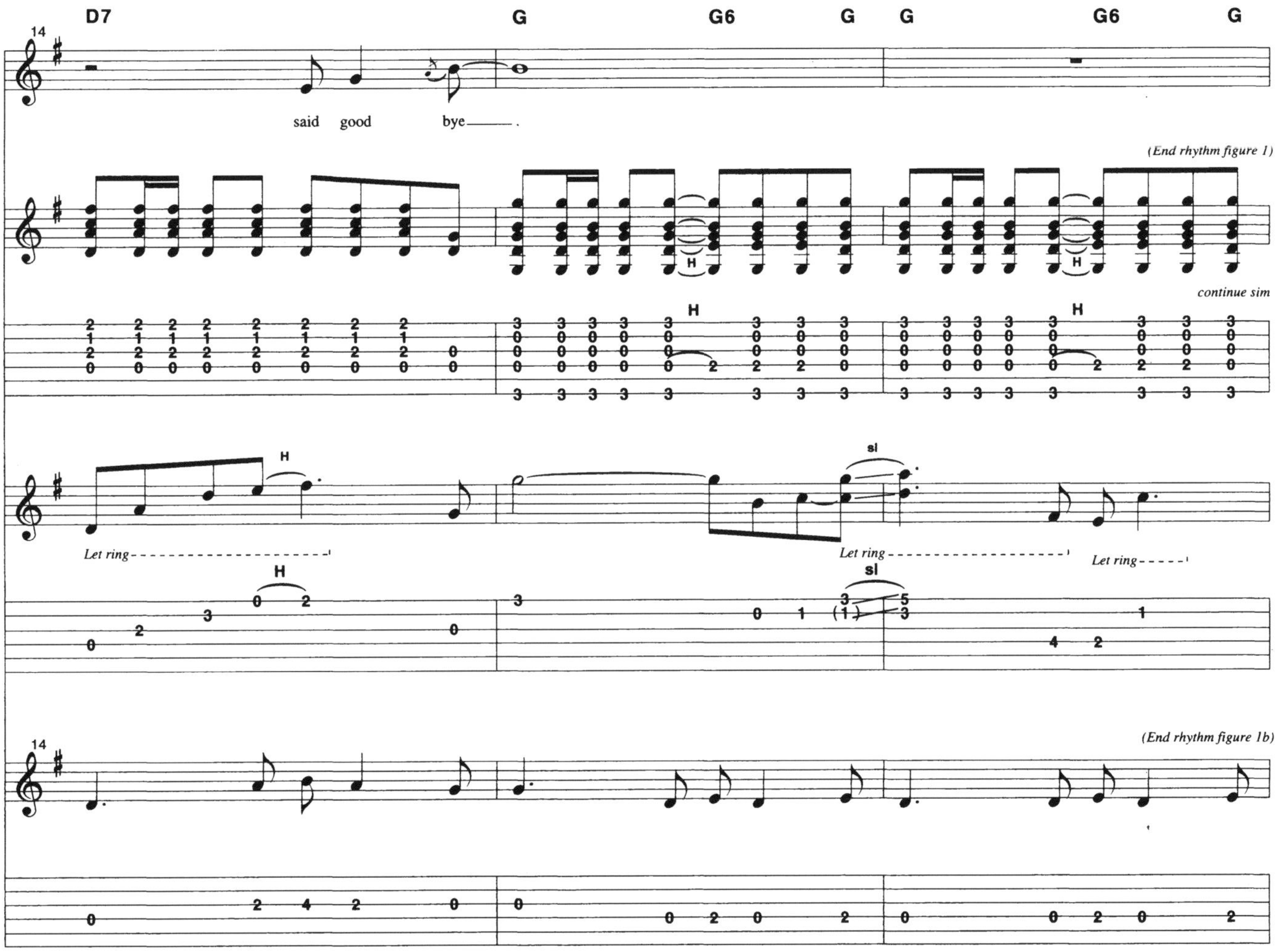

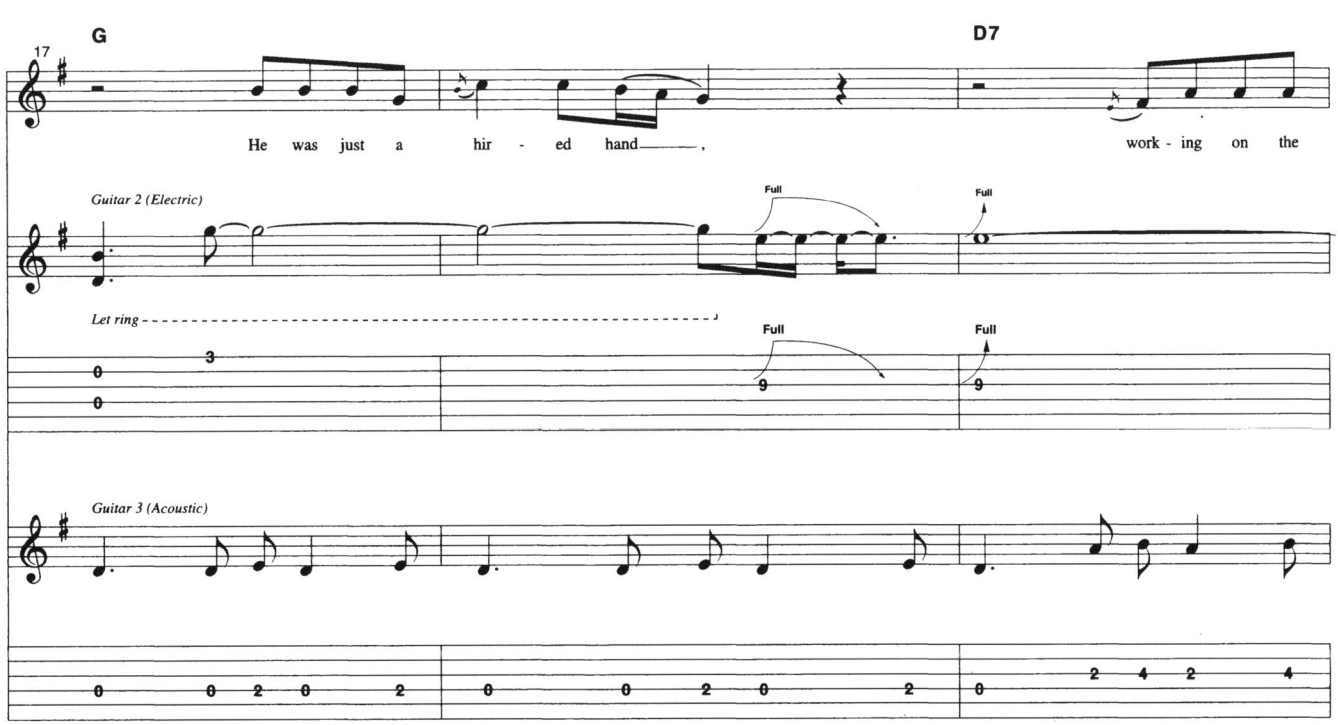

Chorus:

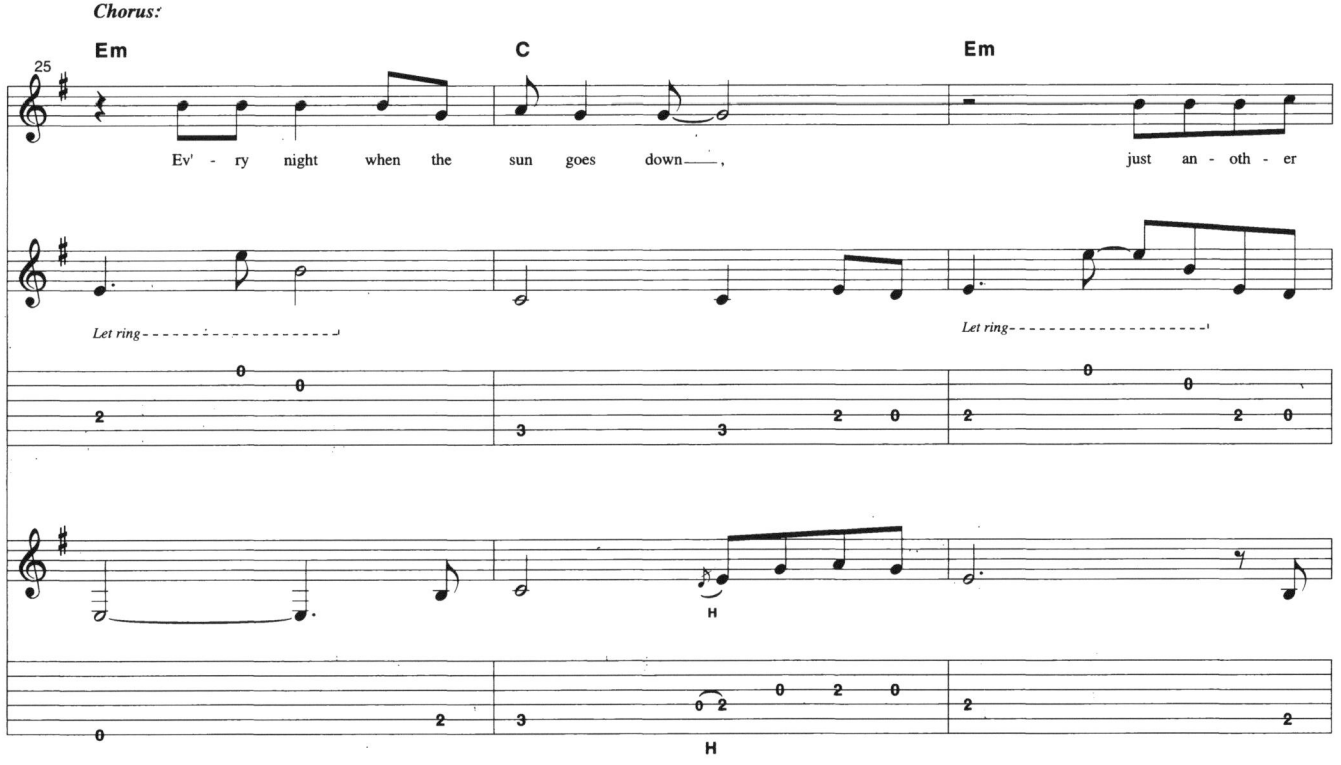

69

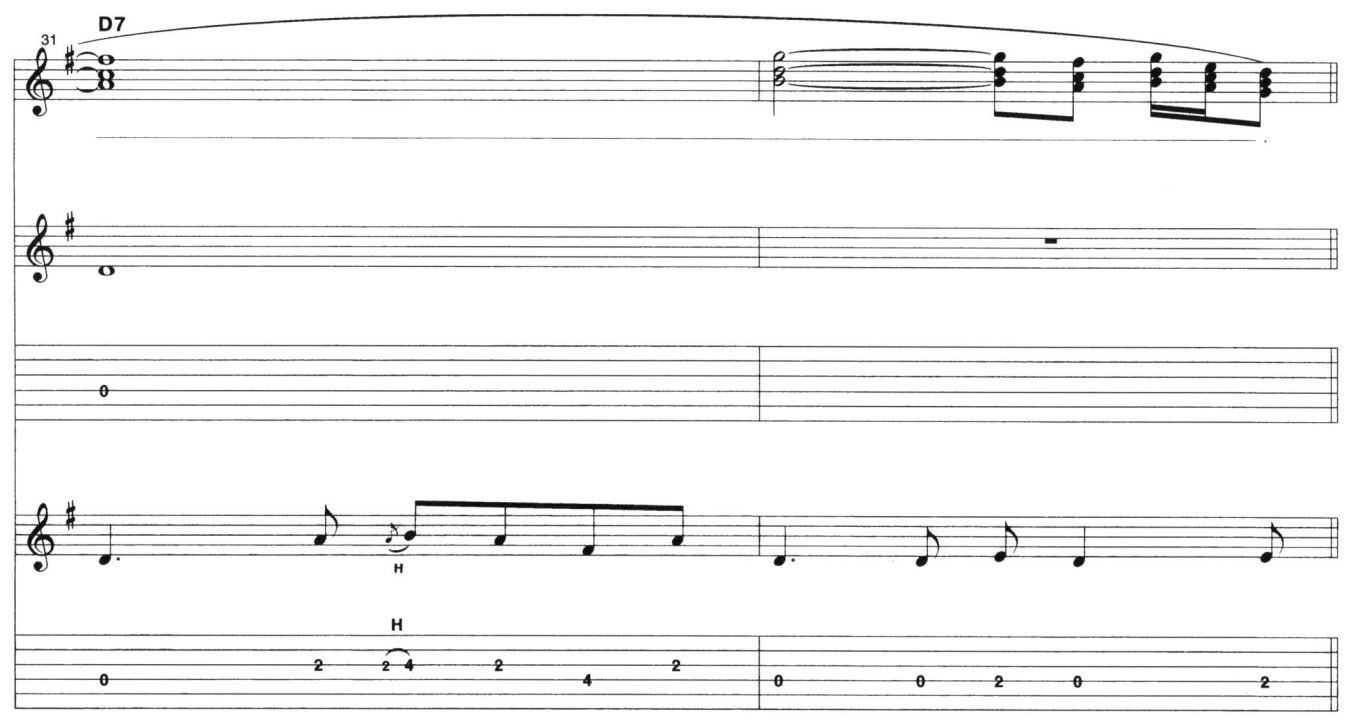

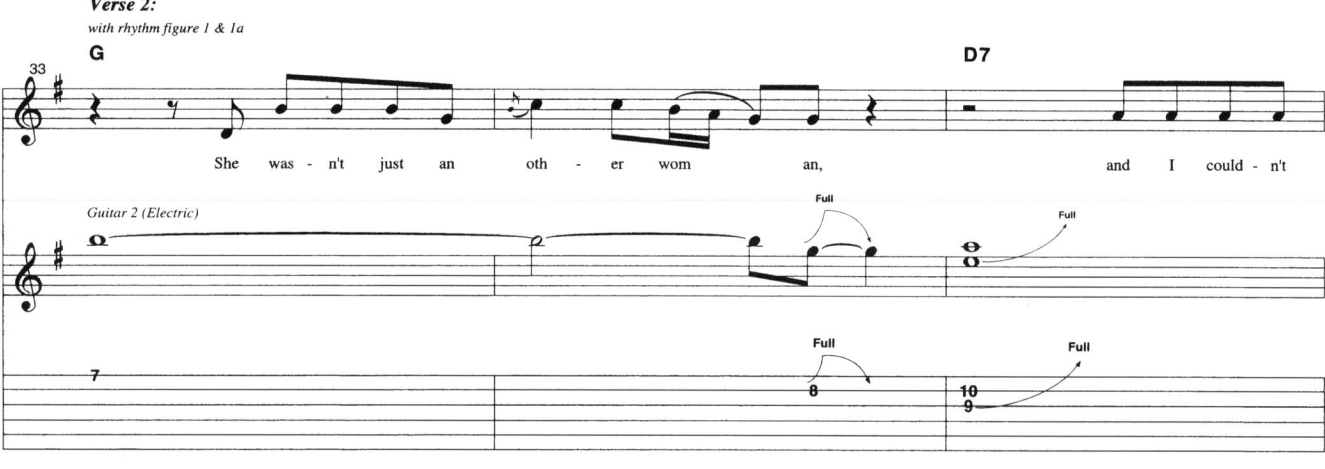

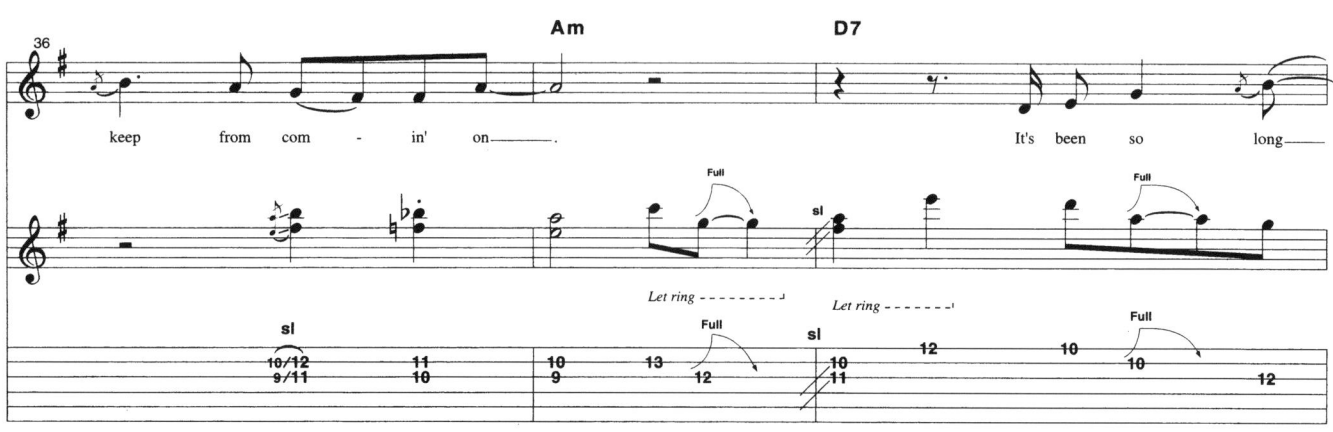

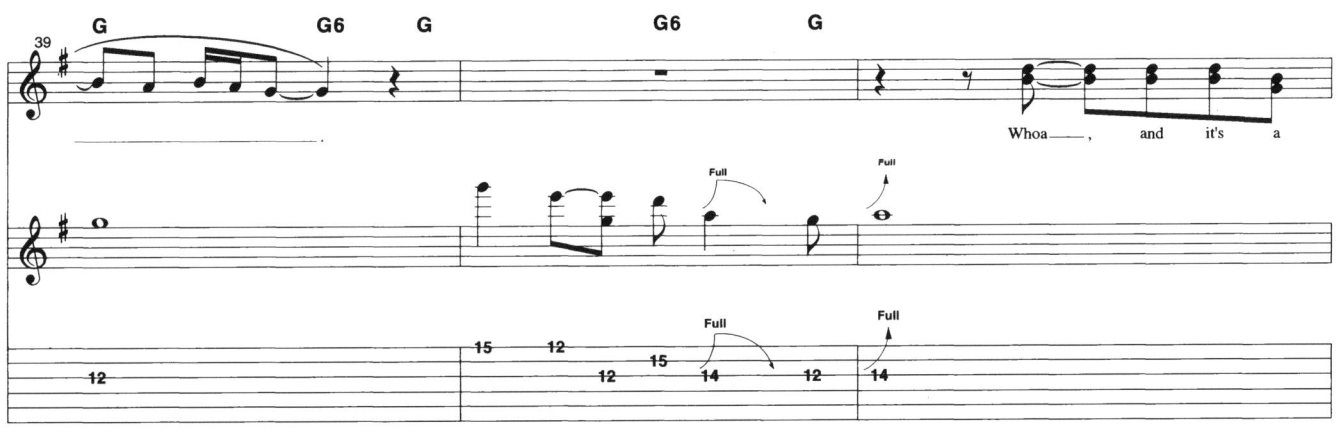
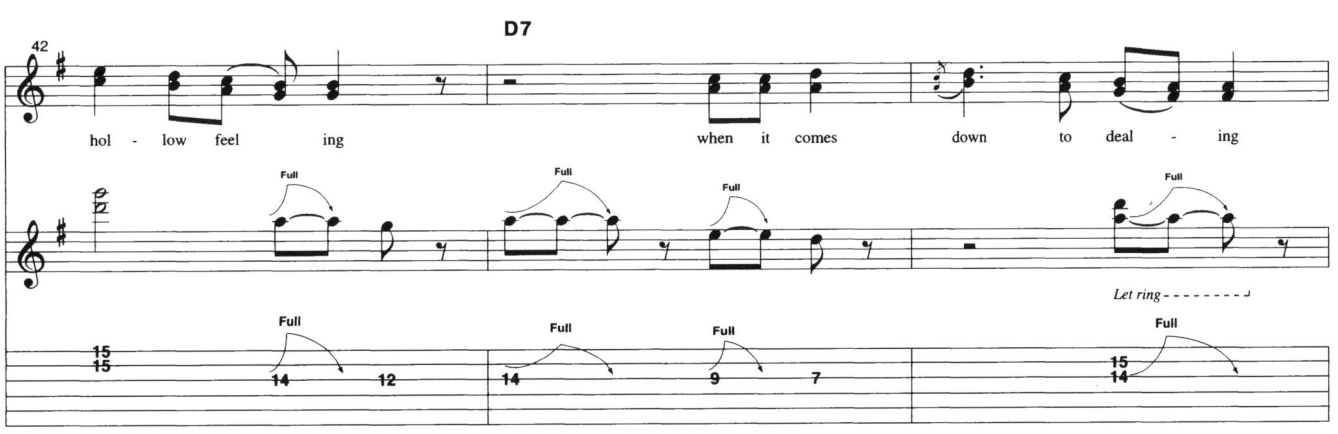

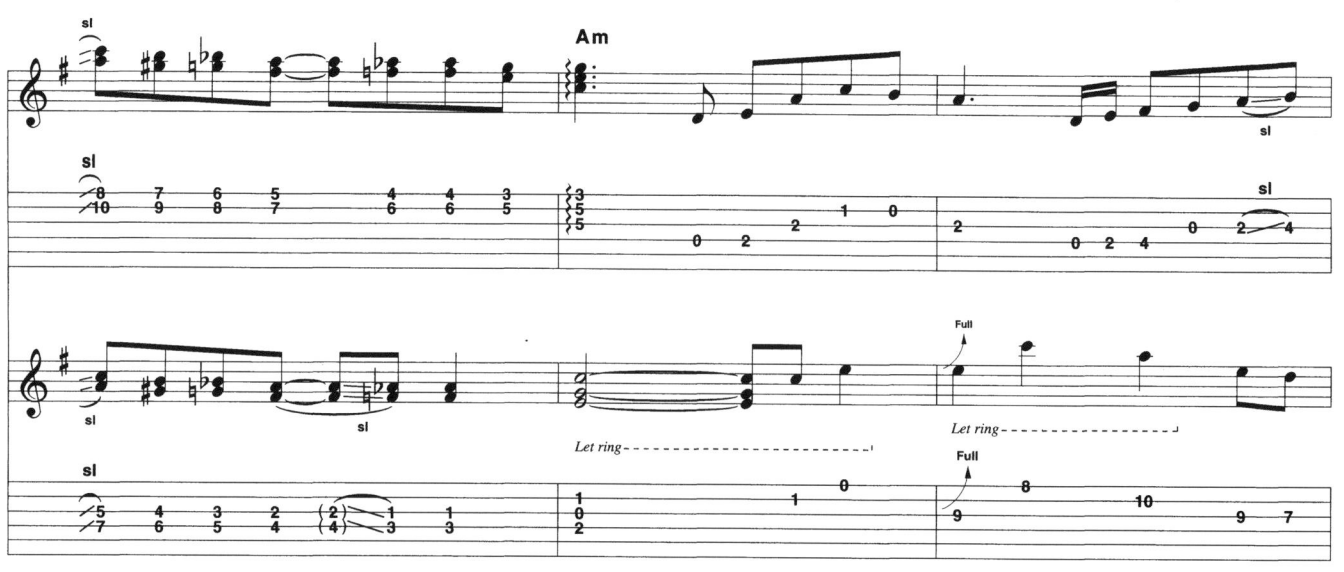

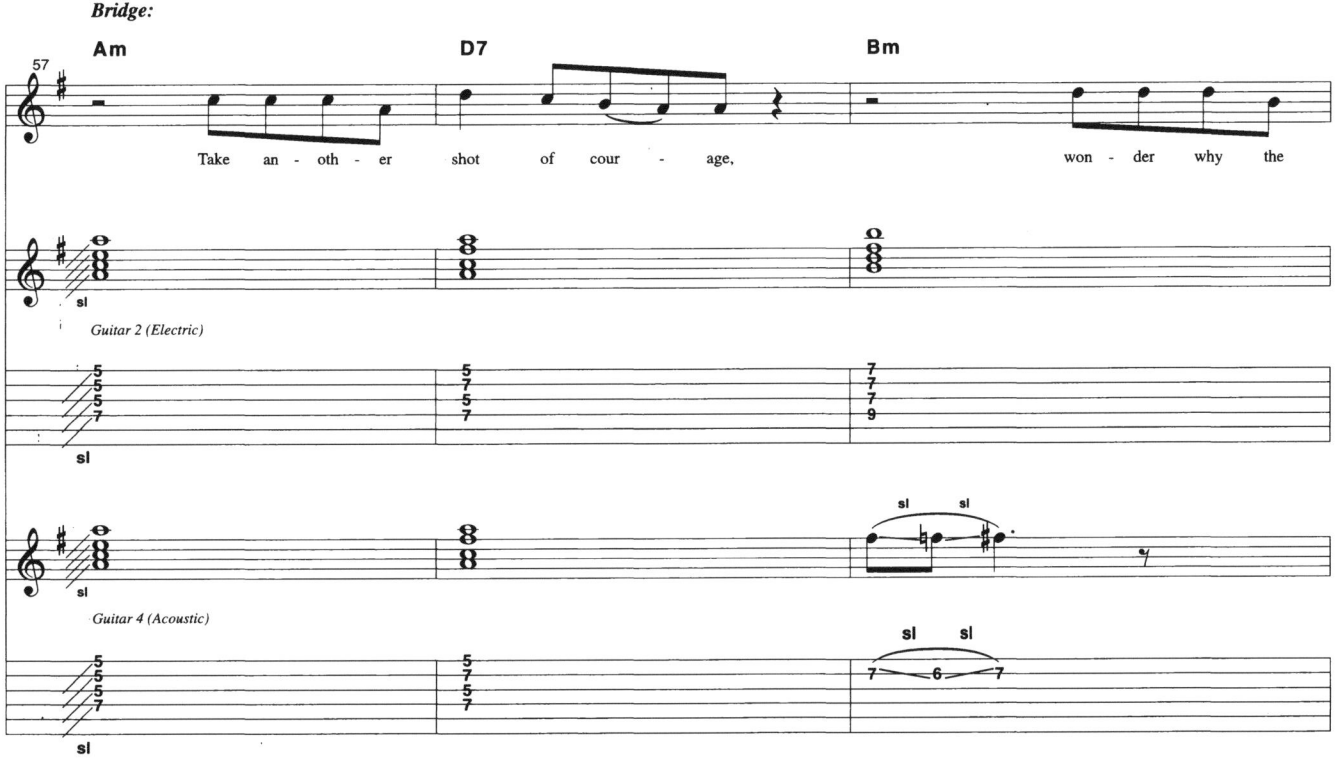
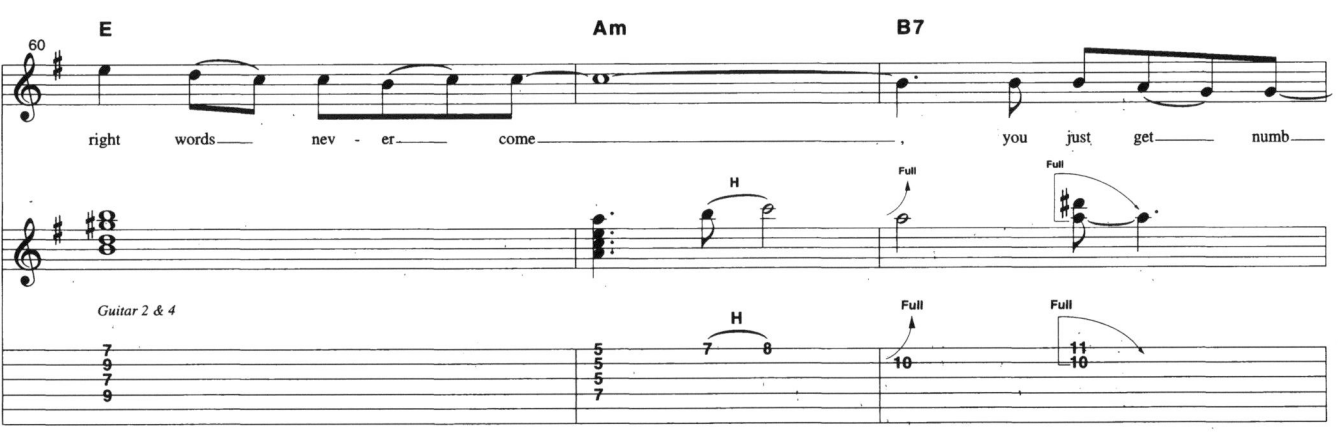
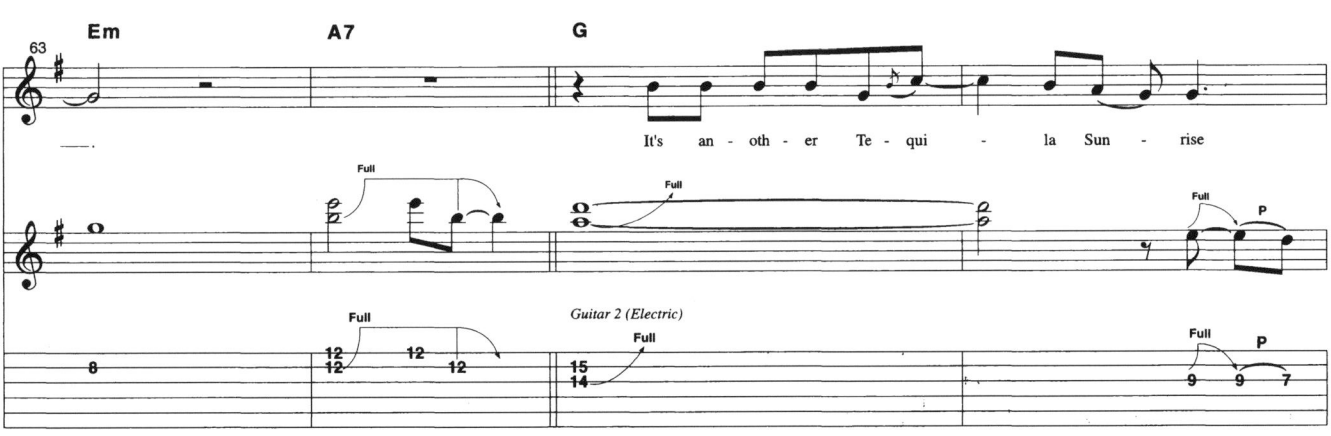

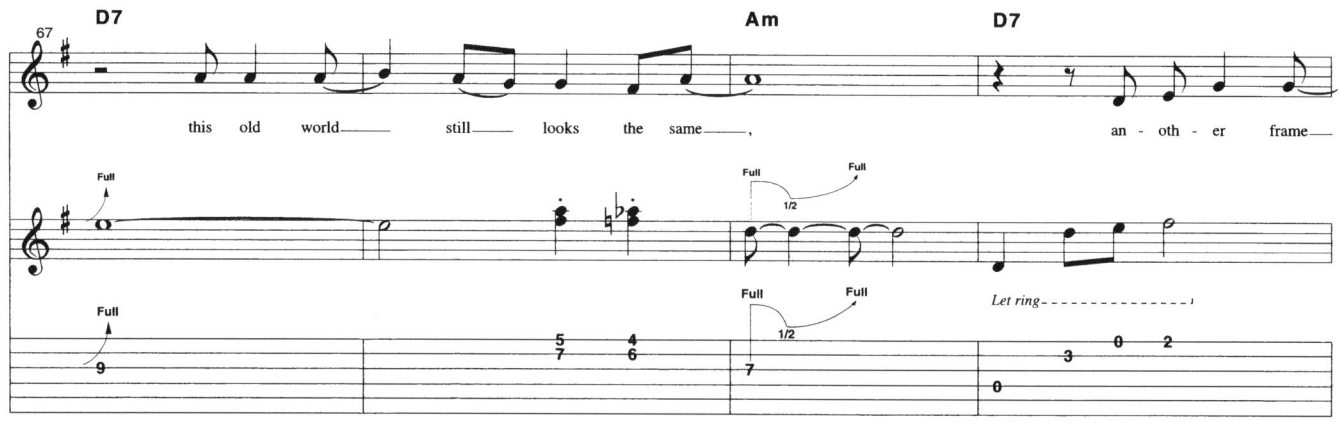

75

New Kid In Town

Words and Music by DAVID JOHN SOUTHER, DON HENLEY and GLENN FREY

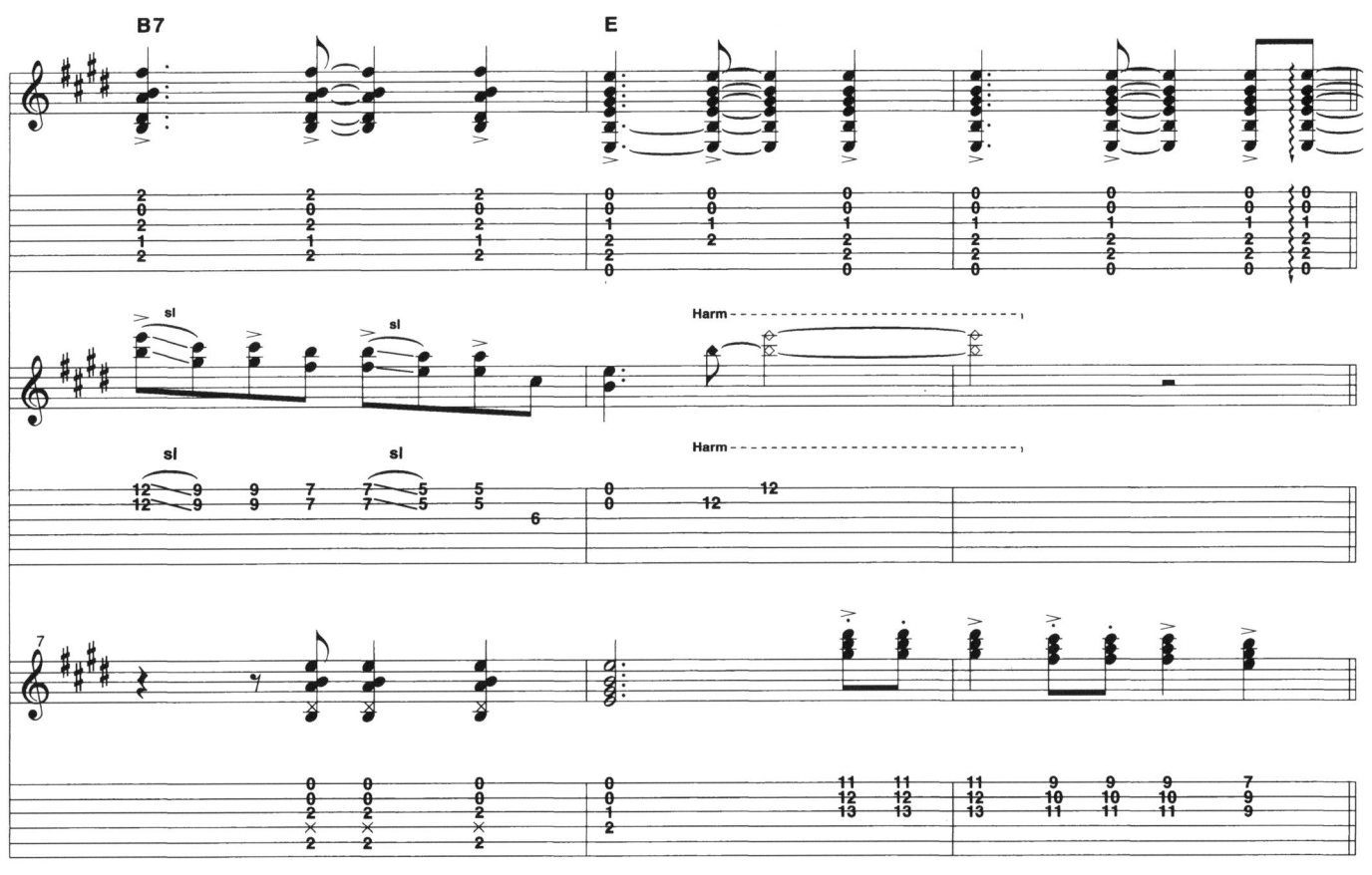

Verse 1:

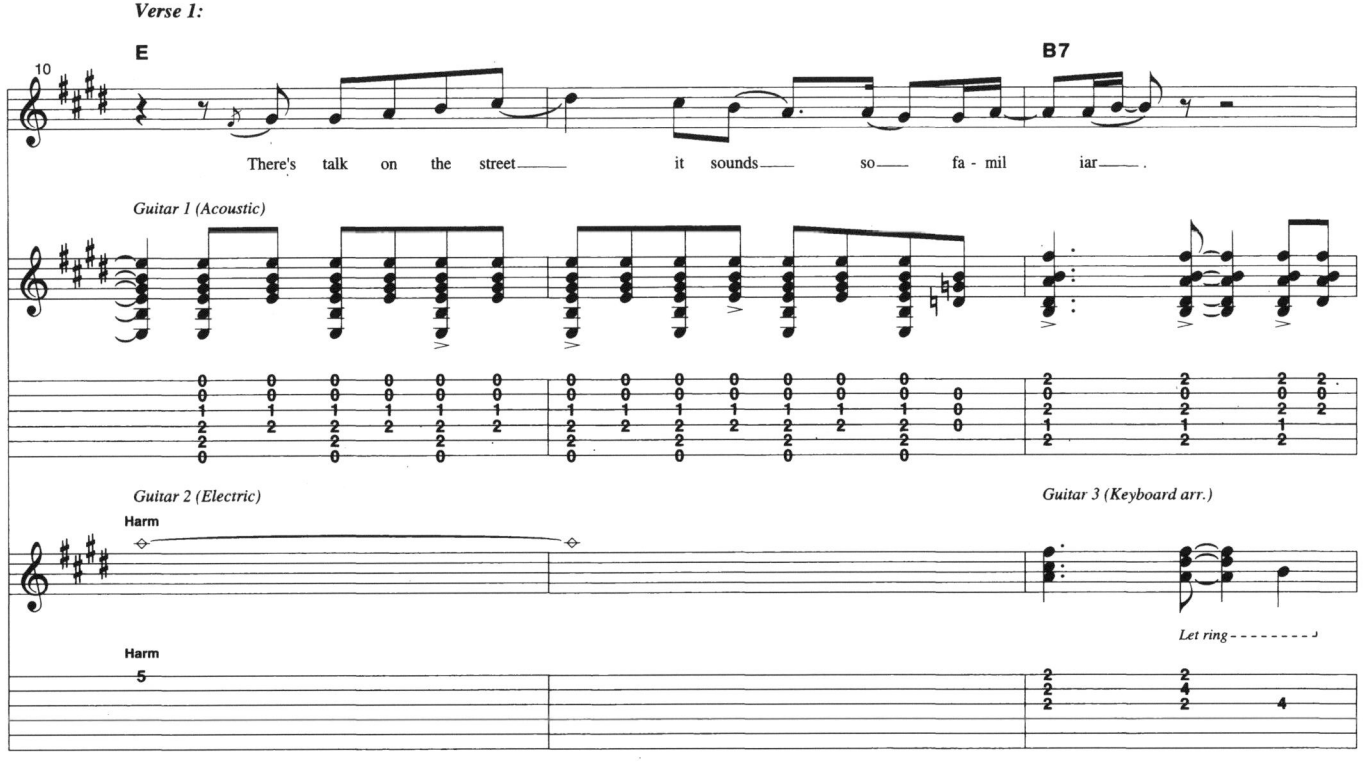

There's talk on the street it sounds so fa-mil-iar.

Guitar 1 (Acoustic)

Guitar 2 (Electric)

Guitar 3 (Keyboard arr.)

77

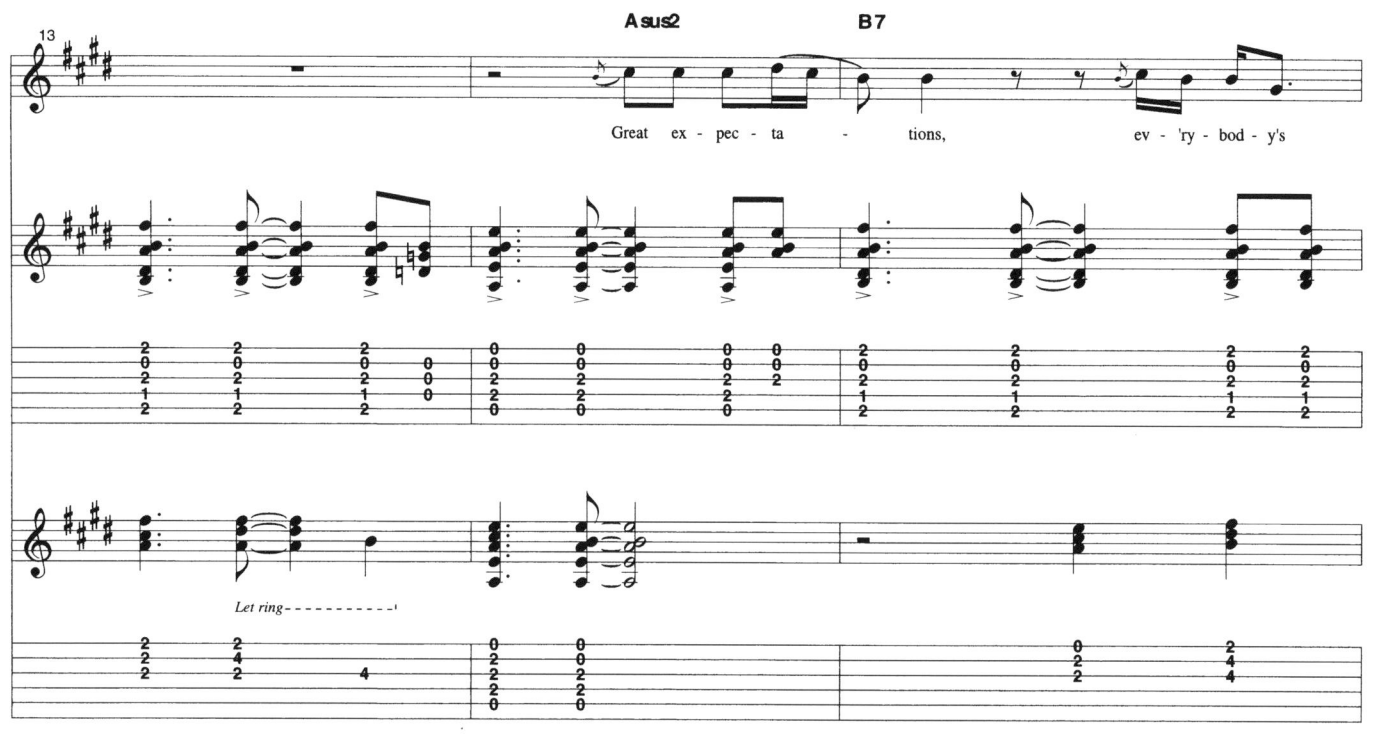
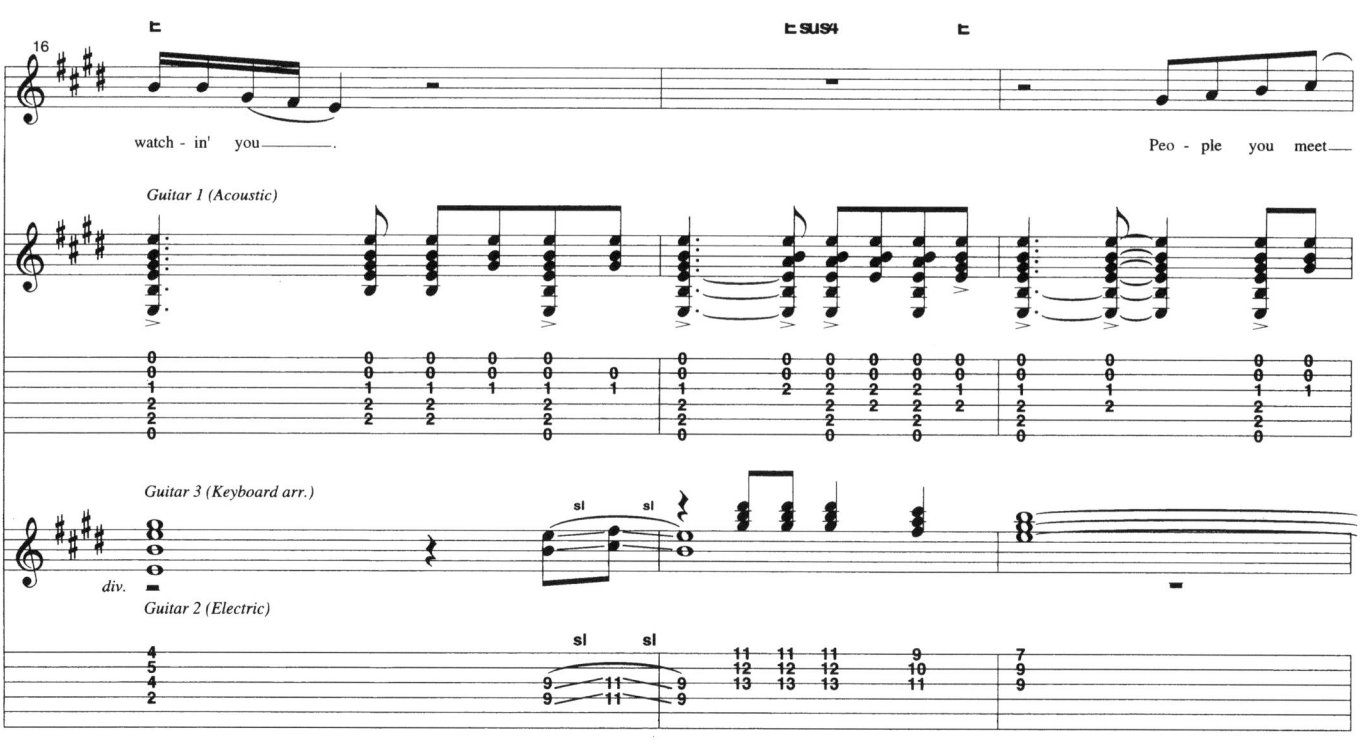

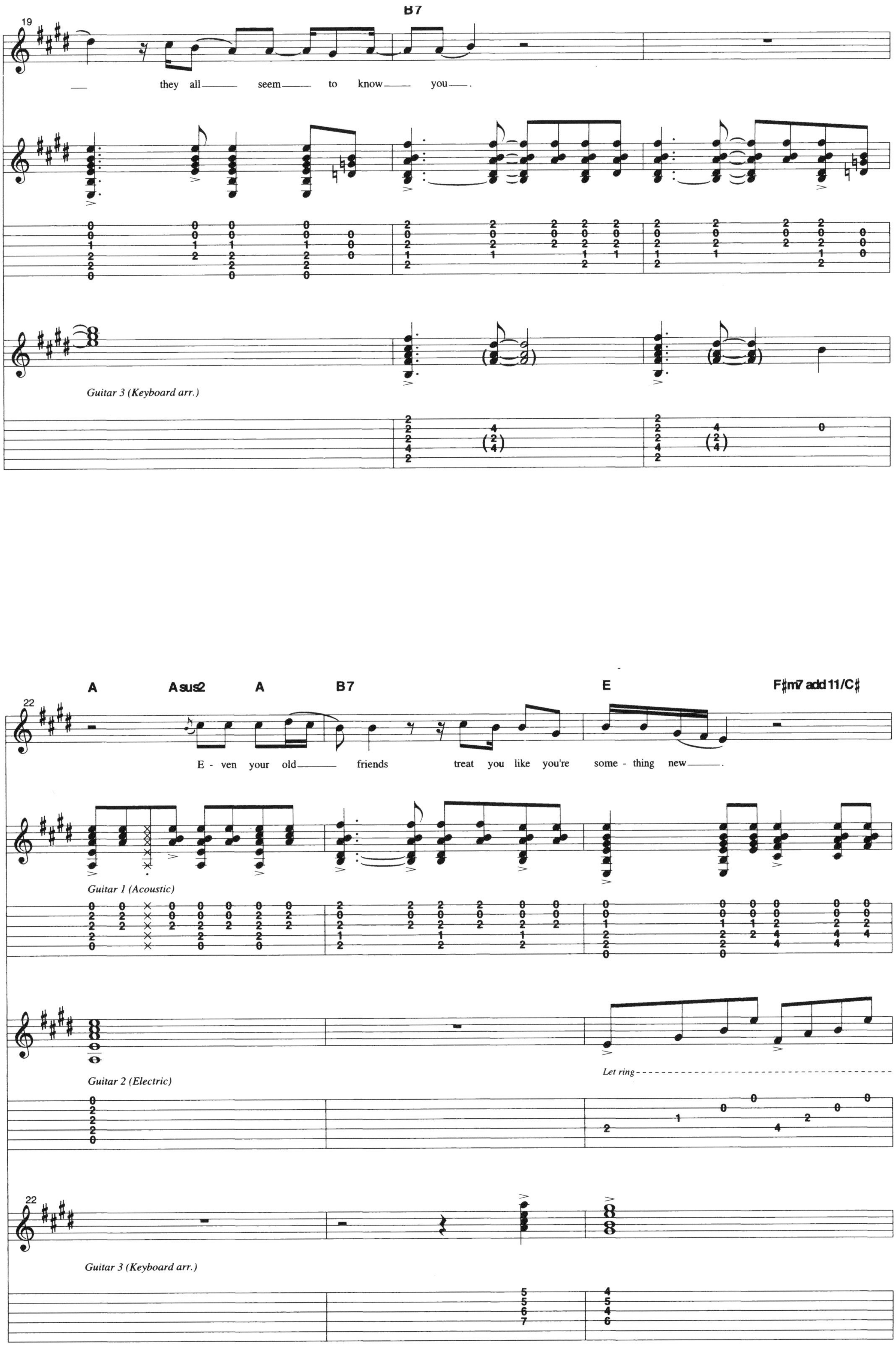
19
B7
they all seem to know you.
Guitar 3 (Keyboard arr.)
22
A Asus2 A B7 E F♯m7 add 11/C♯
E - ven your old friends treat you like you're some - thing new.
Guitar 1 (Acoustic)
Guitar 2 (Electric)
Let ring
22
Guitar 3 (Keyboard arr.)

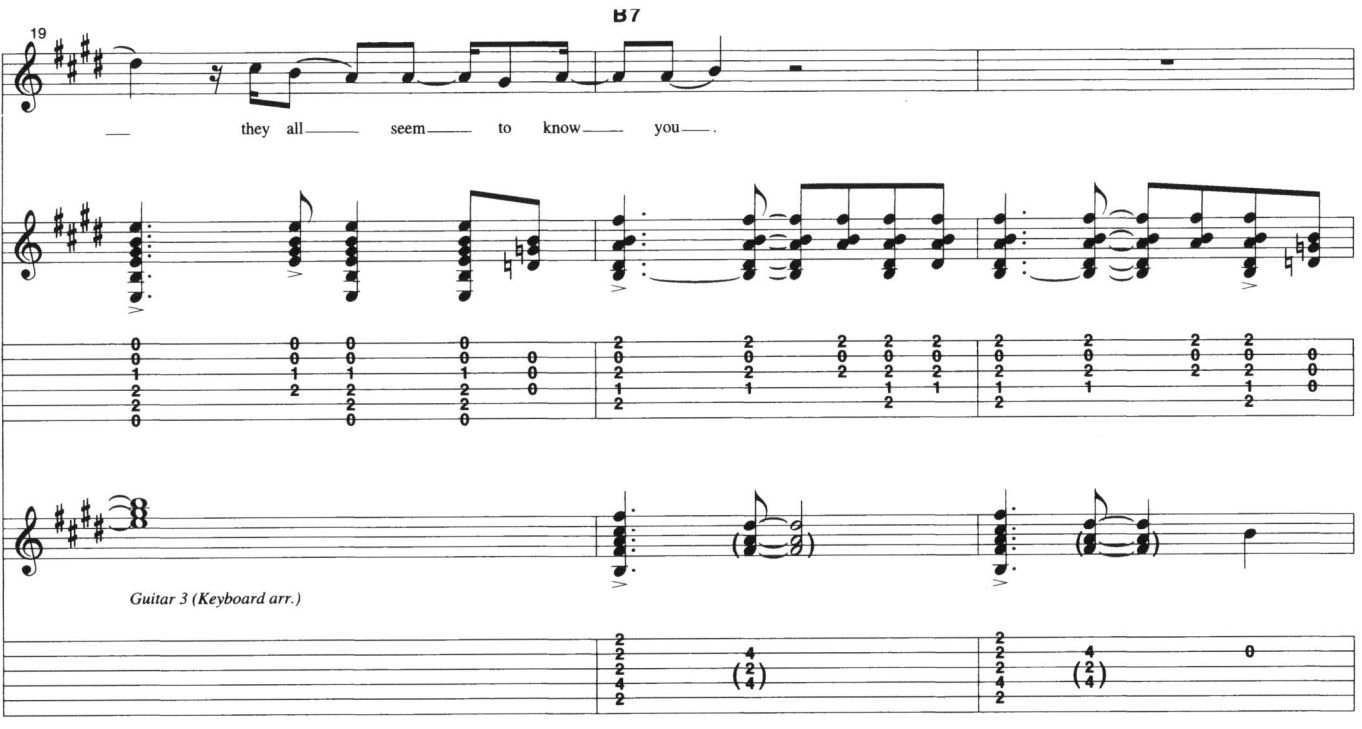

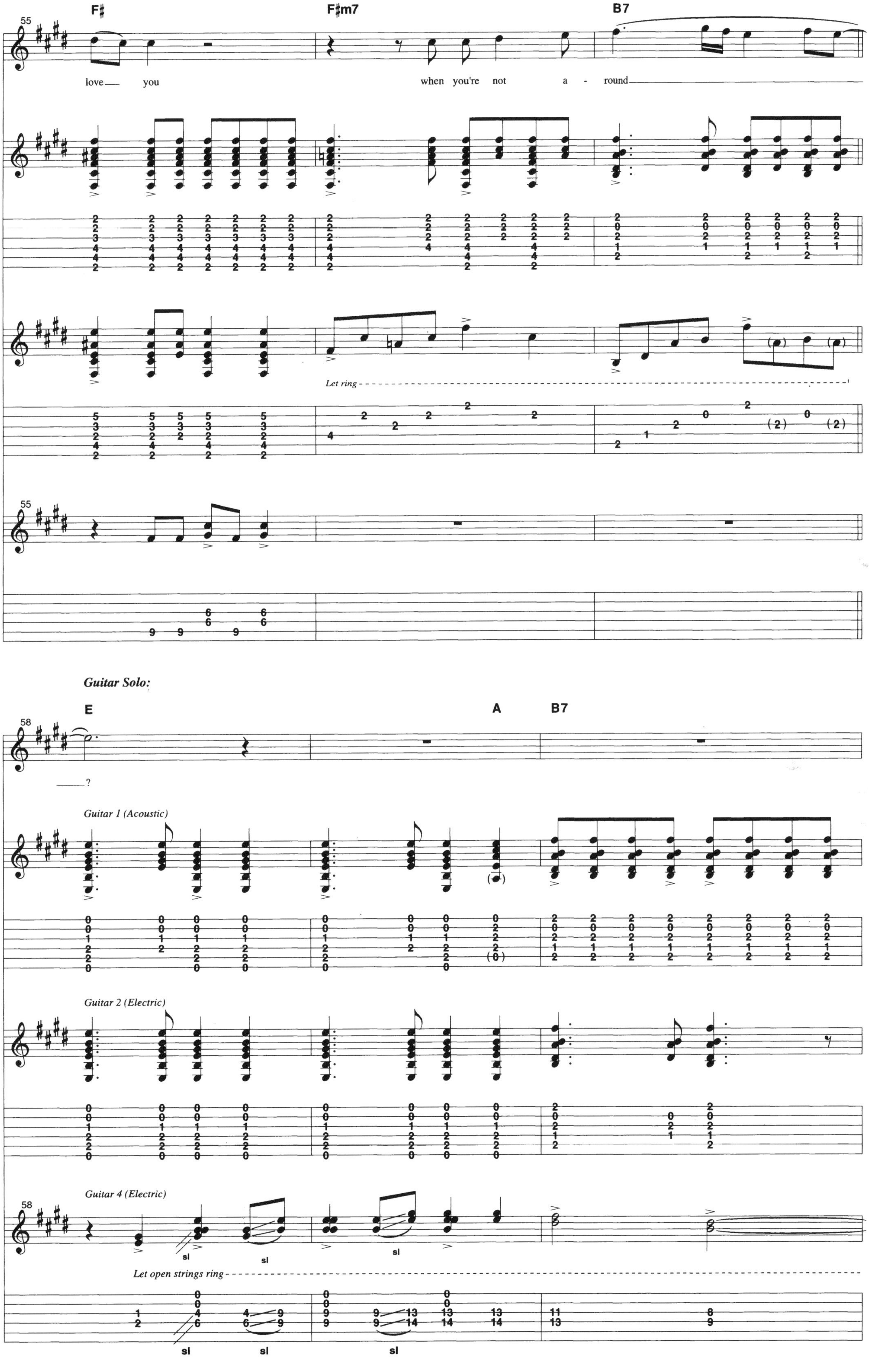
55
F♯
F♯m7
B7
love you when you're not a - round
Let ring
Guitar Solo:
58
E
A
B7
?
Guitar 1 (Acoustic)
Guitar 2 (Electric)
Guitar 4 (Electric)
Let open strings ring
sl

A
B7
sl
61
P
Full
64
E
A
E/G♯
F♯m
B7
3
There's so man - y
8va

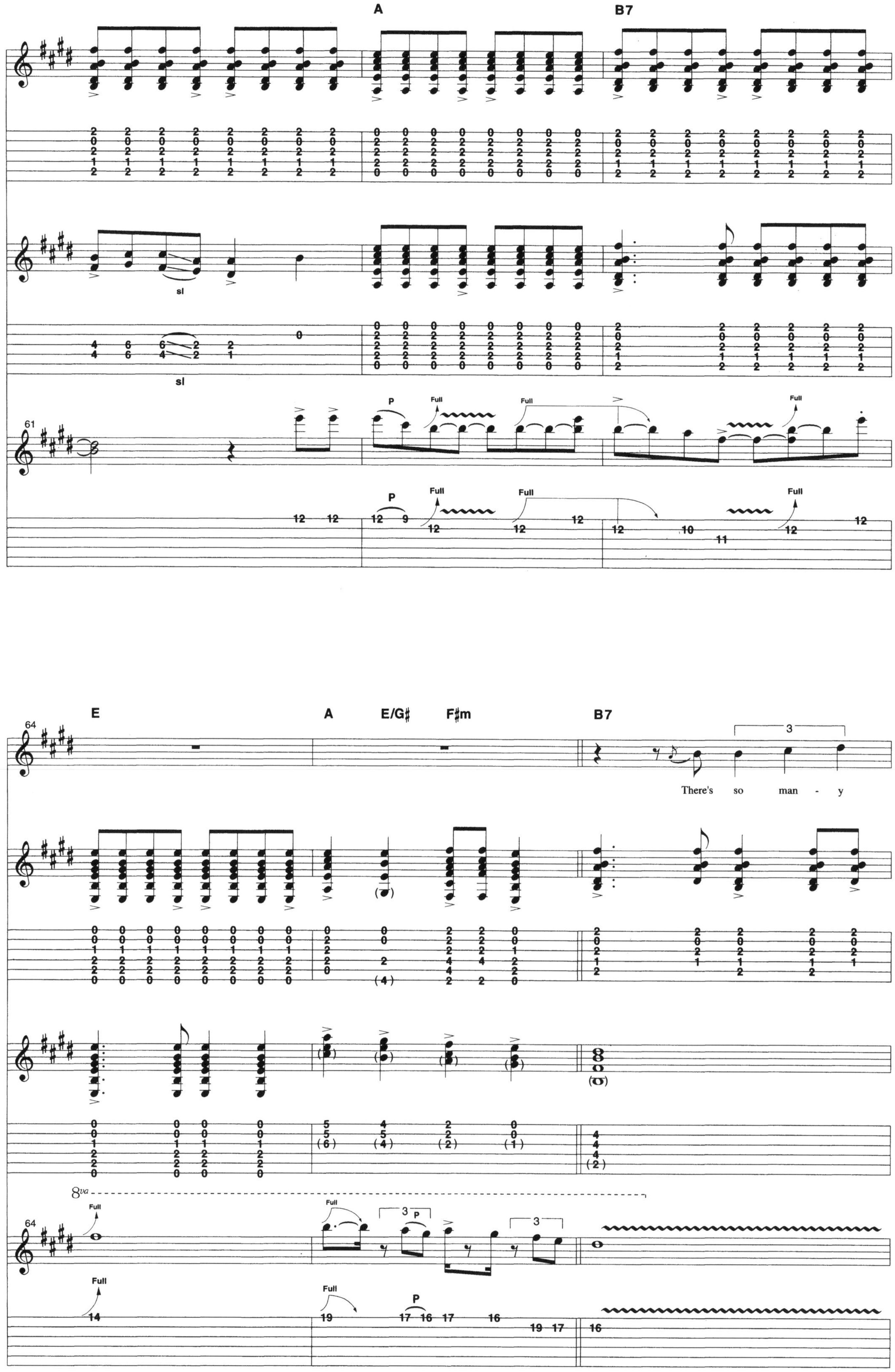

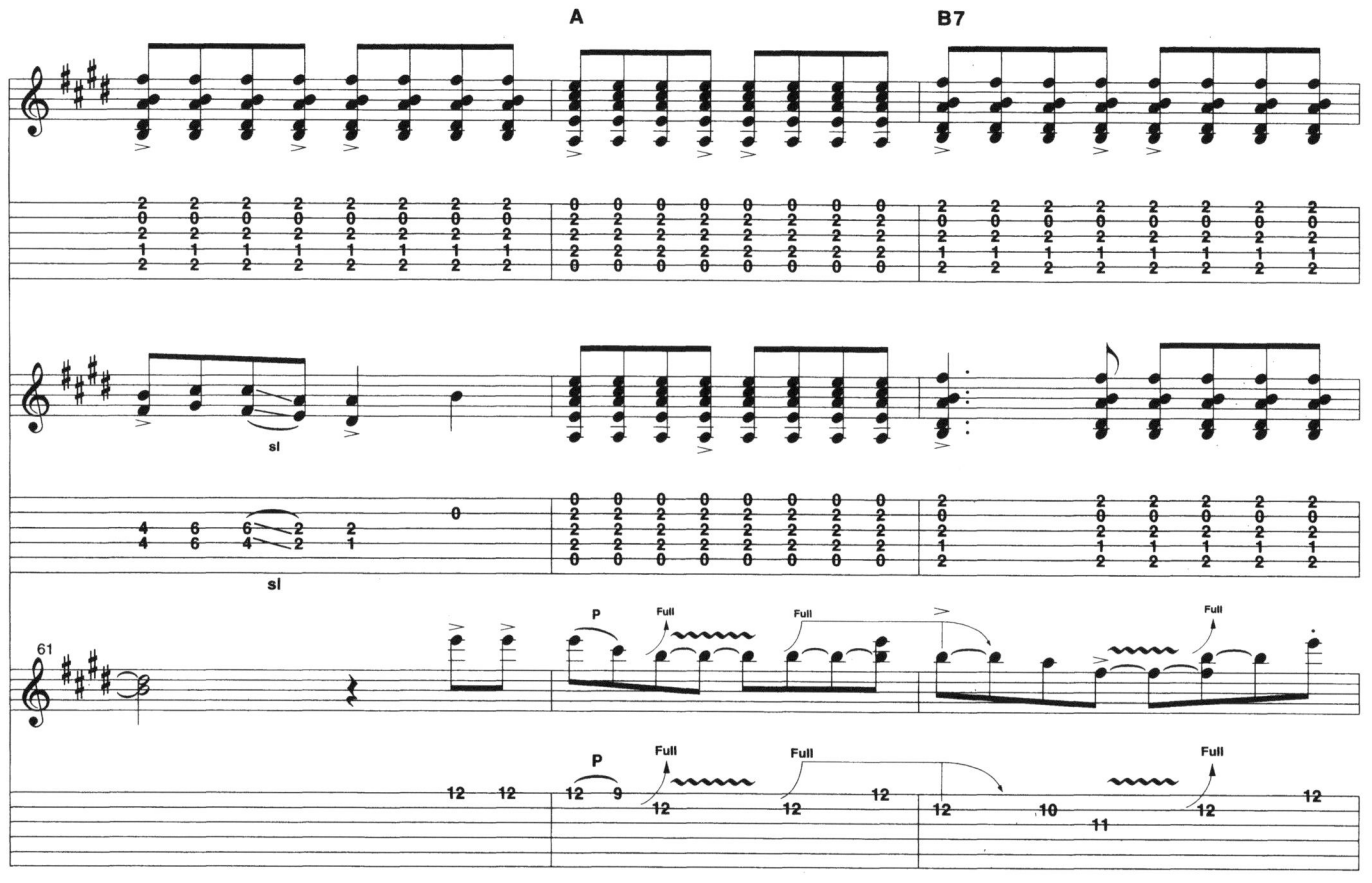

F♯
Am7
C/D
D7
hold her. Tears on your shoulder.
Verse 3:
G
Am7
D
There's talk on the street it's there to re - mind you
Guitar 1 (Acoustic)
Continued simile
Guitar 2 (Electric)
Guitar 4 (Electric)

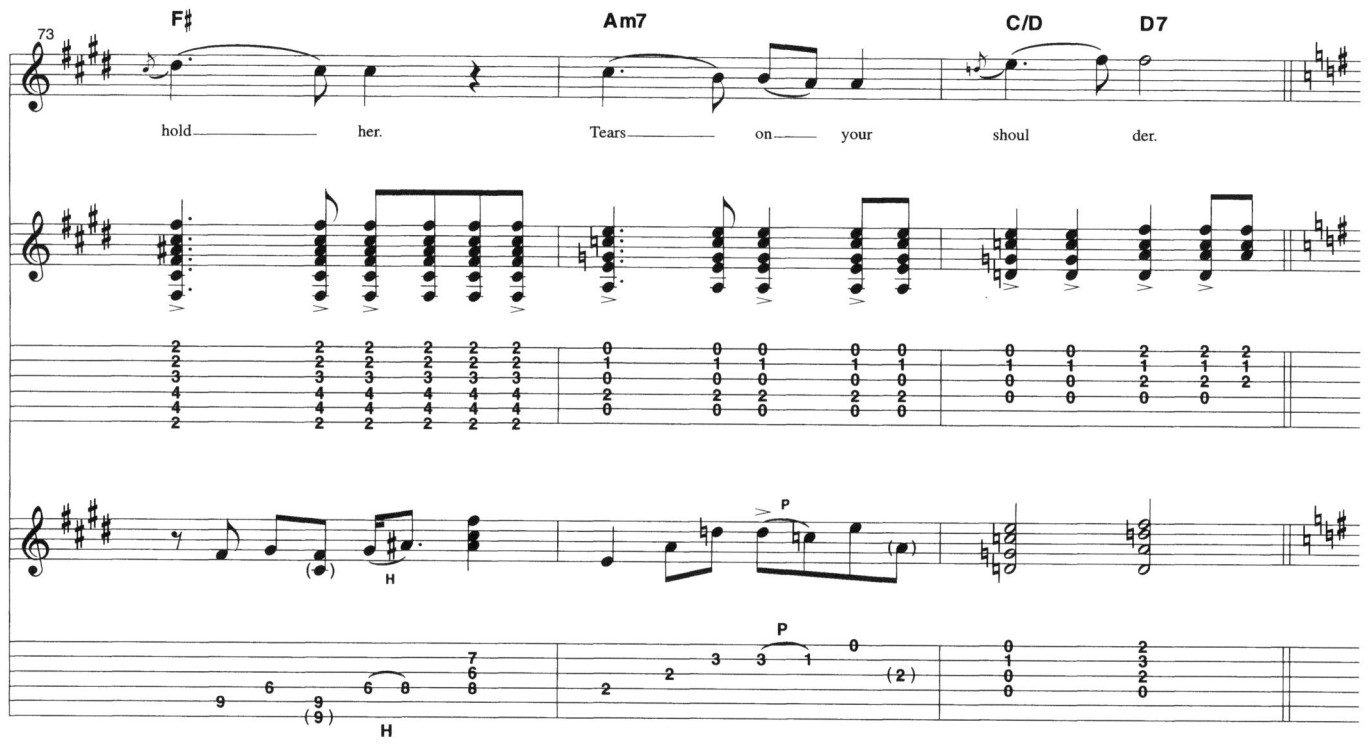

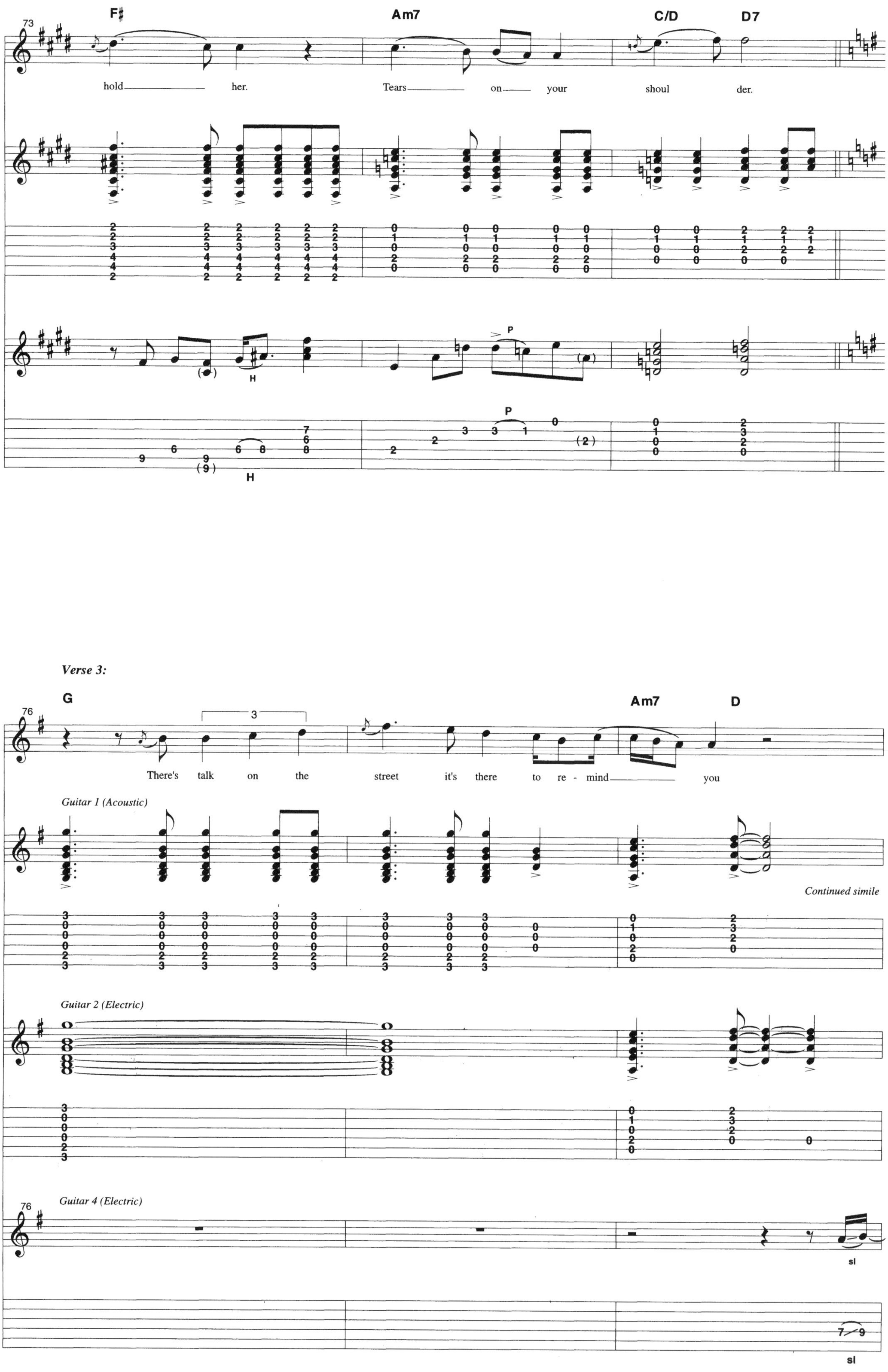

79
Am7
D
C
D
G
that it does - n't real - ly mat ter which side
Guitar 2 (Electric)
Guitar 4 (Electric)
sl
P

82
Am7
D
G
you're on.
You're walk - in' a - way
Guitar 3 (Keyboard arr.)
Guitar 2 (Electric)
Guitar 4 (Electric)
Full
1/2
sl
P

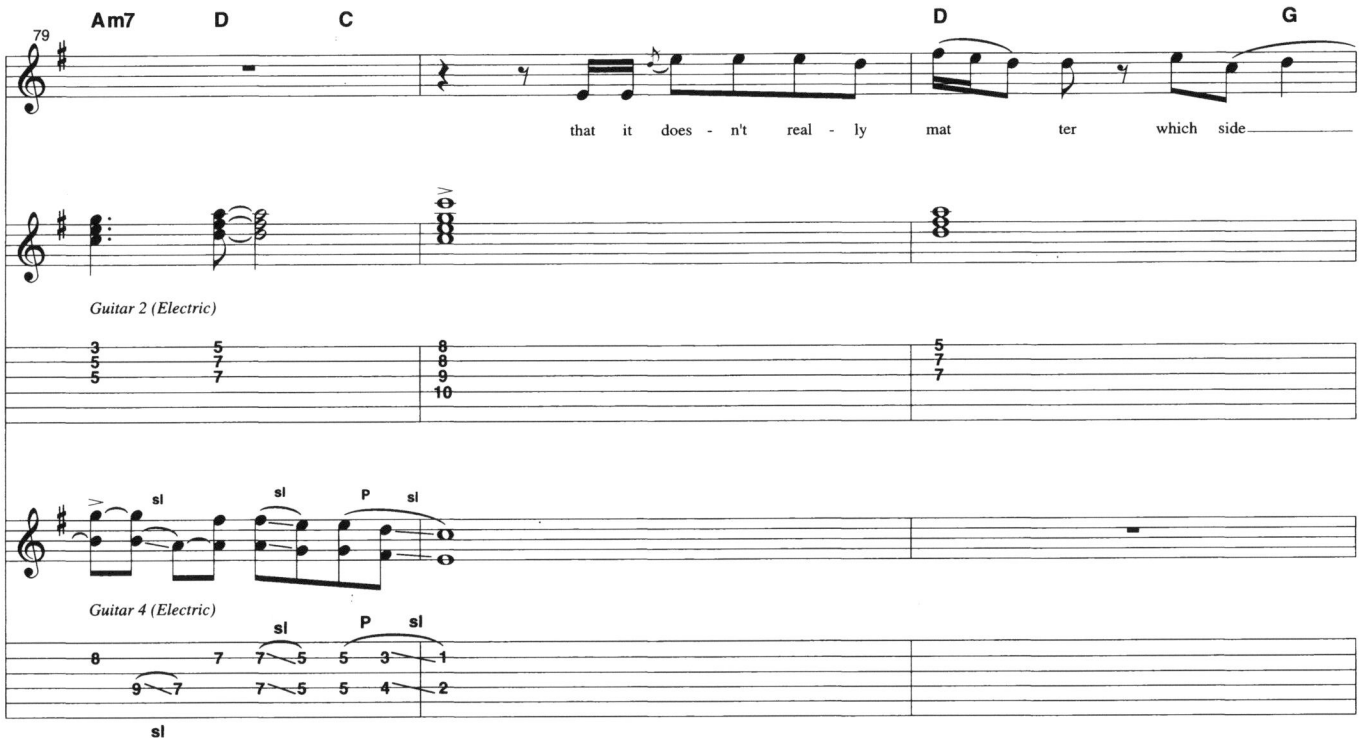

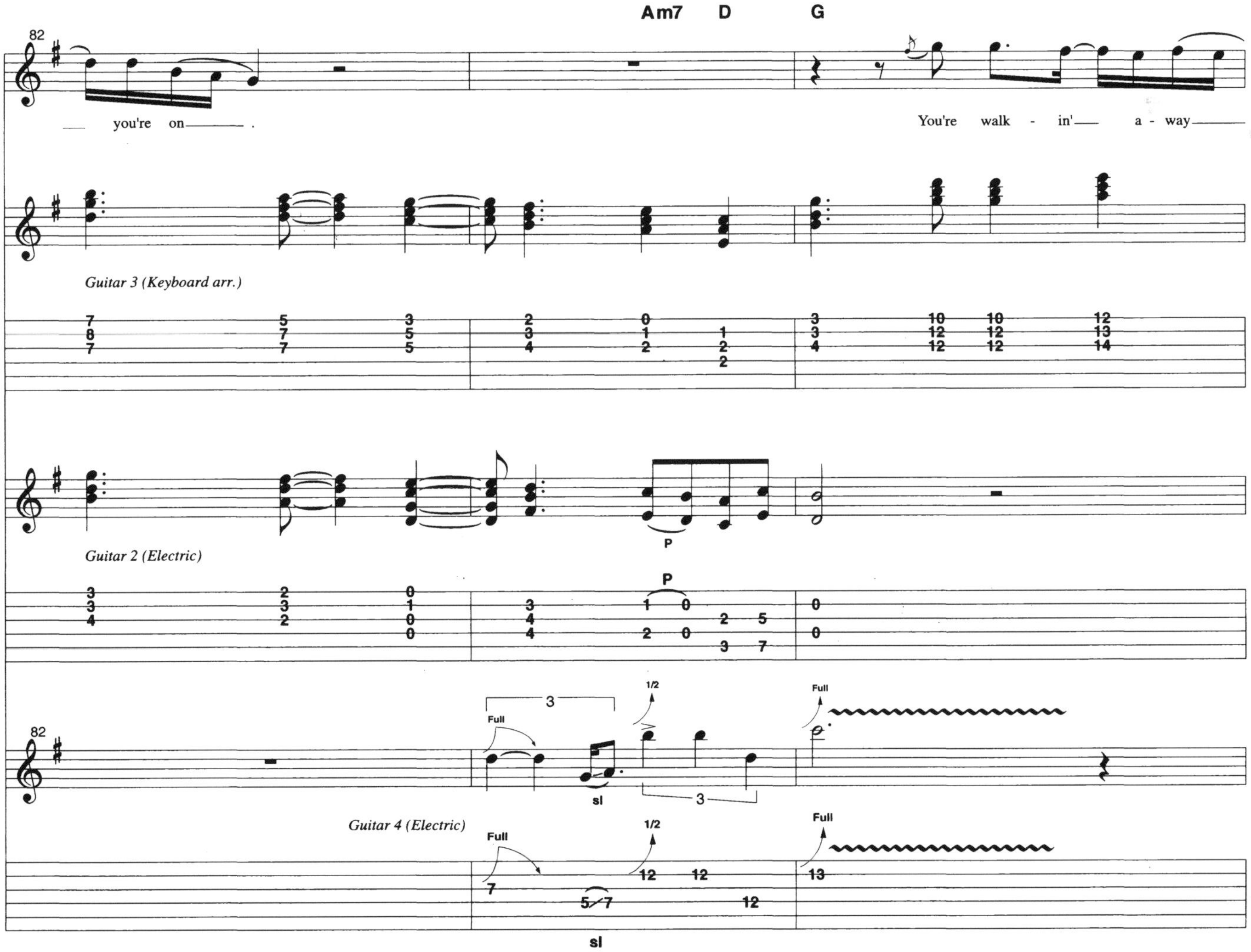

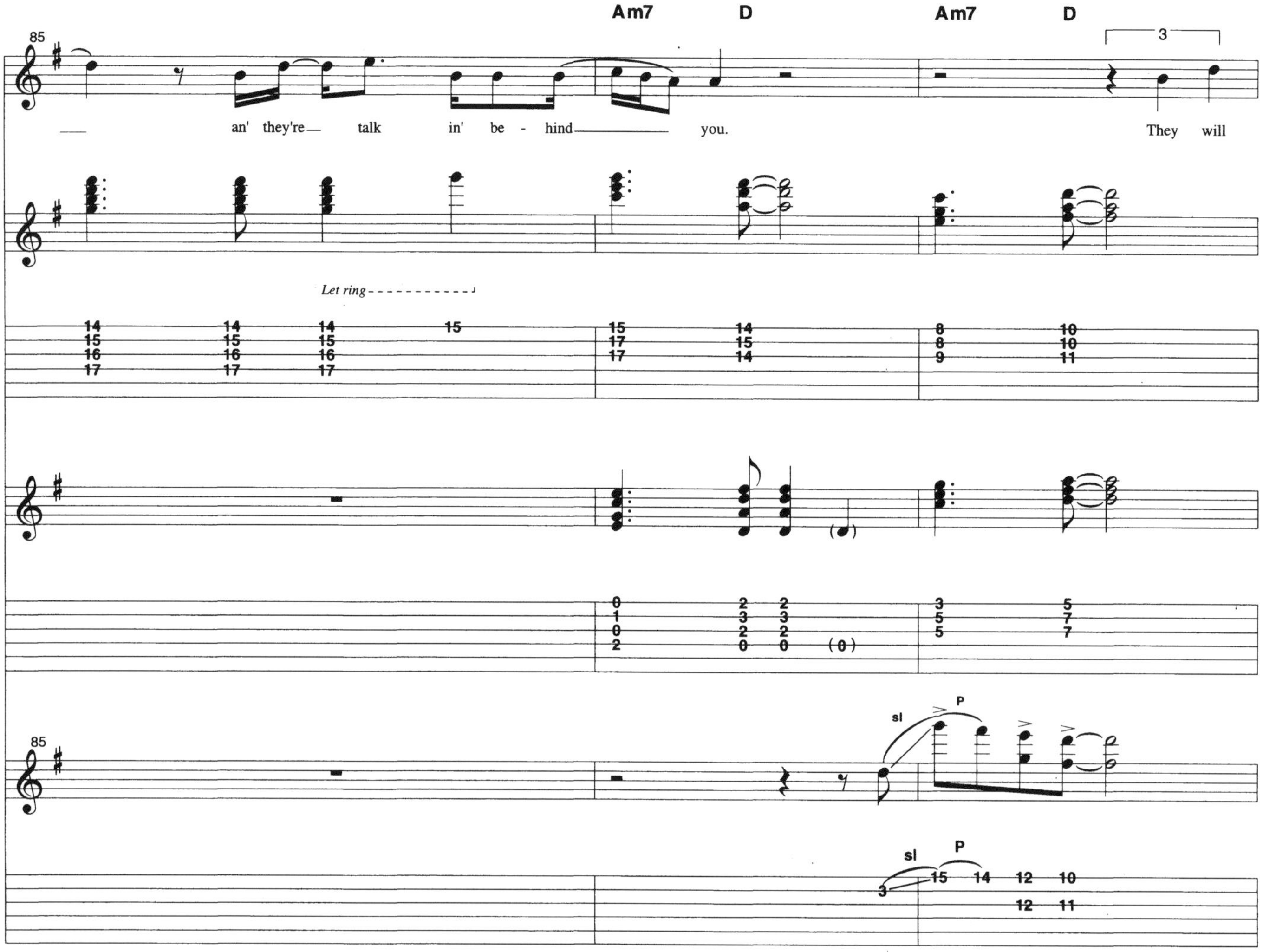
Am7 D Am7 D
85
an' they're talk in' be - hind you. They will
Let ring
sl P

C D G
88
nev - er for - get you til' some - bod - y new comes a long.
Guitar 3 (Keyboard arr.)
Guitar 2 (Electric)
sl

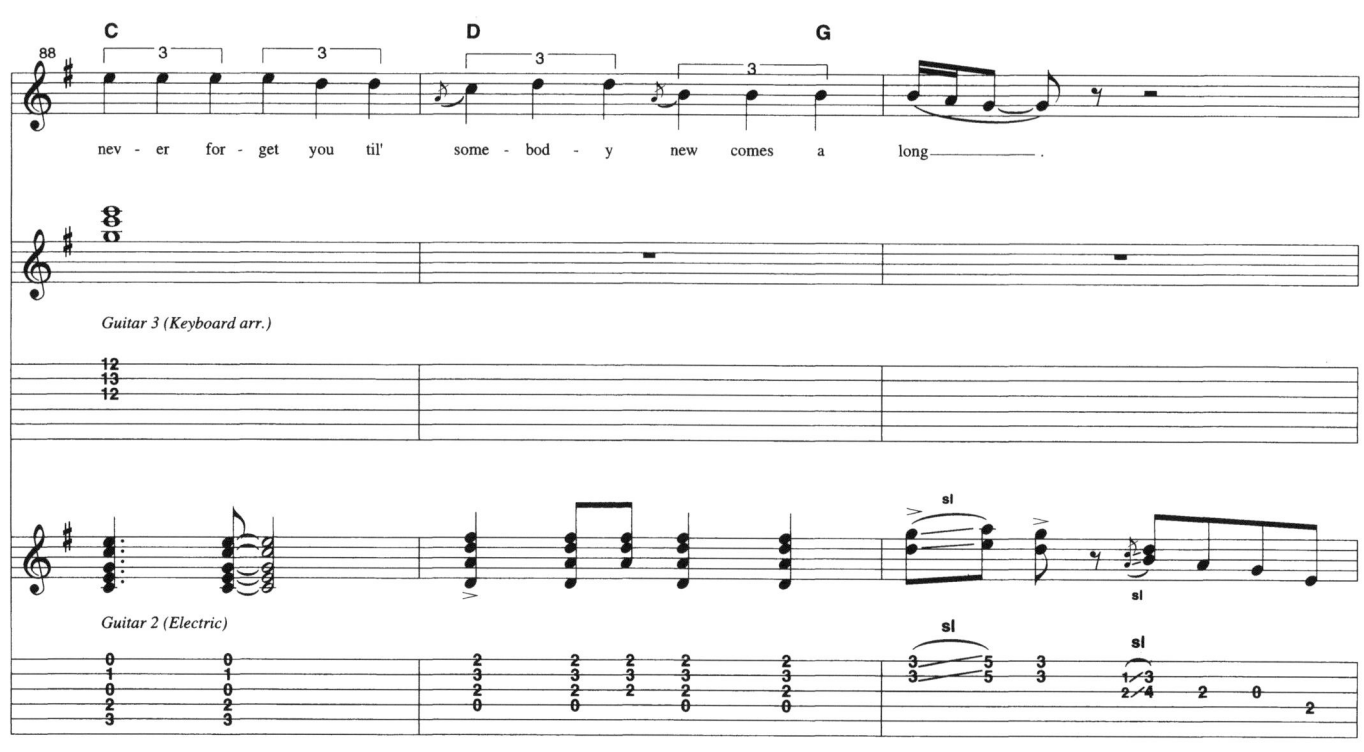

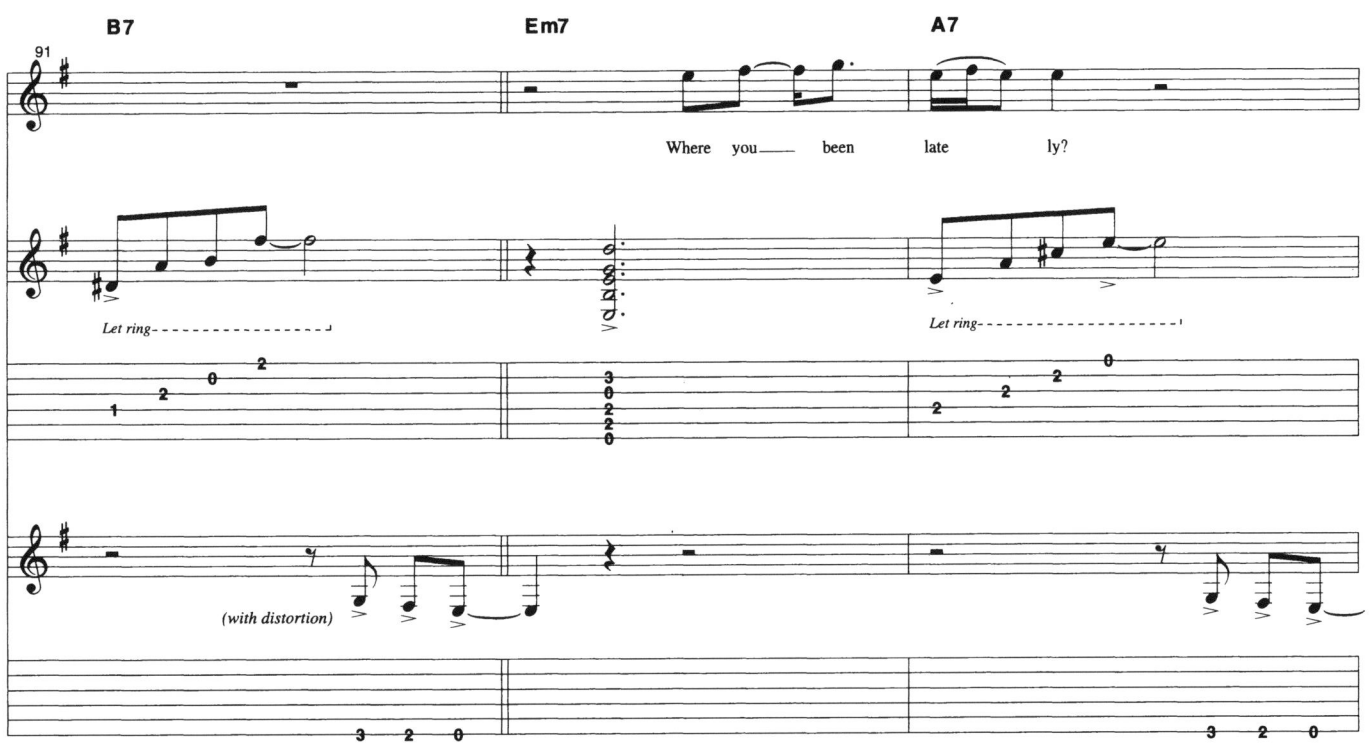

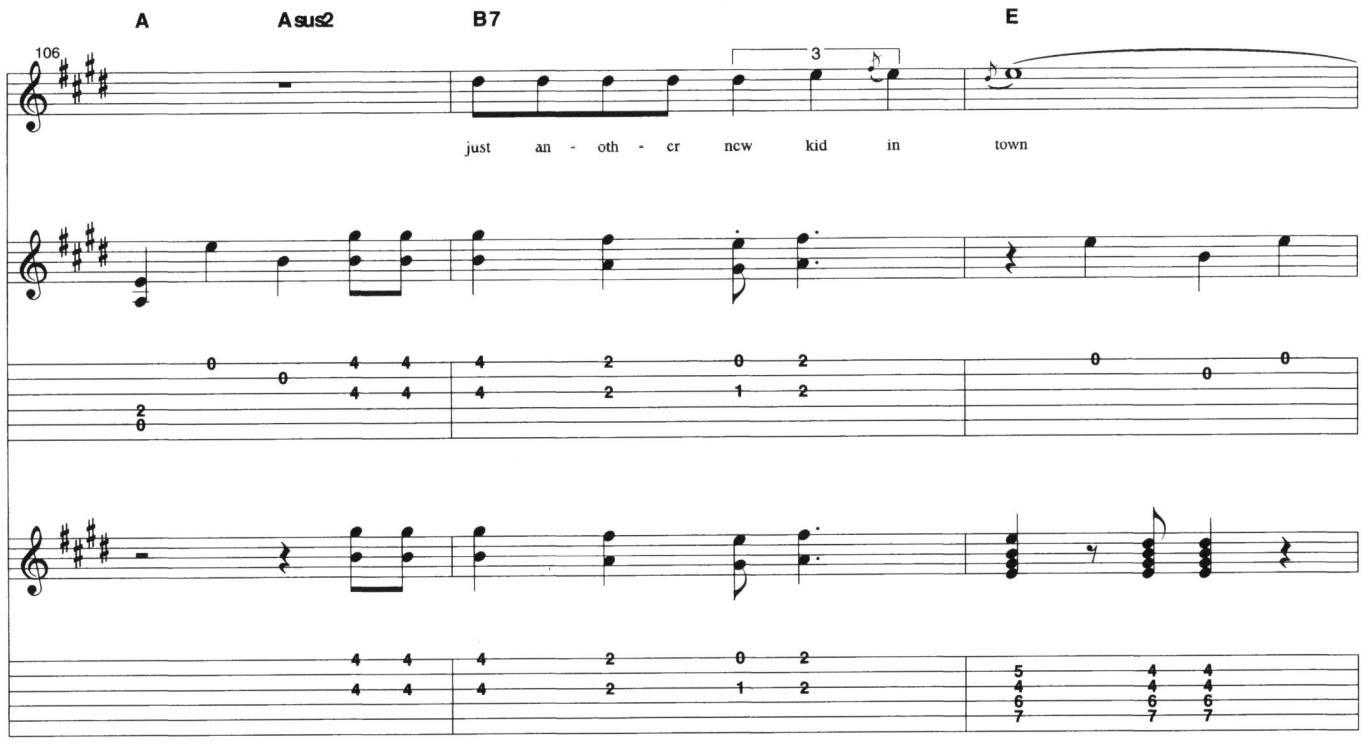
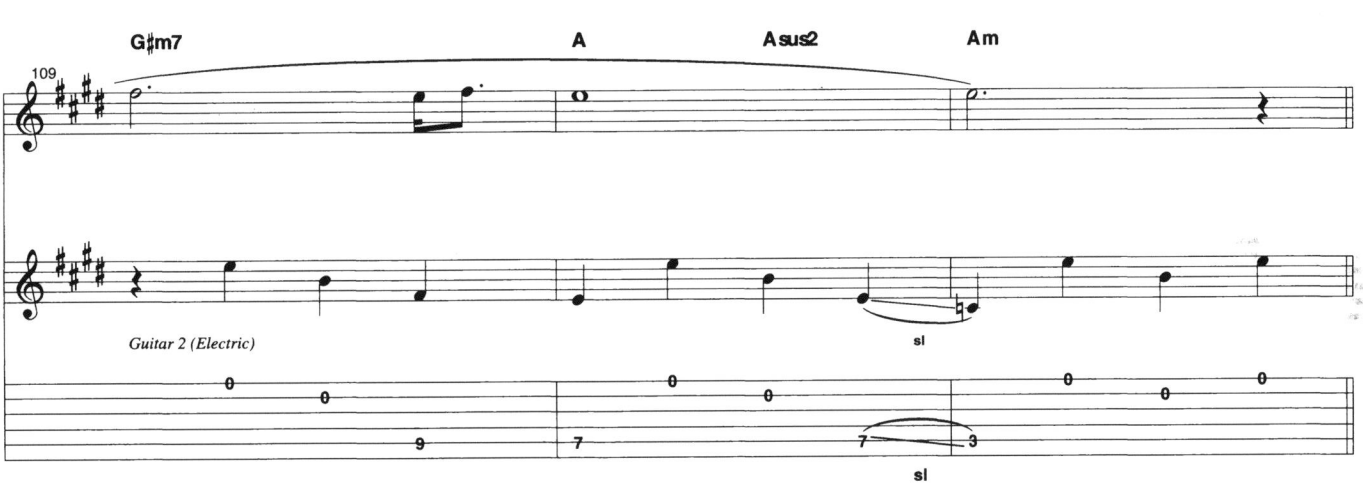

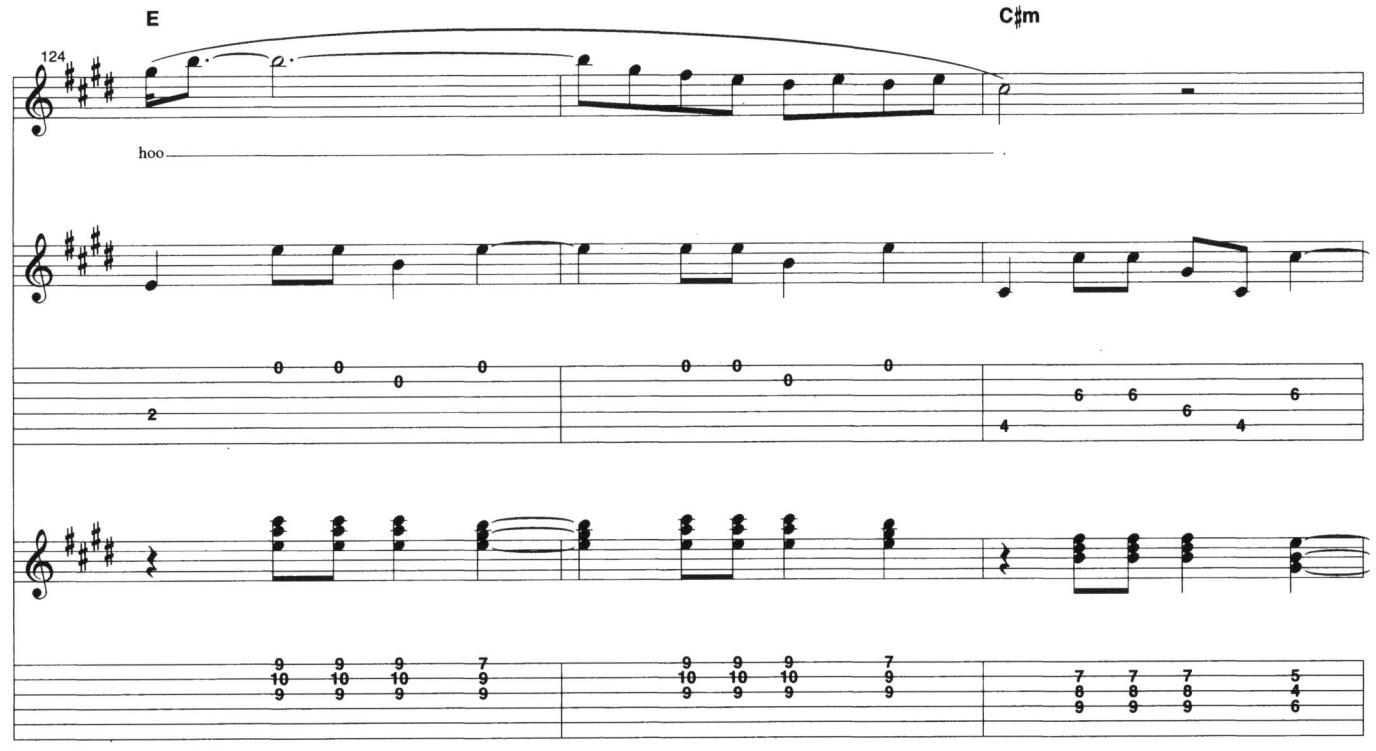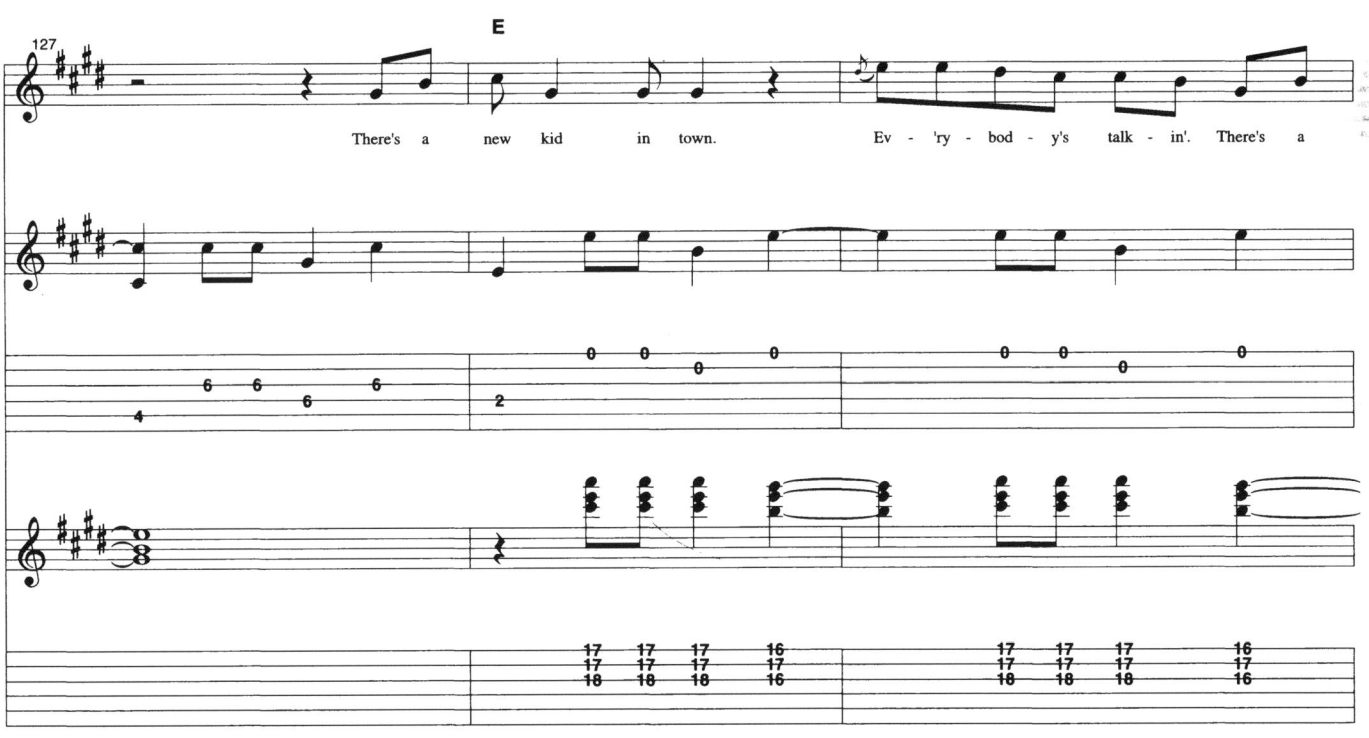

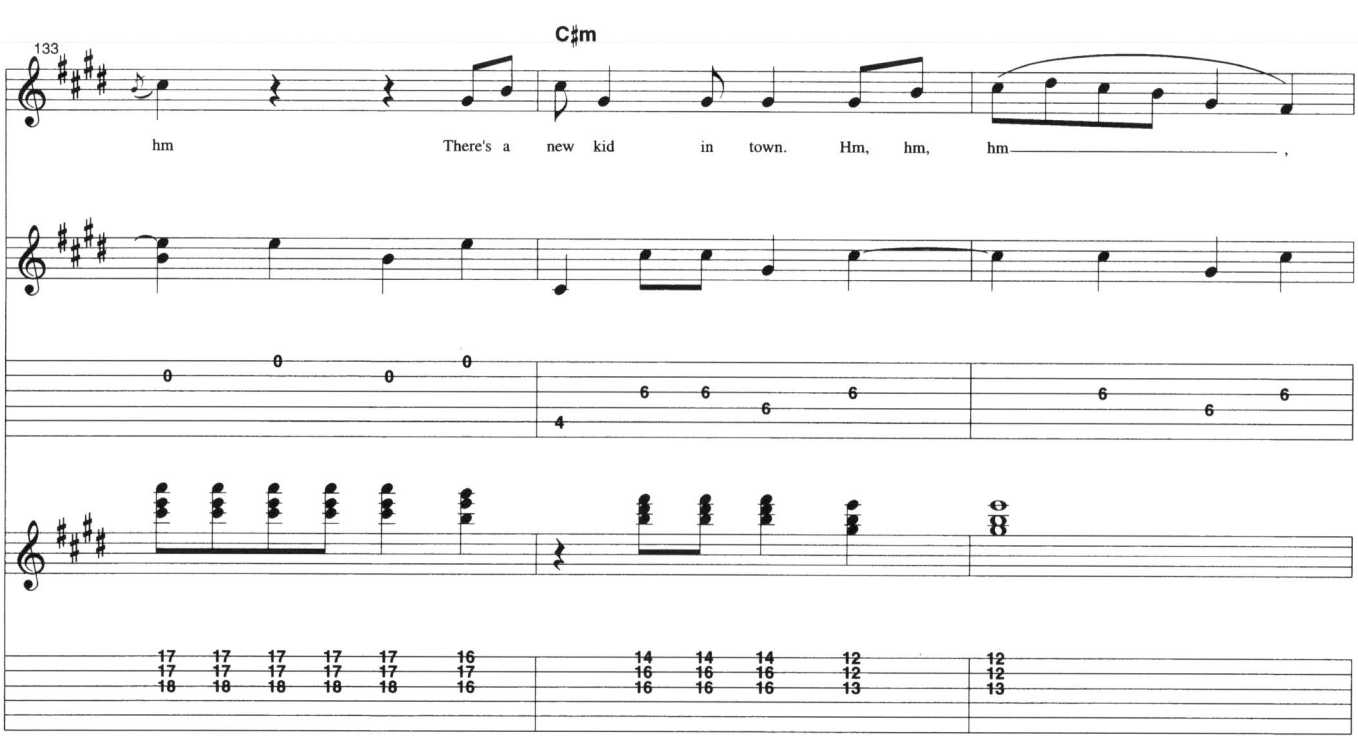

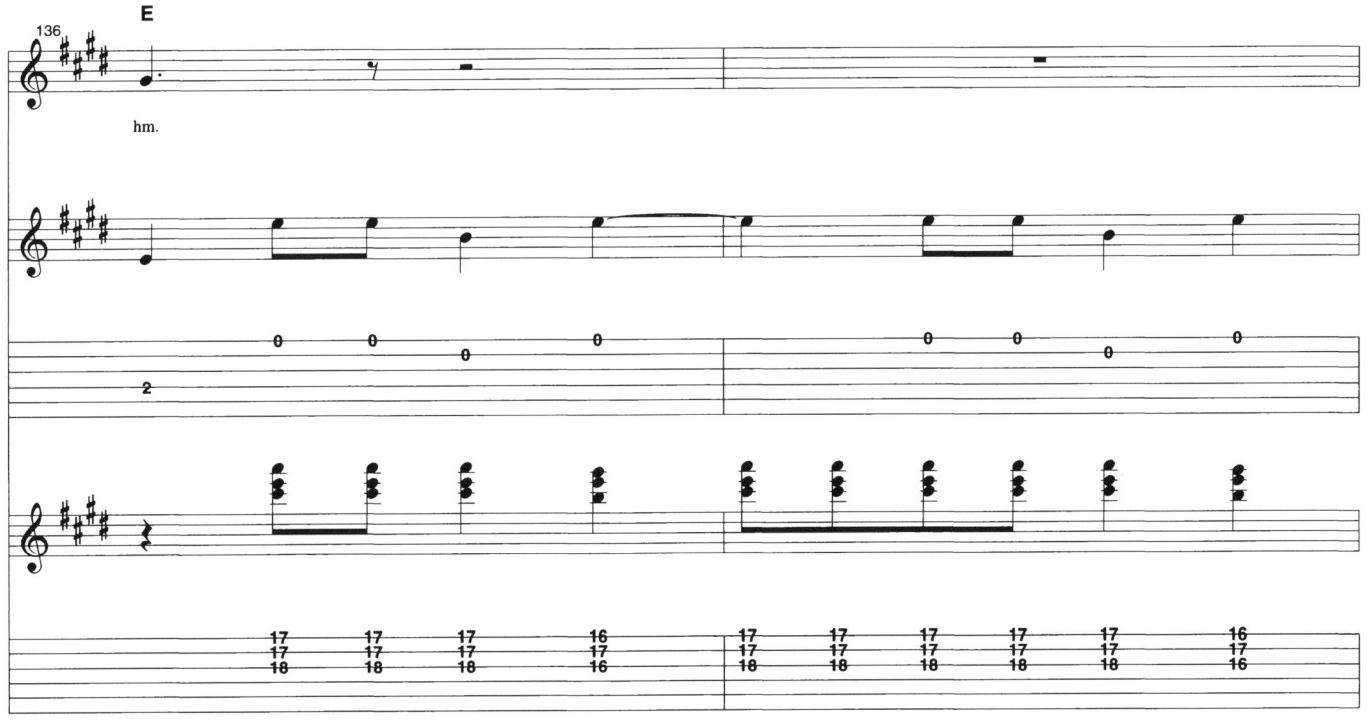
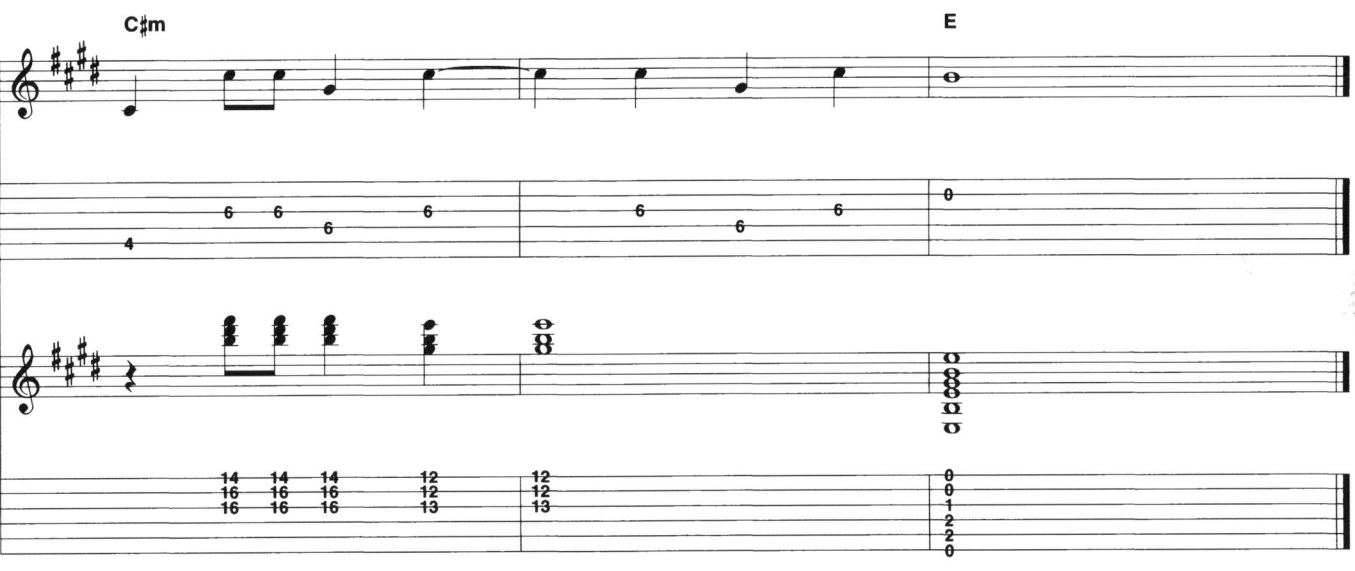

97

Lyin' Eyes

Words and Music by DON HENLEY and GLENN FREY

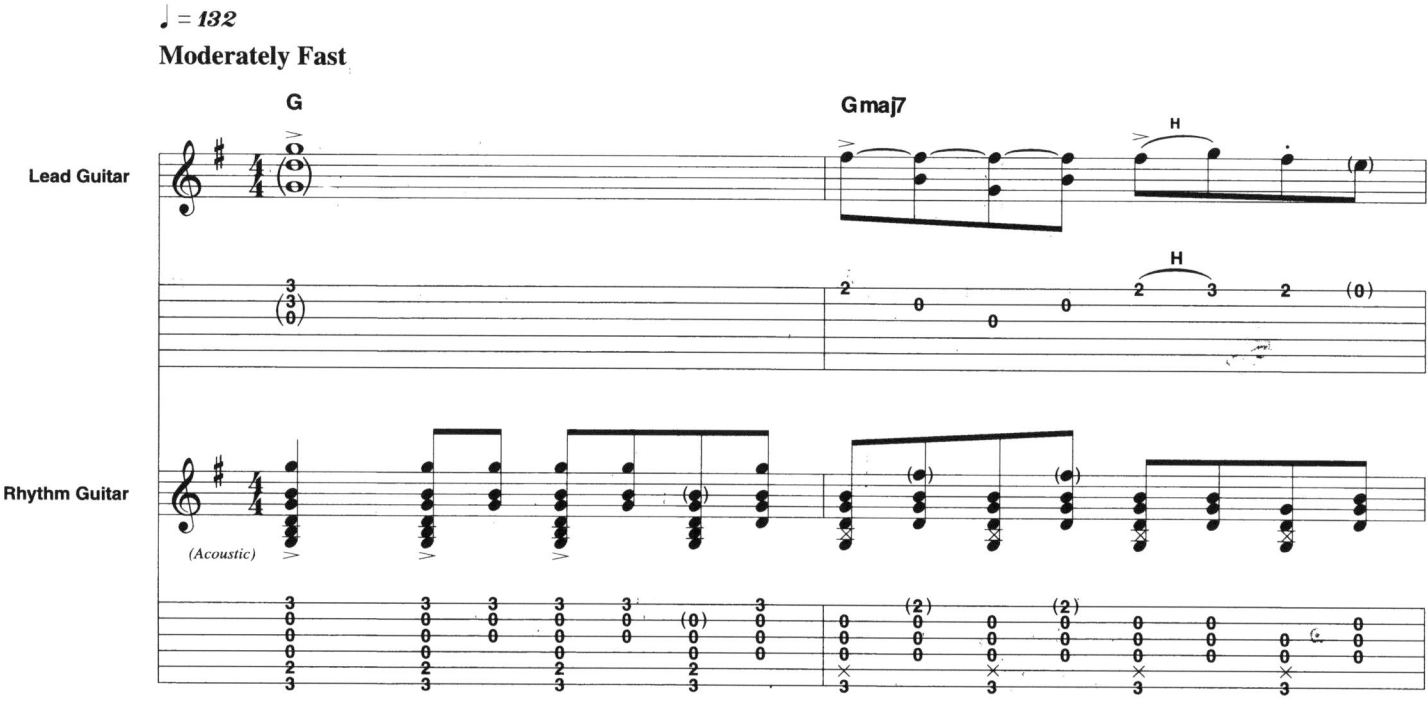

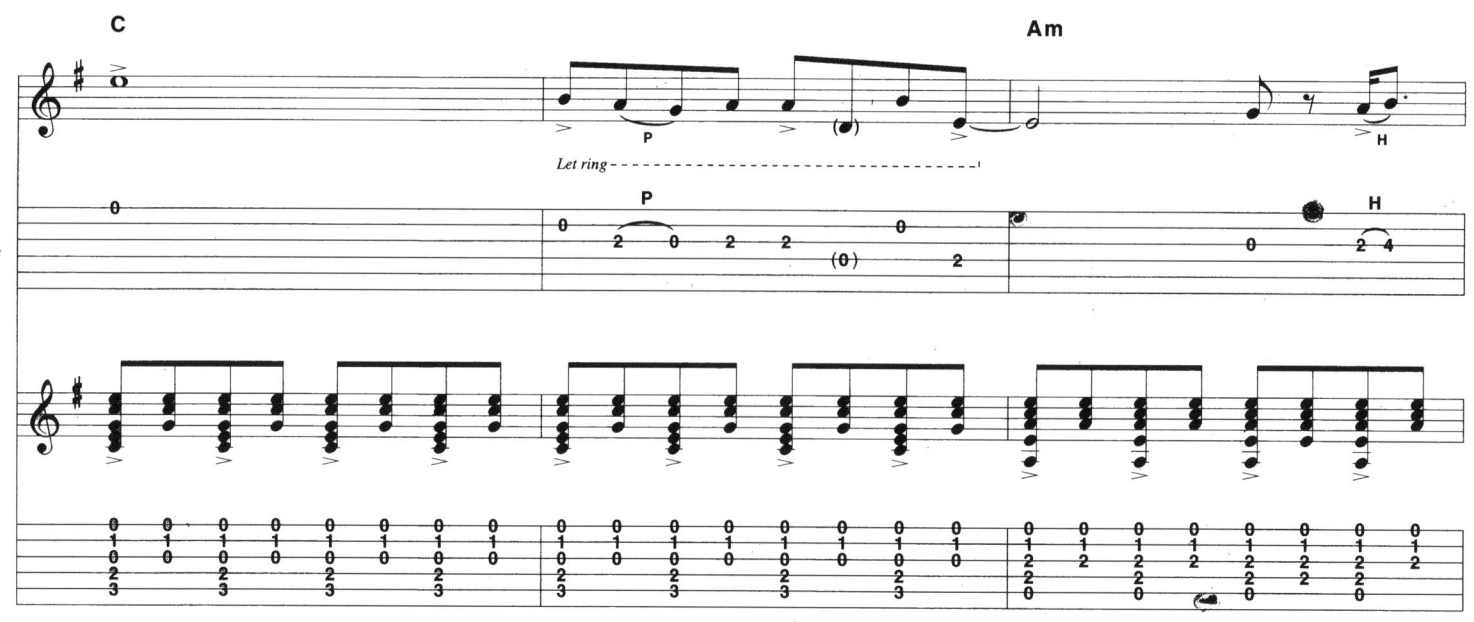

© 1975 & 1996 Benchmark Music and Kicking Bear Music, USA
Warner/Chappell Music Ltd, London W1Y 3FA

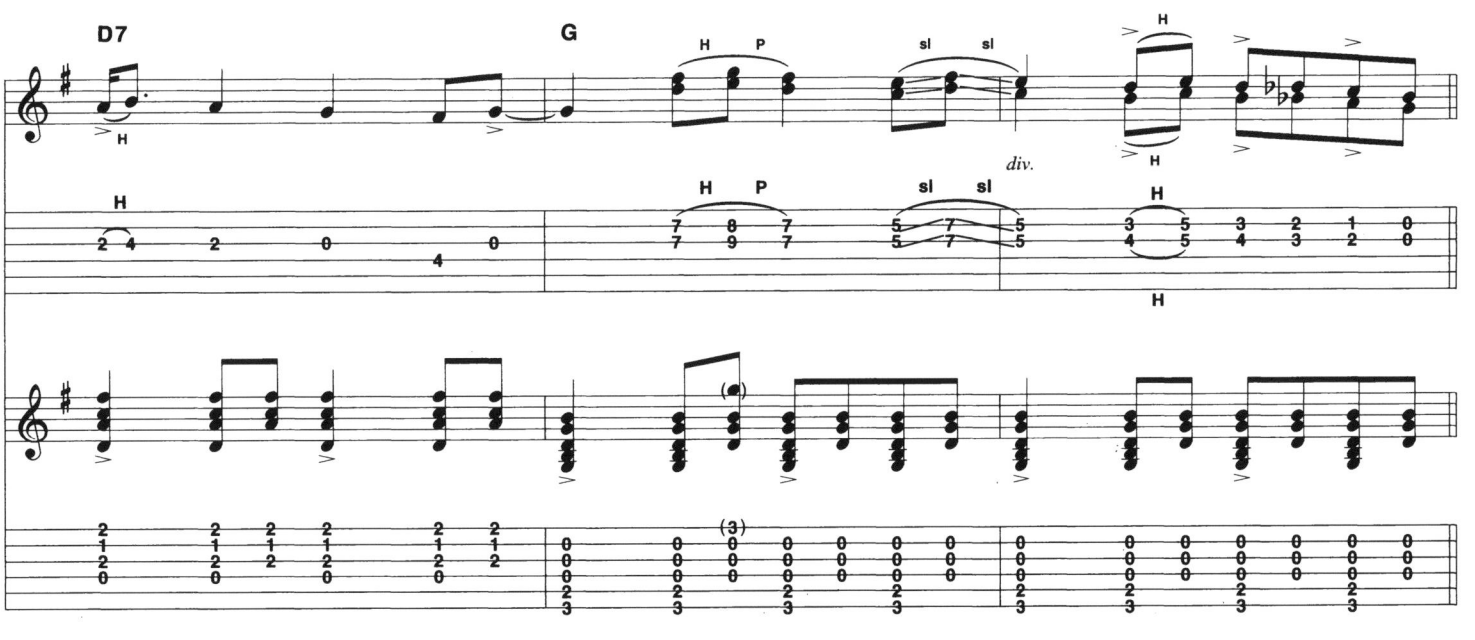

Verse 1:

City girls just seem to find out early how to open doors with just a smile

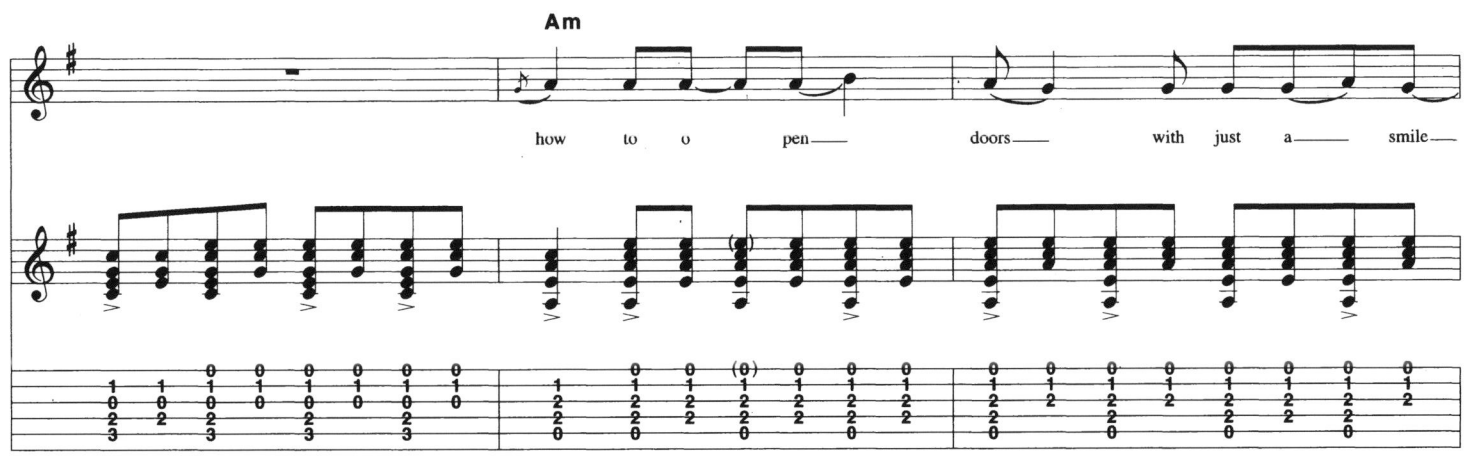

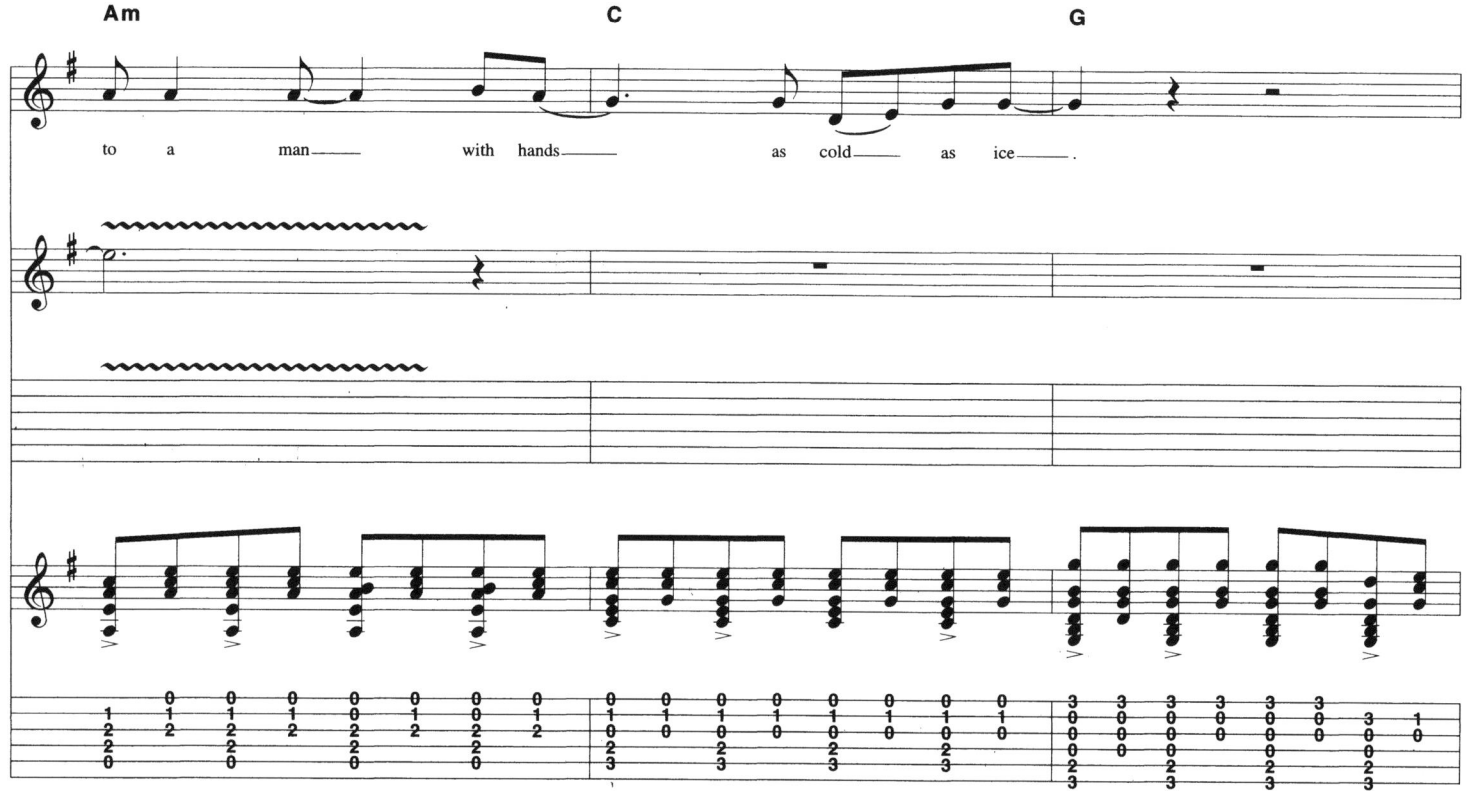

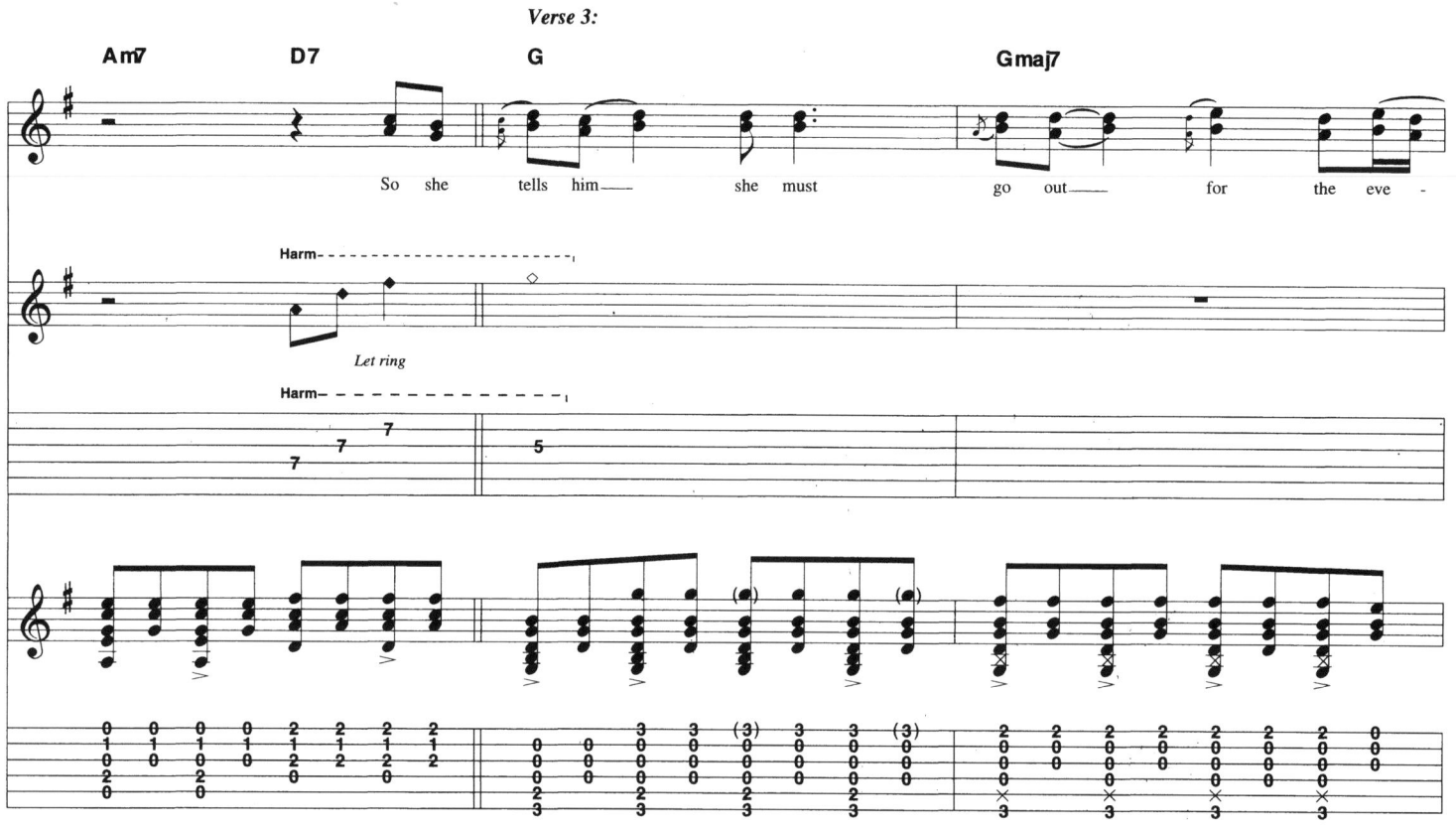

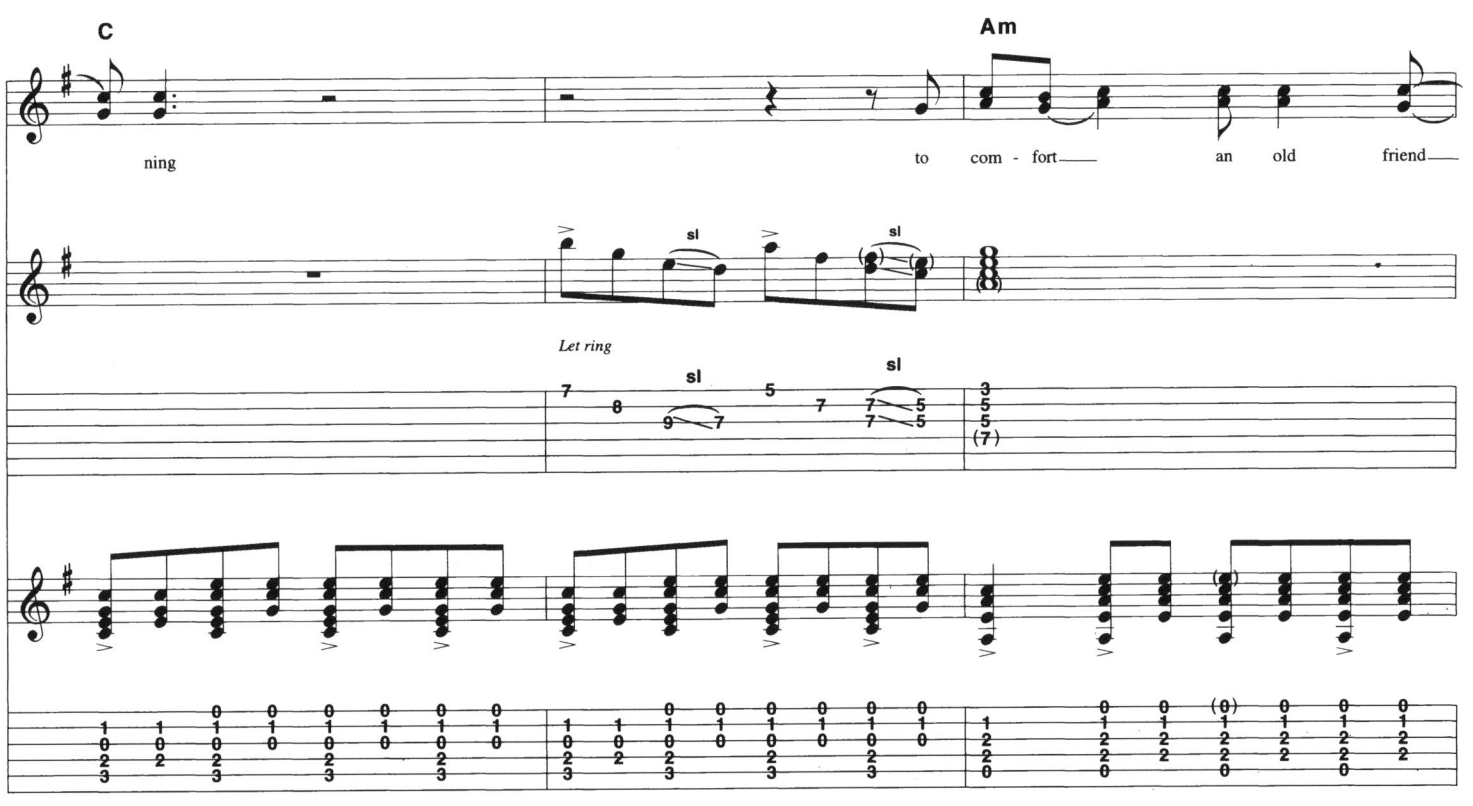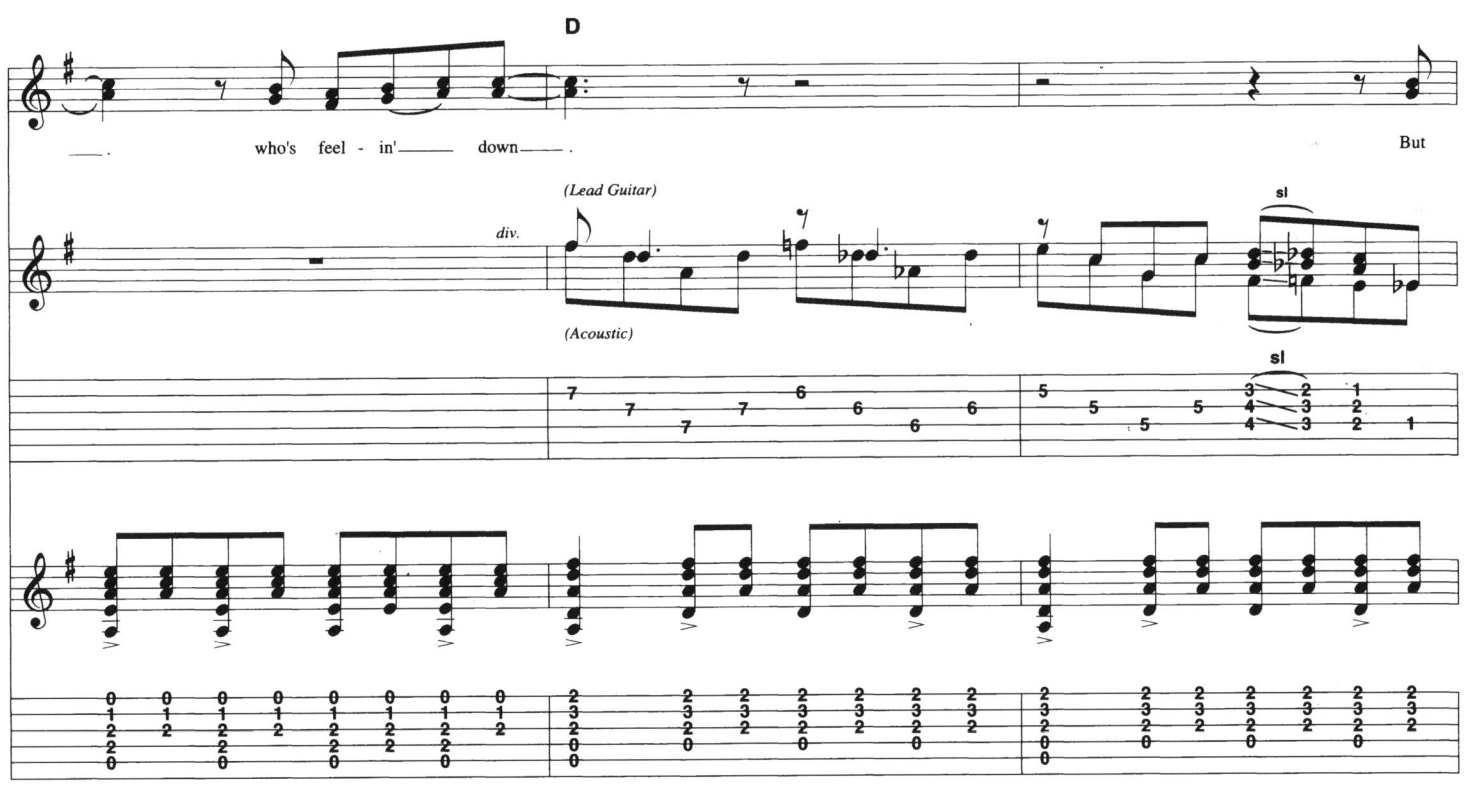

103

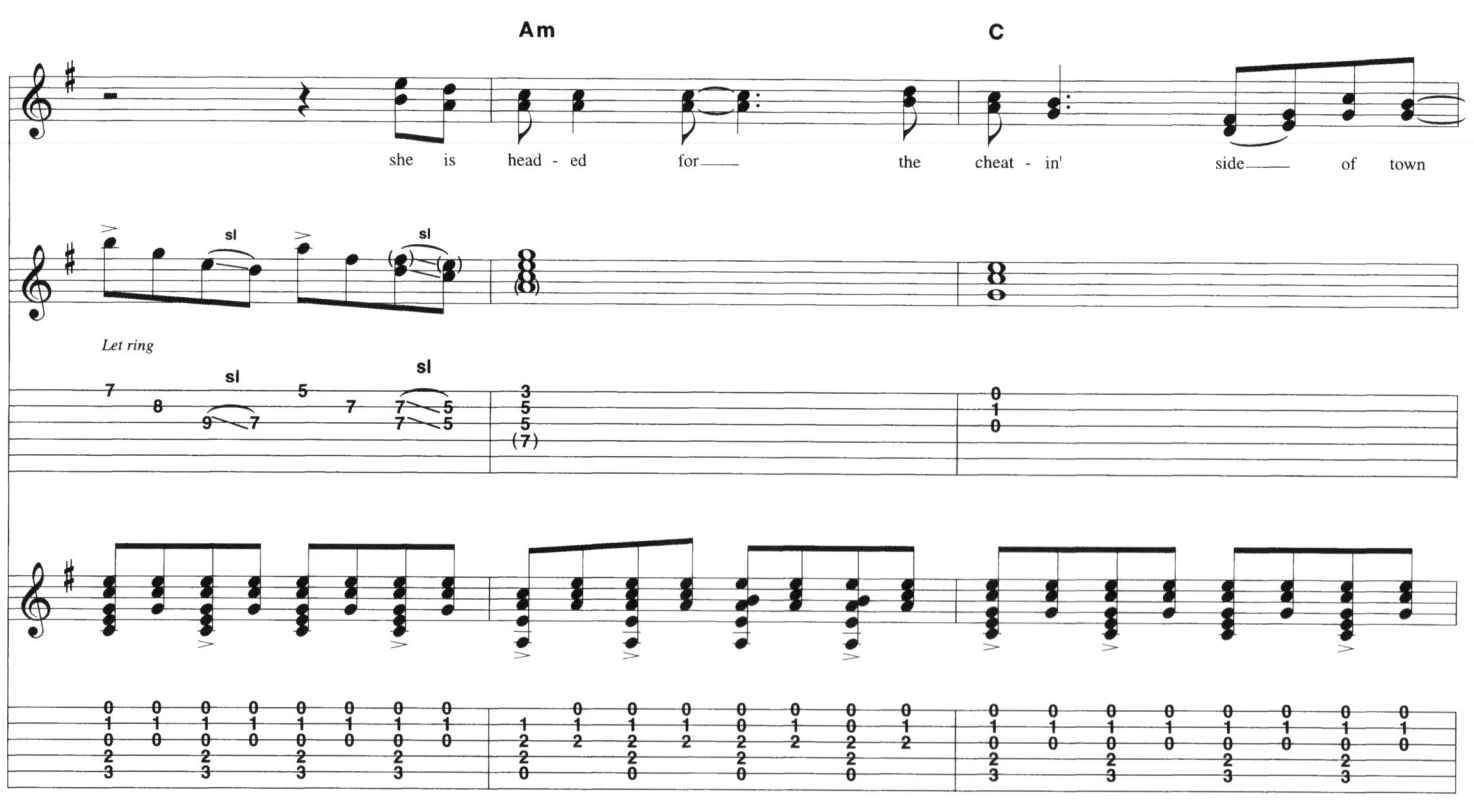

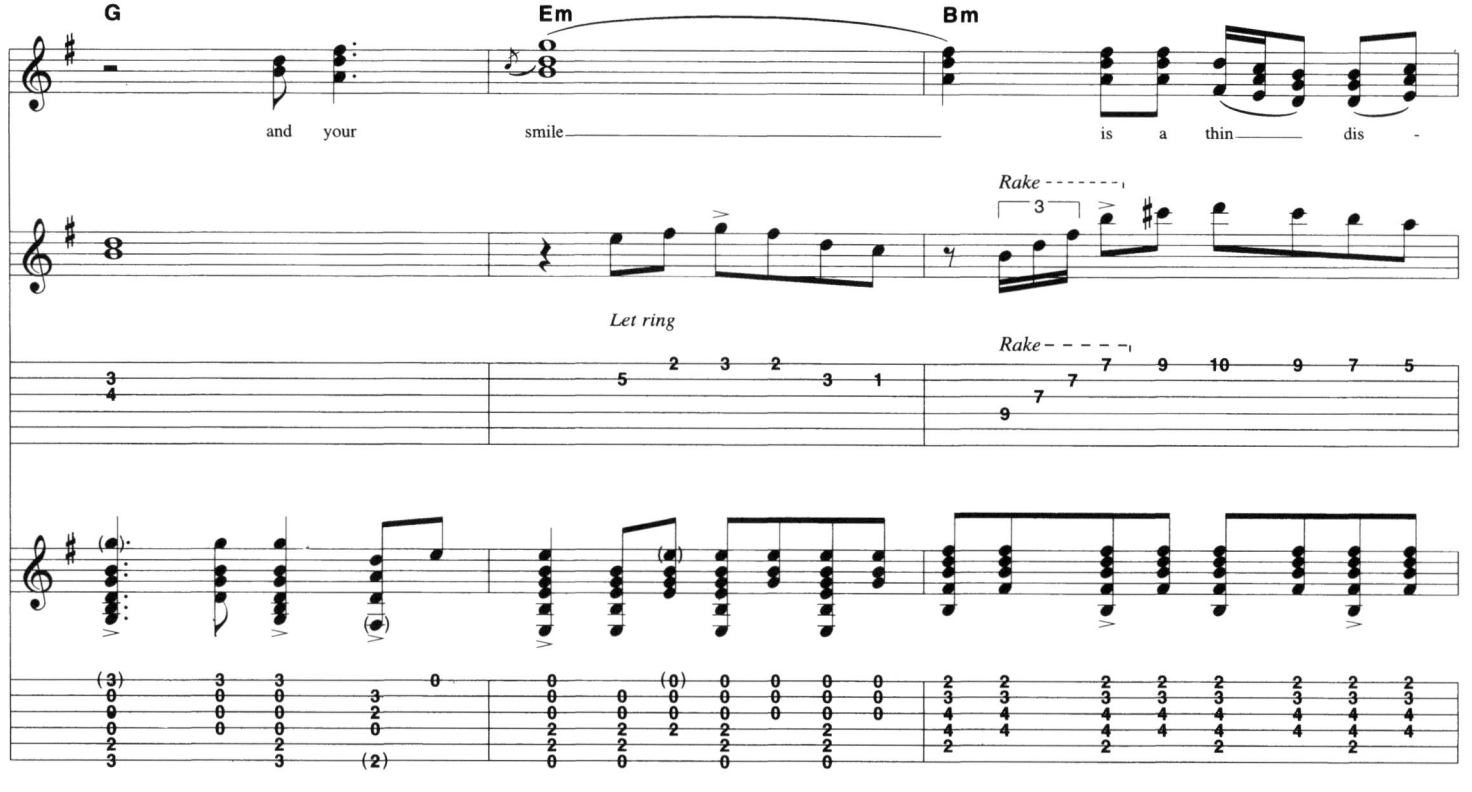

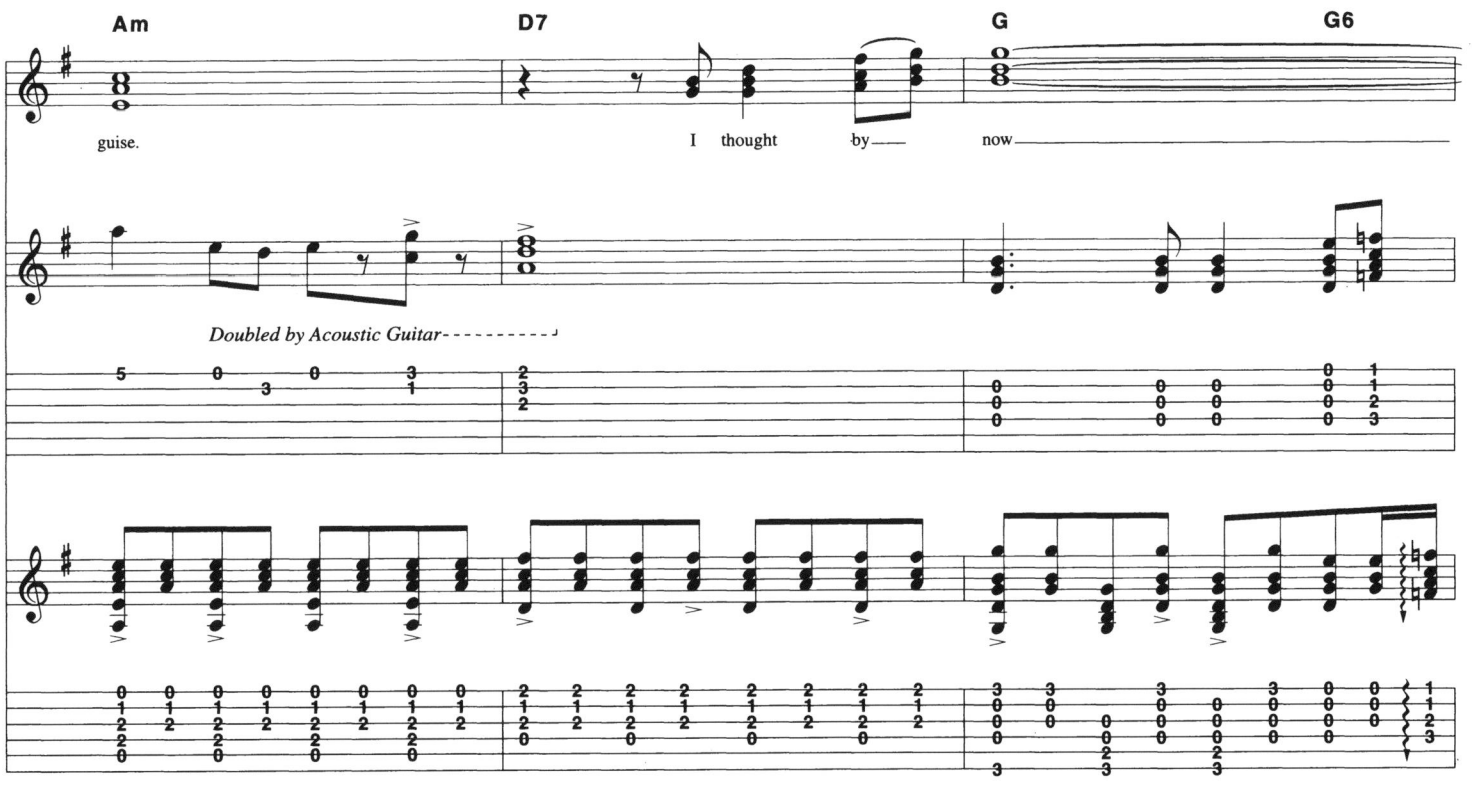
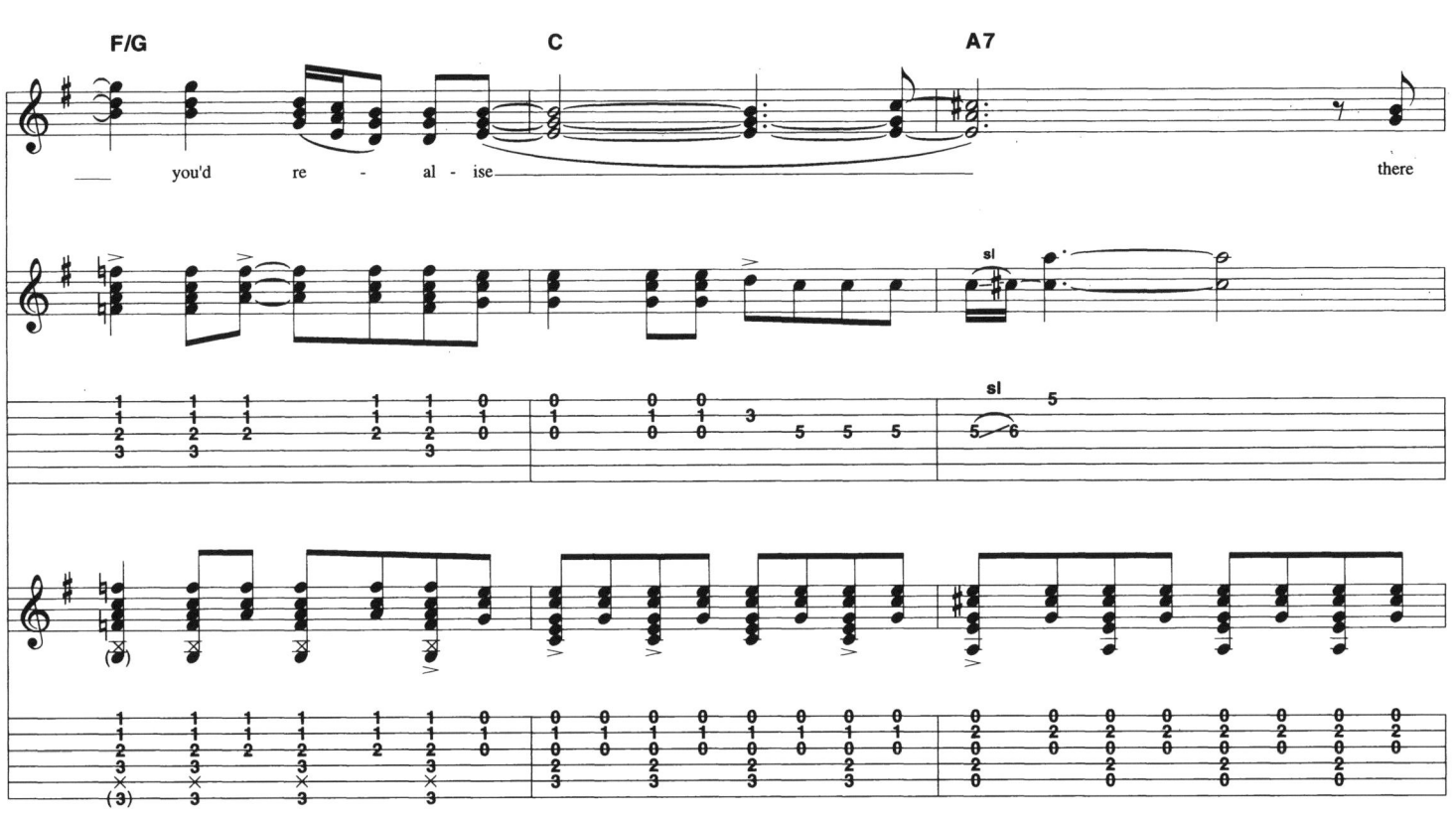

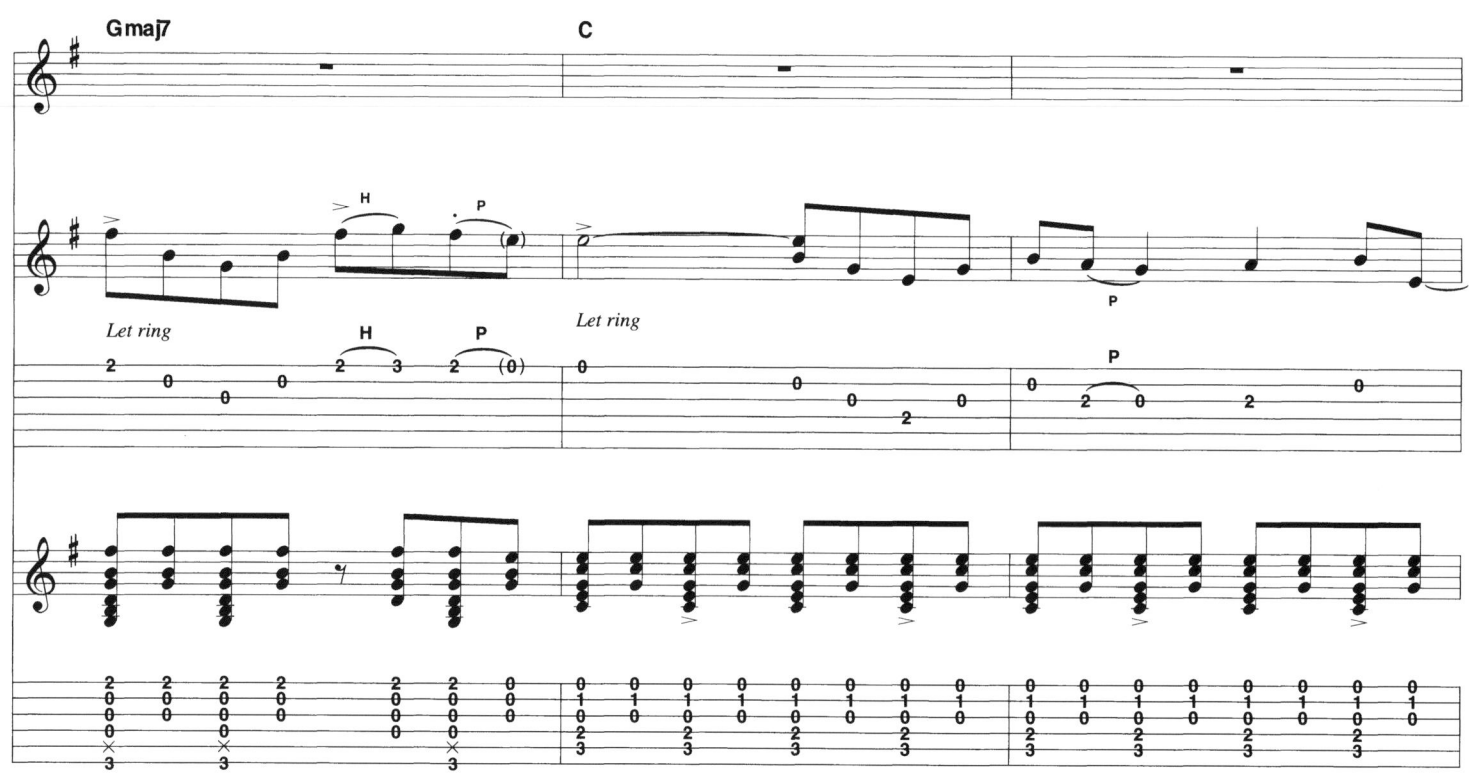

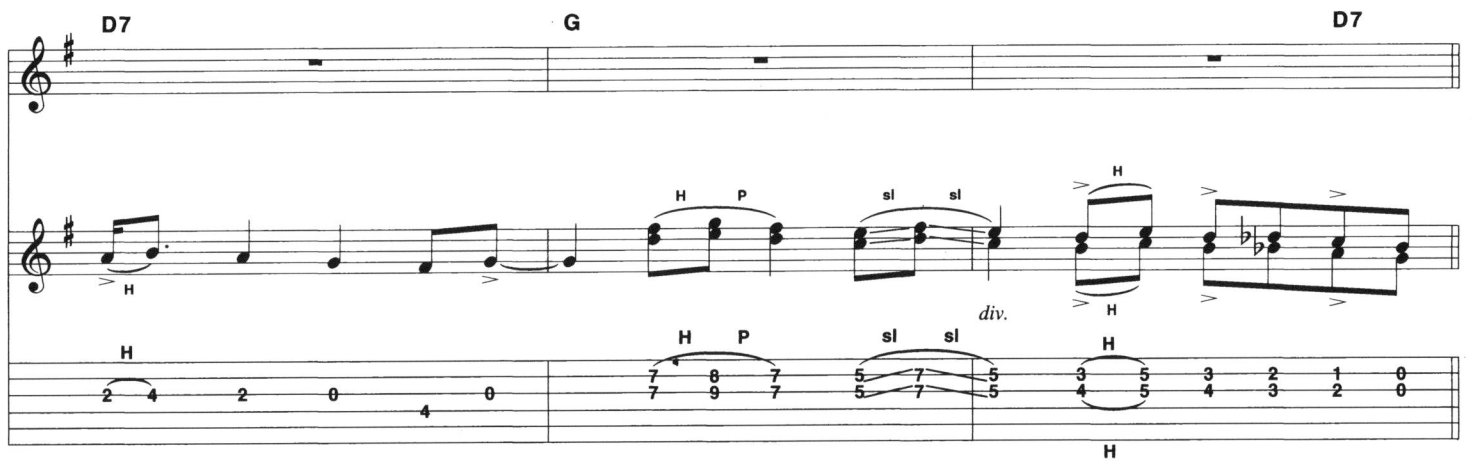

Verse 6:

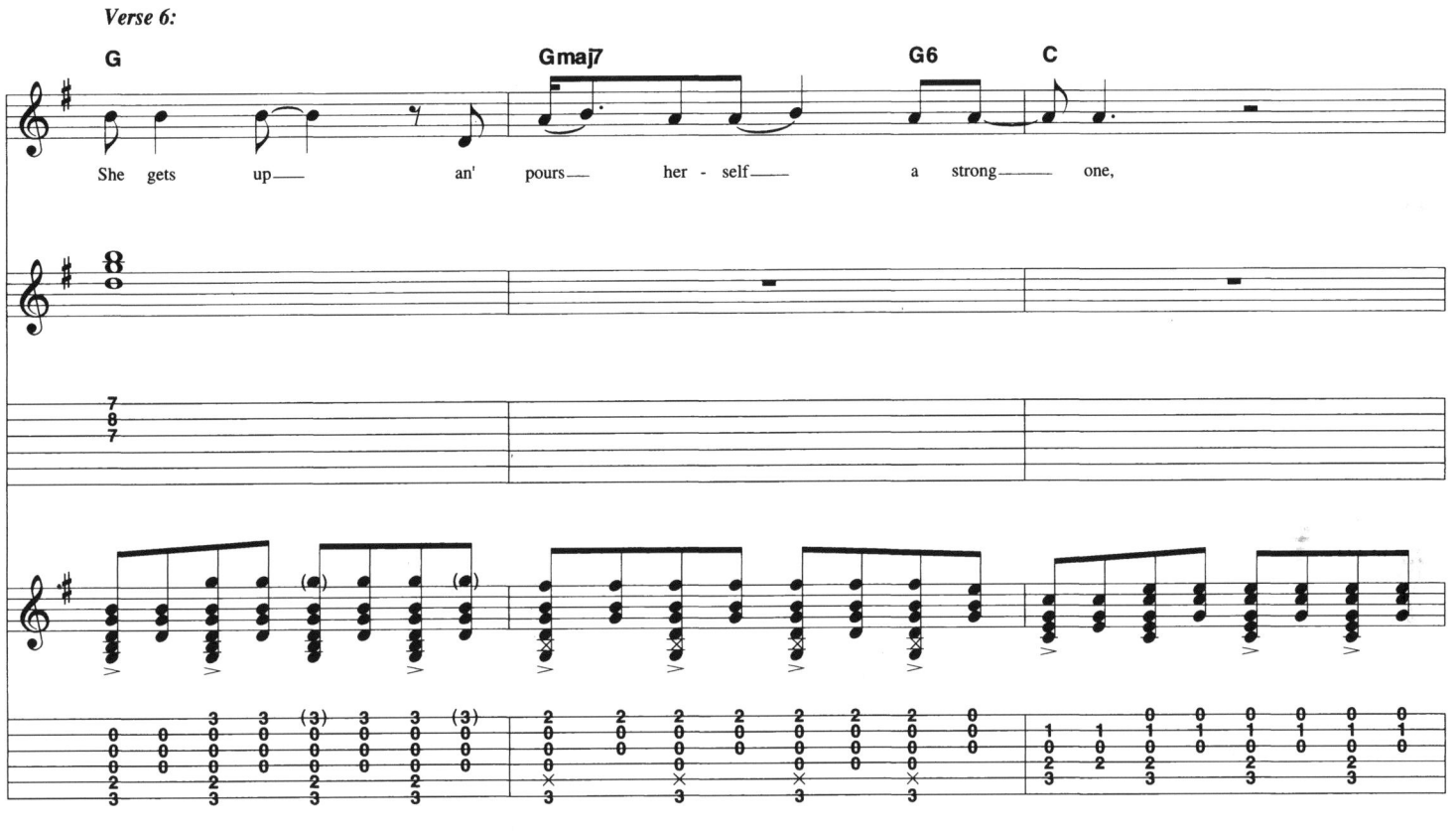

She gets up an' pours herself a strong one,

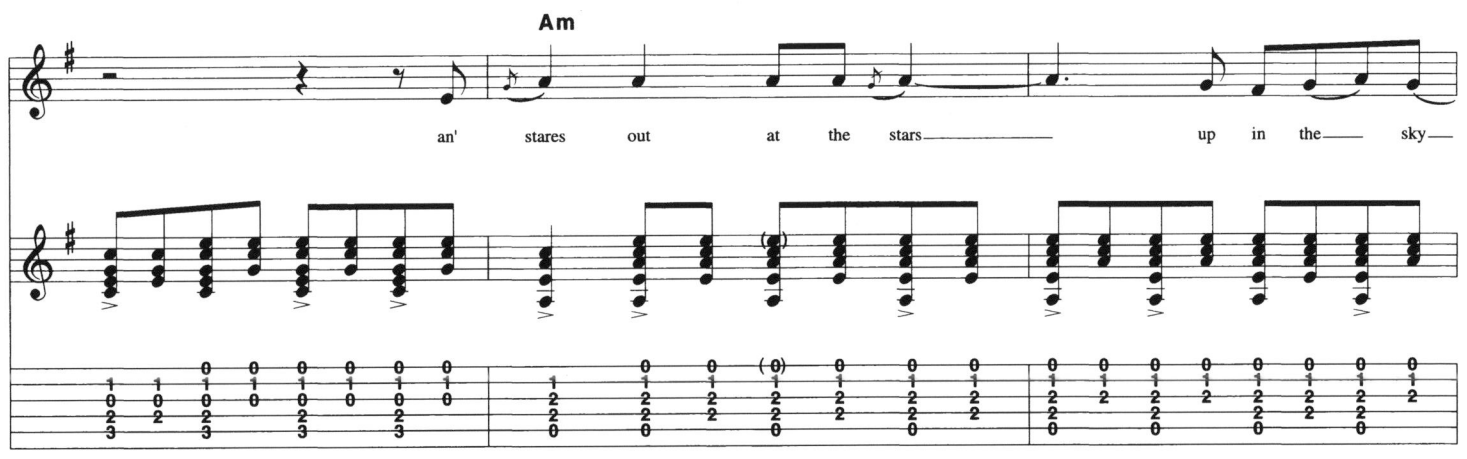

an' stares out at the stars up in the sky

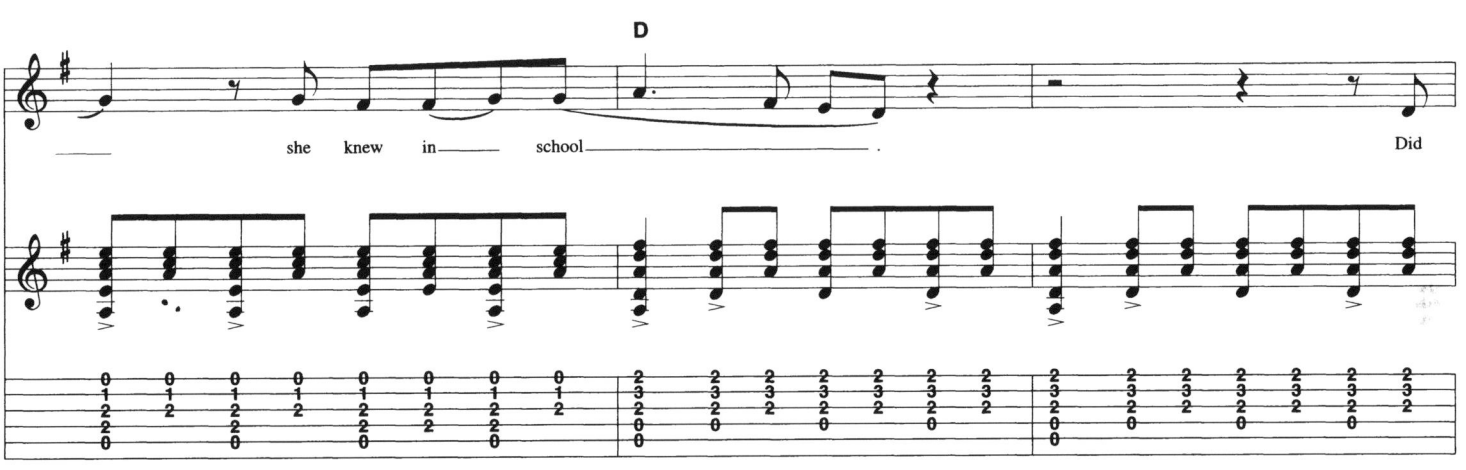

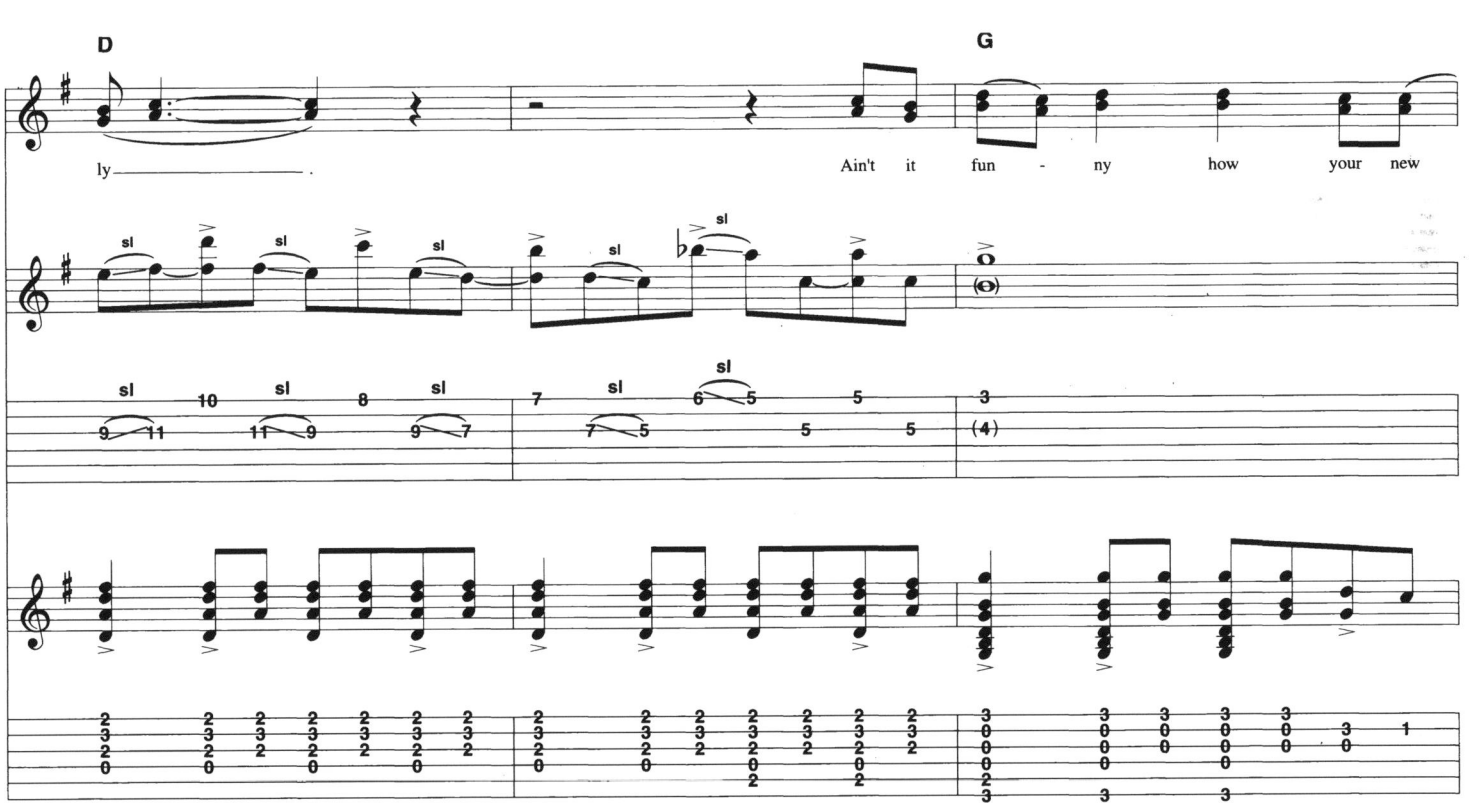

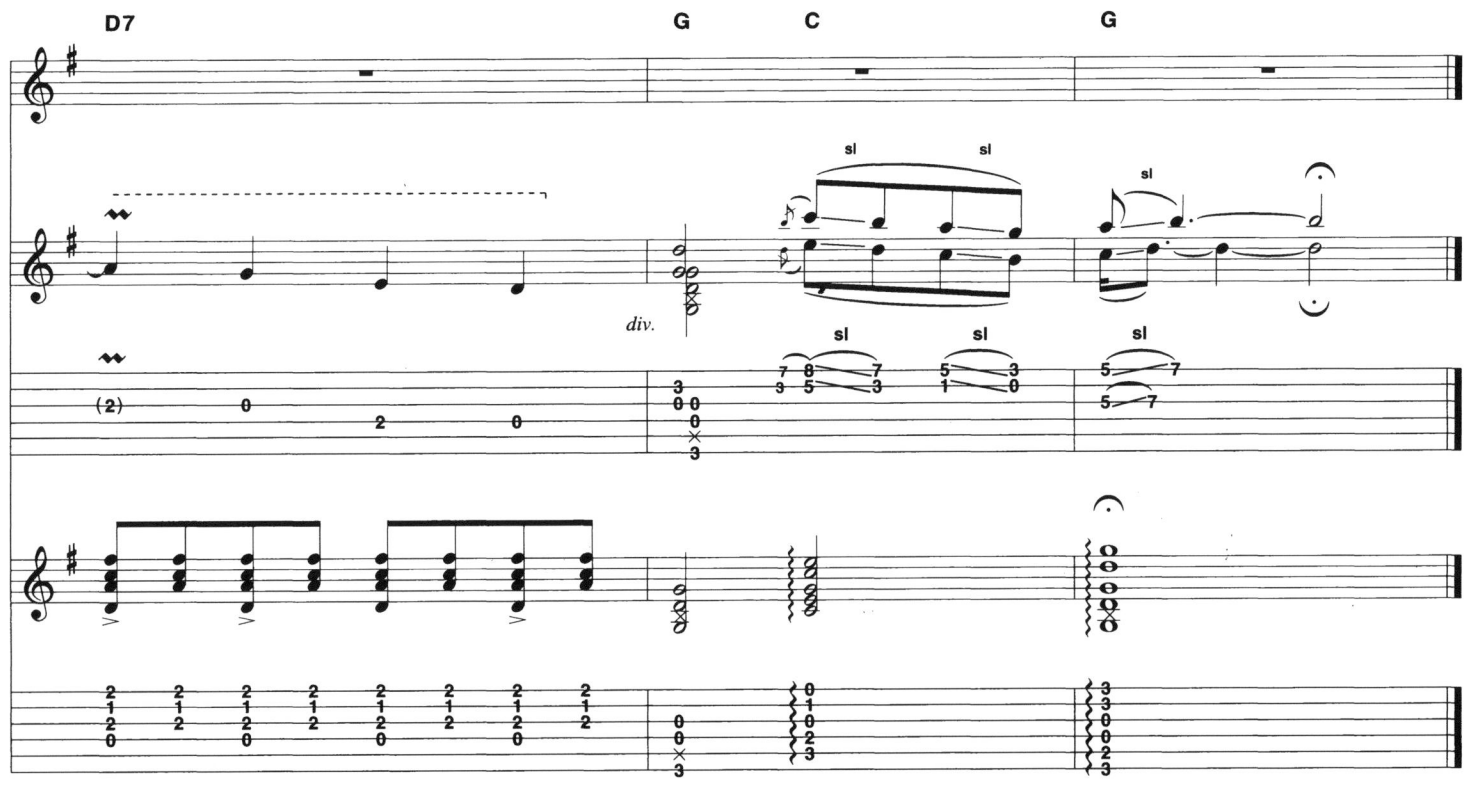

Take It Easy

Words and Music by JACKSON BROWNE and GLENN FREY

♩ = 138
Moderate Country feel

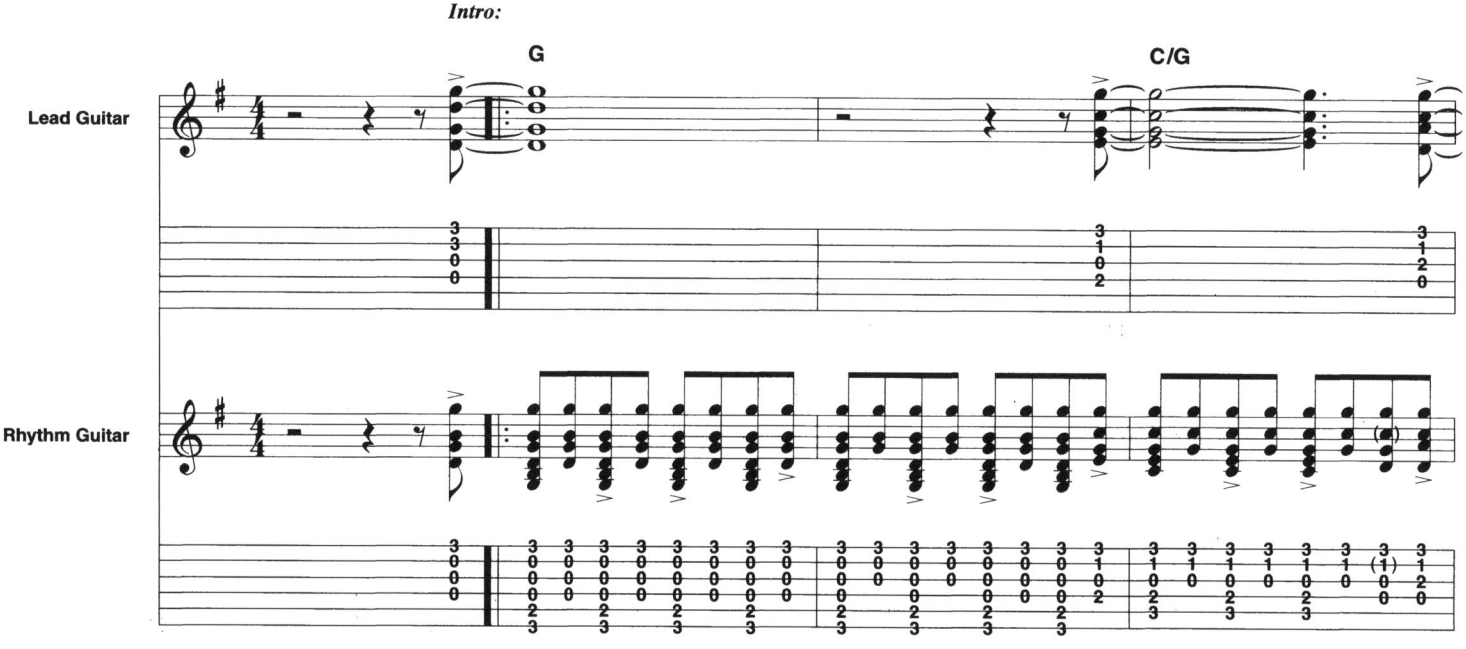

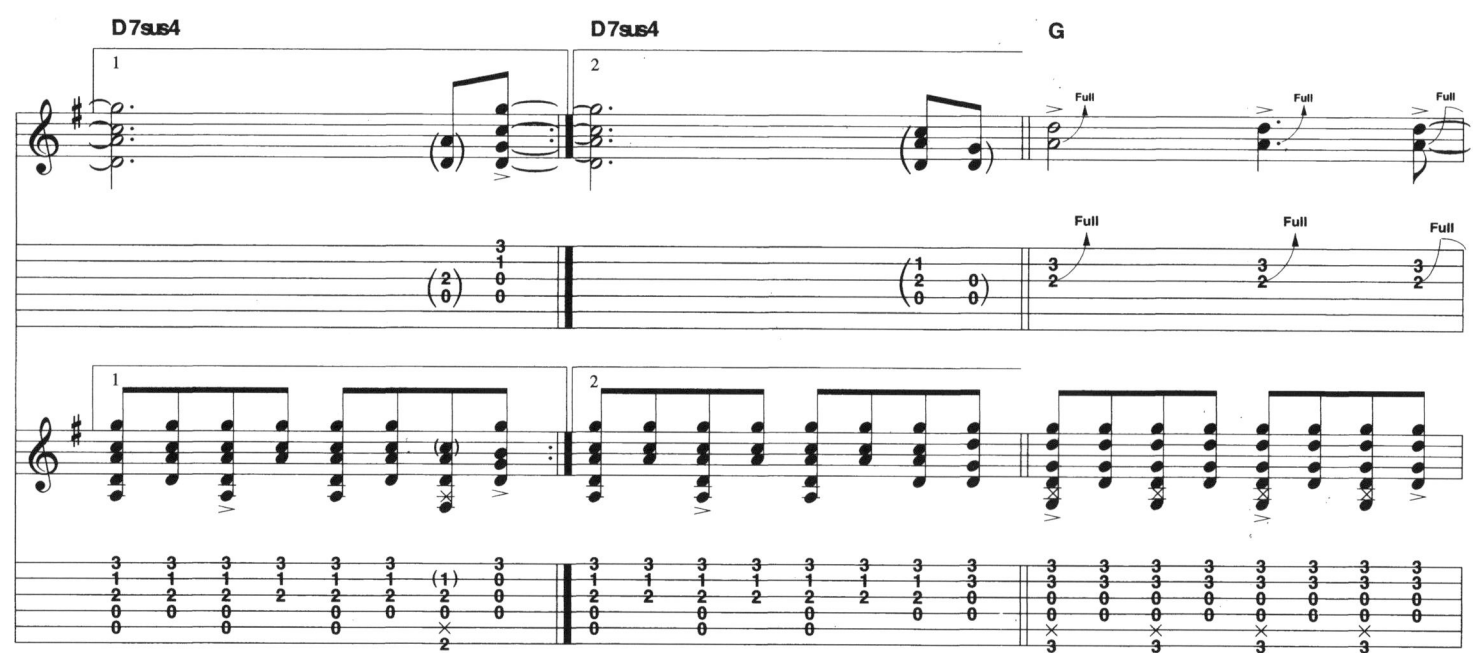

Verse 1:

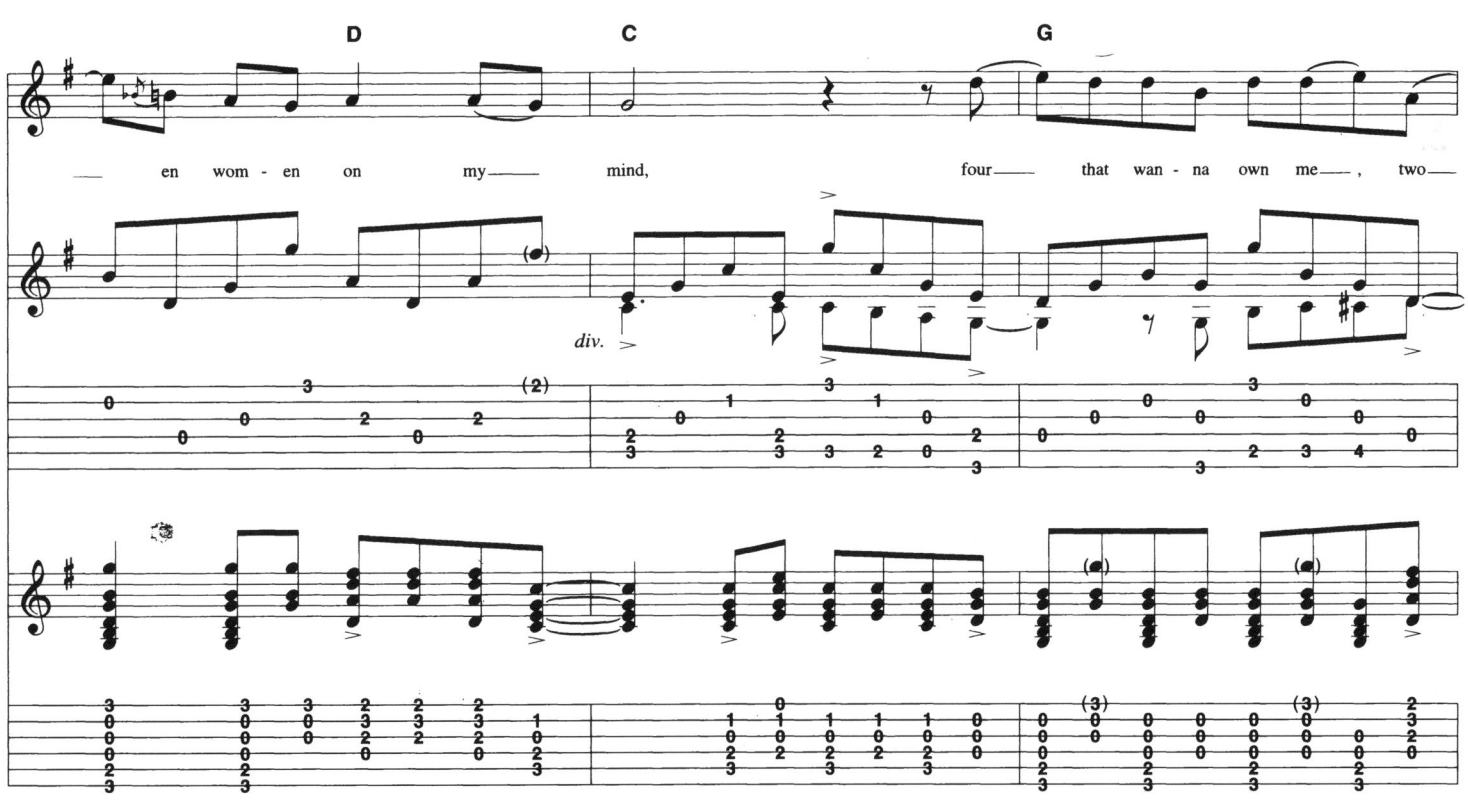

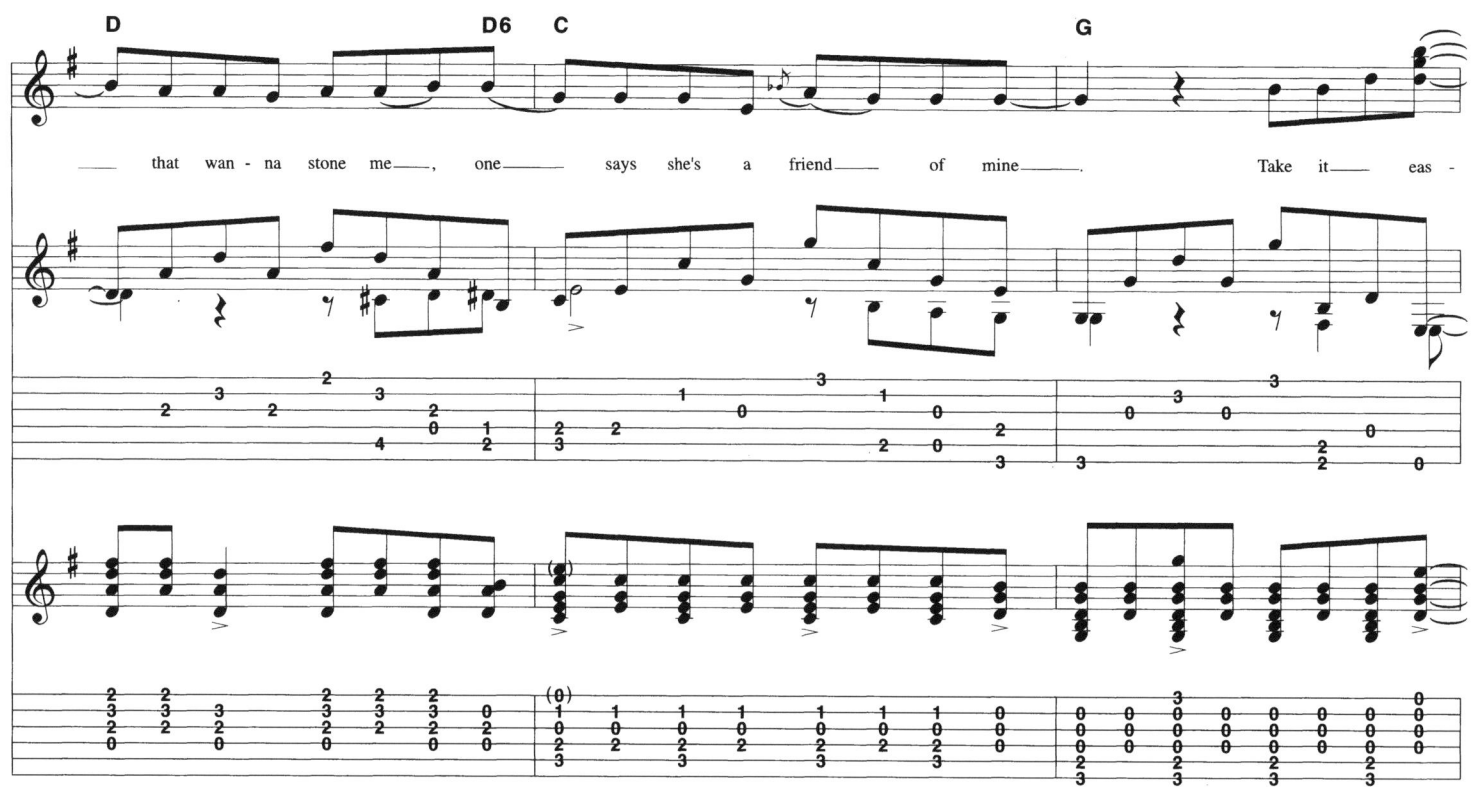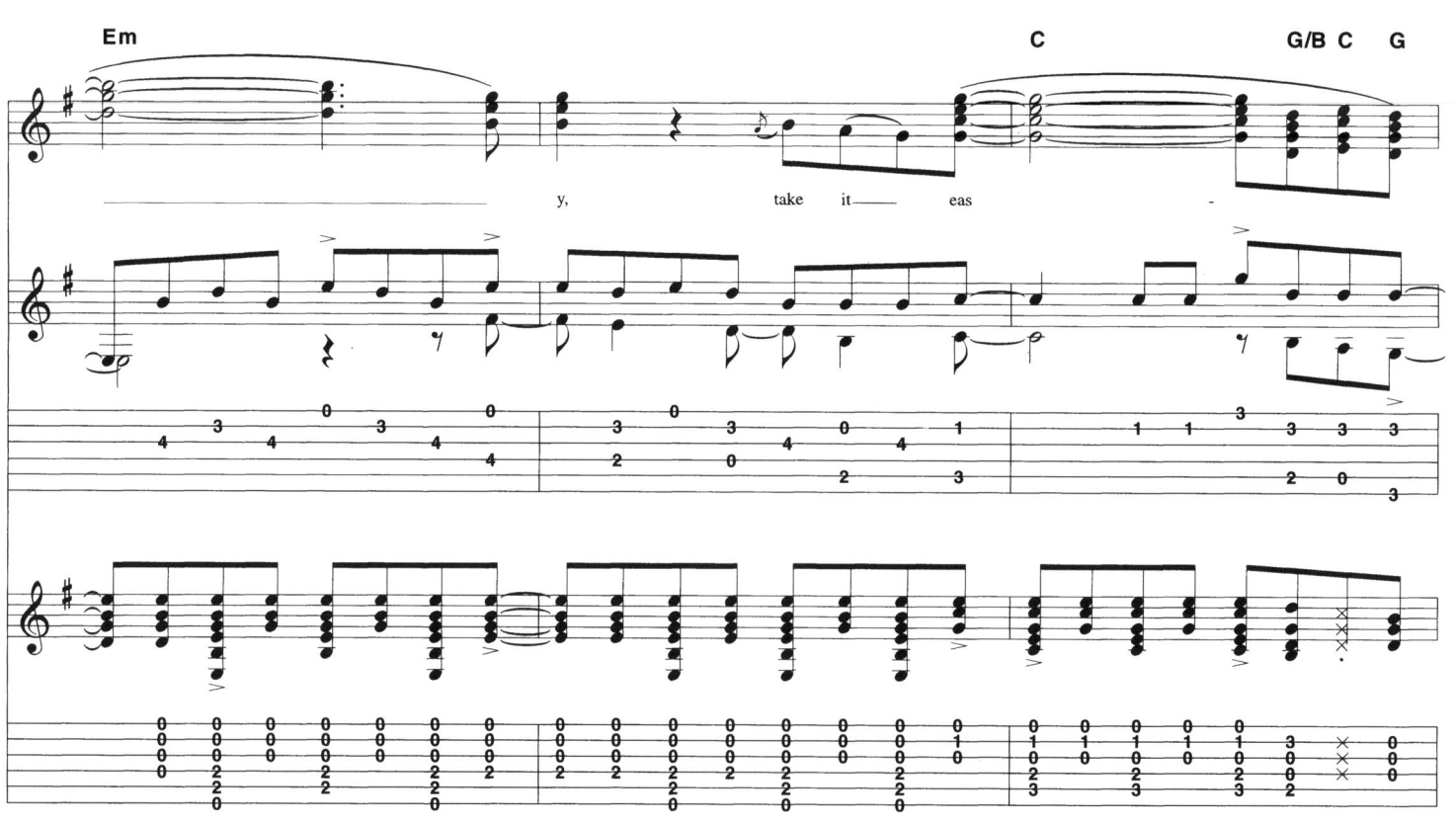

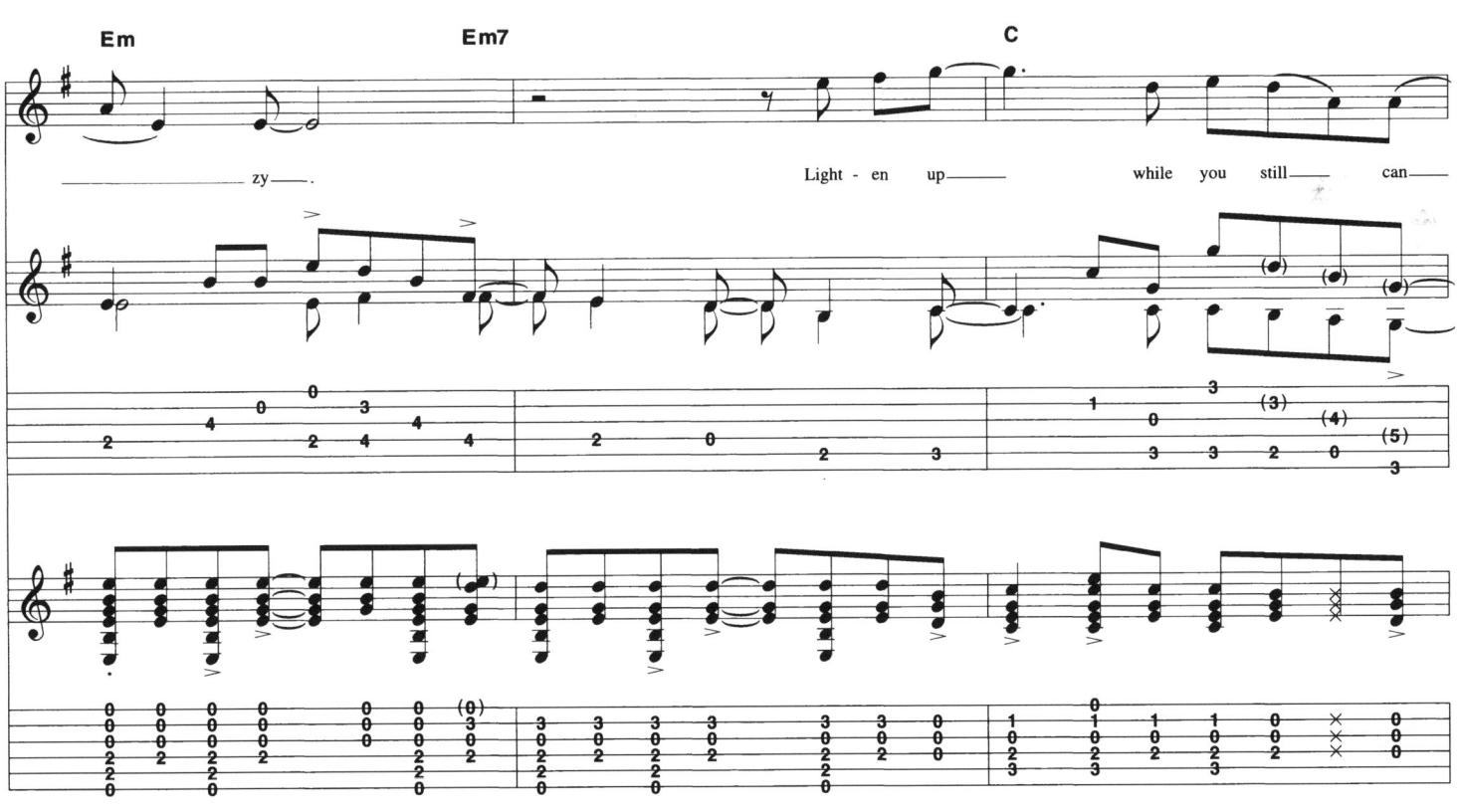

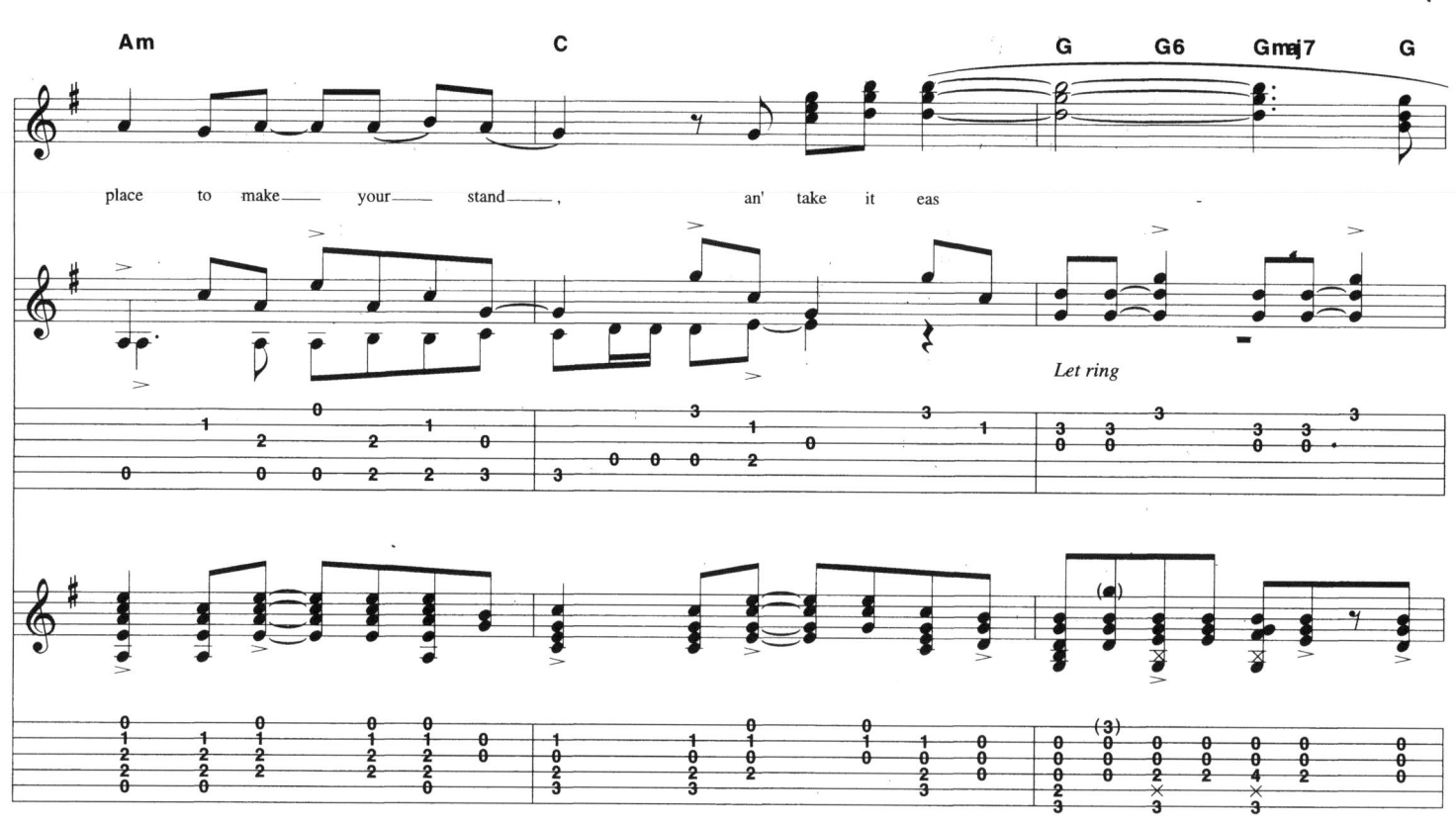

Verse 2:

Acoustic Guitar Continues Sim

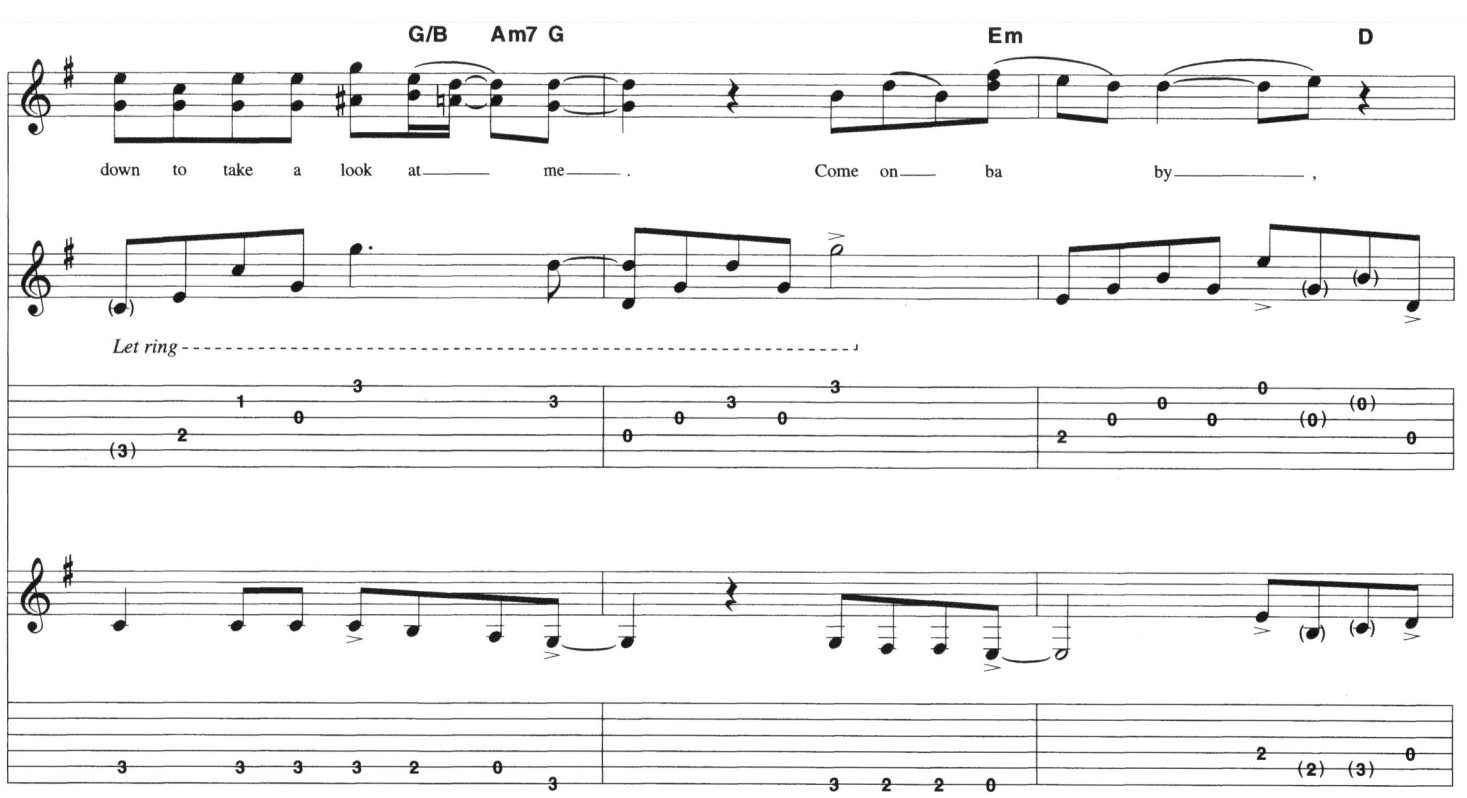

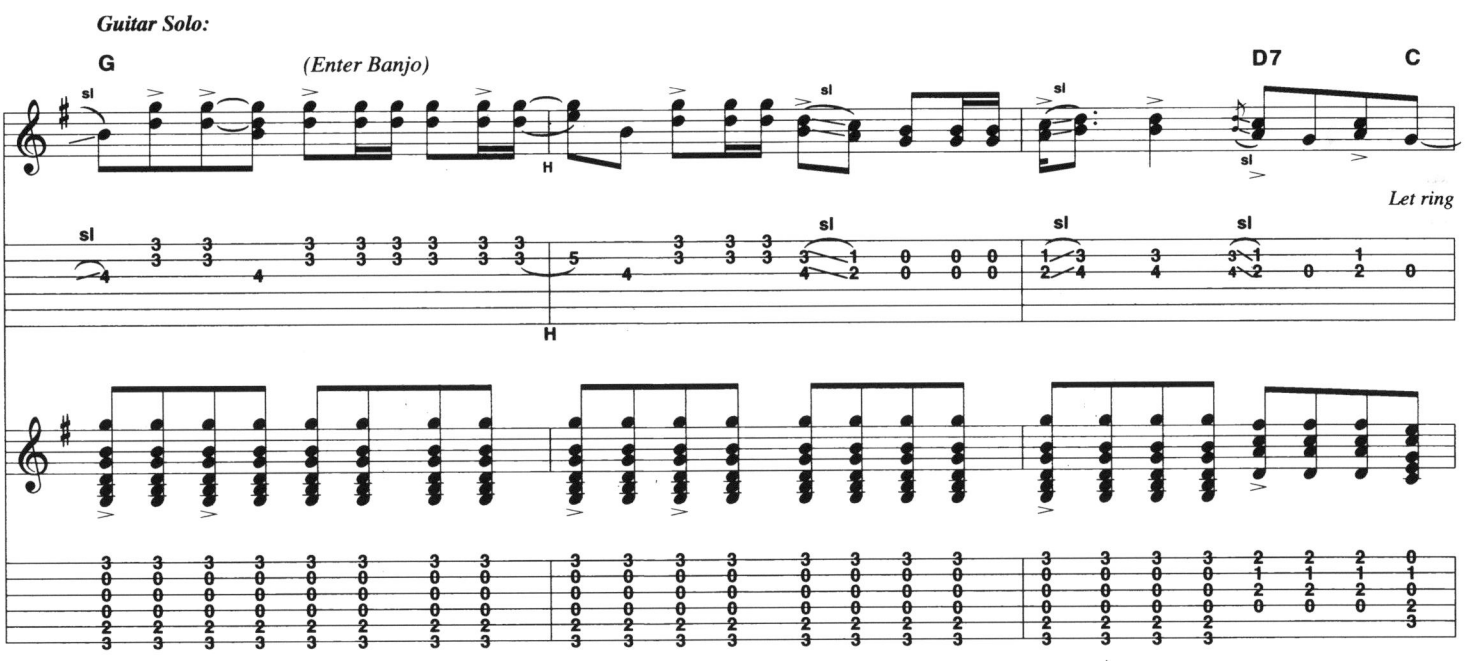

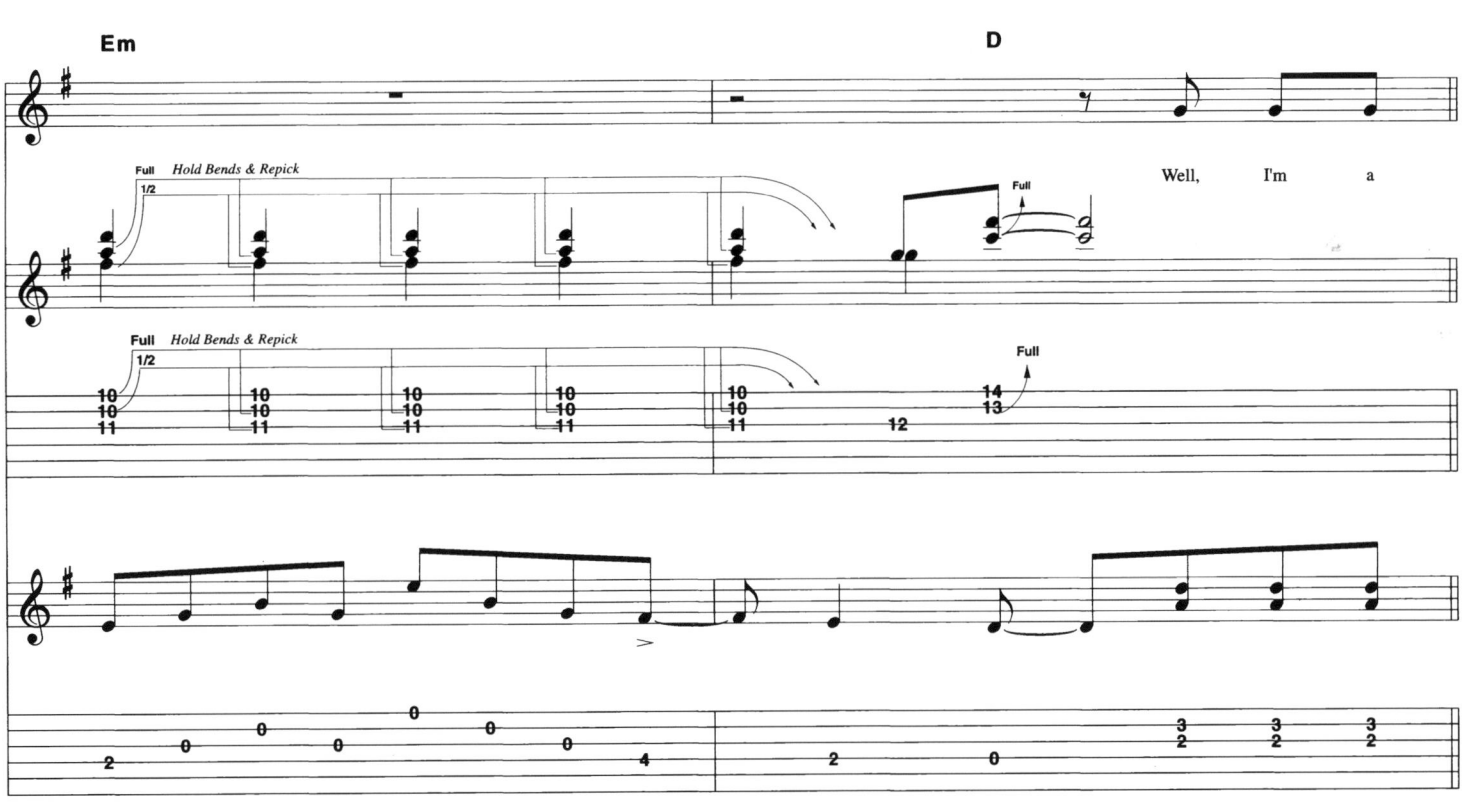

133

Verse 3:

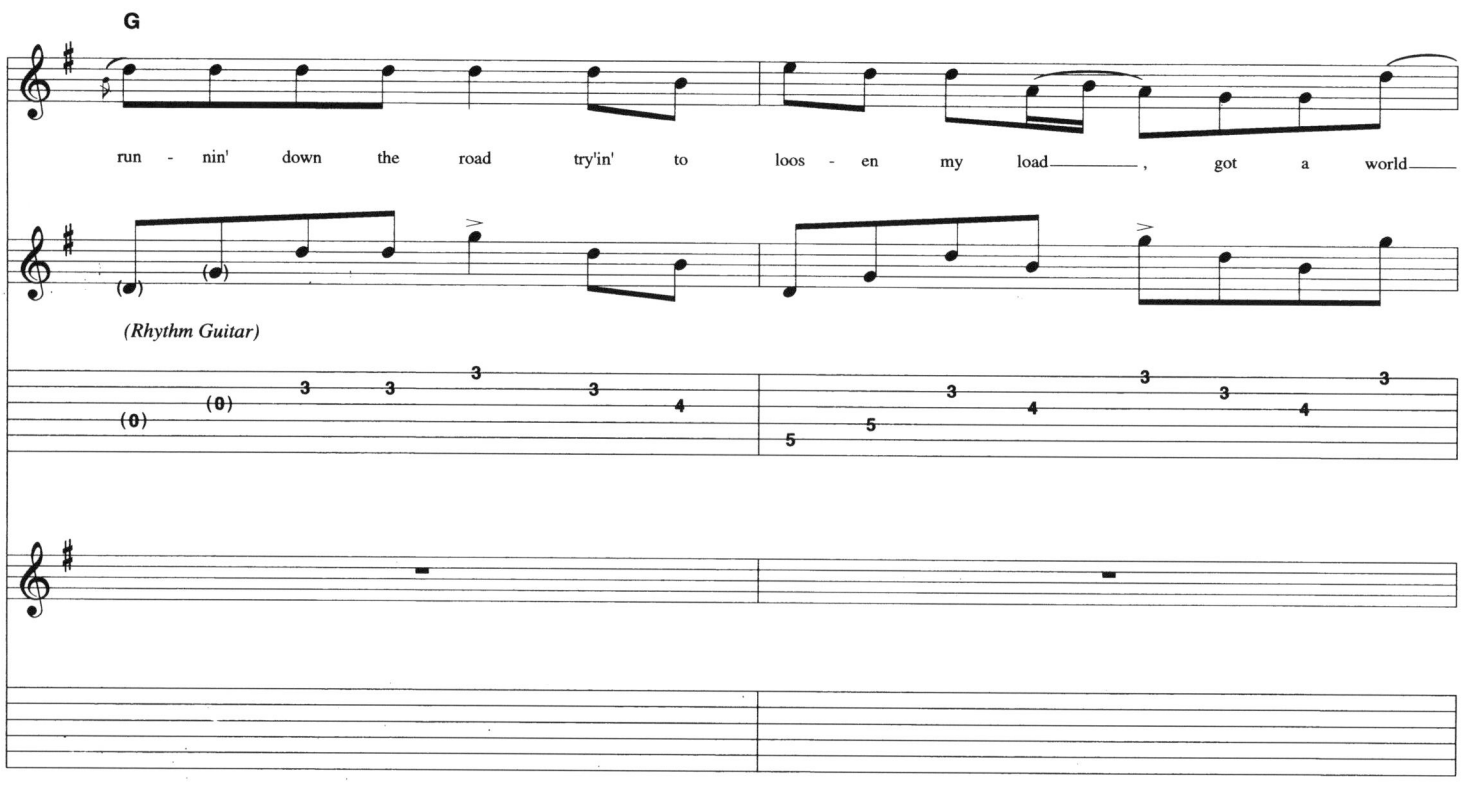

run - nin' down the road try'in' to loos - en my load, got a world of trou - ble on my mind, look - in' for a lov - er who won't

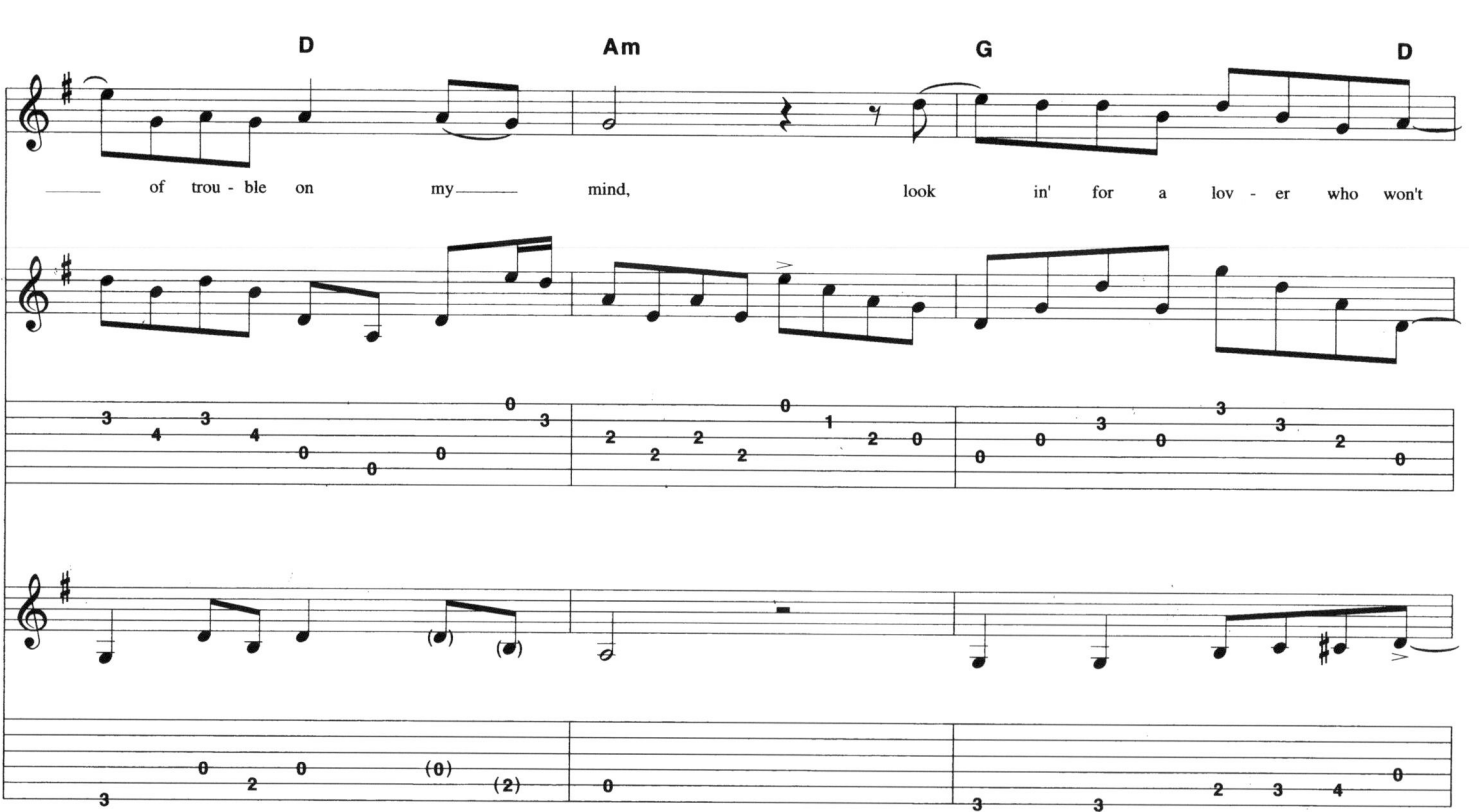

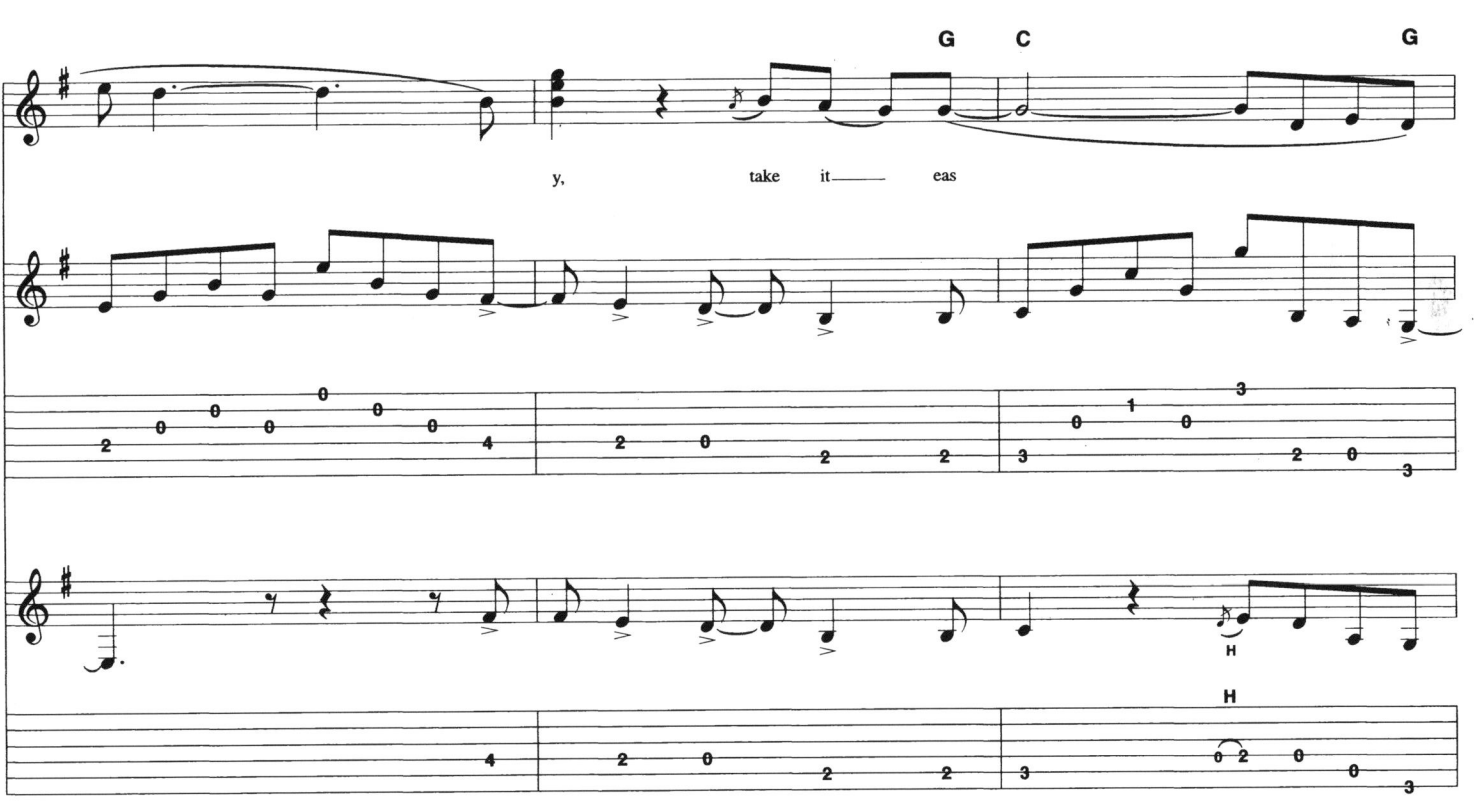

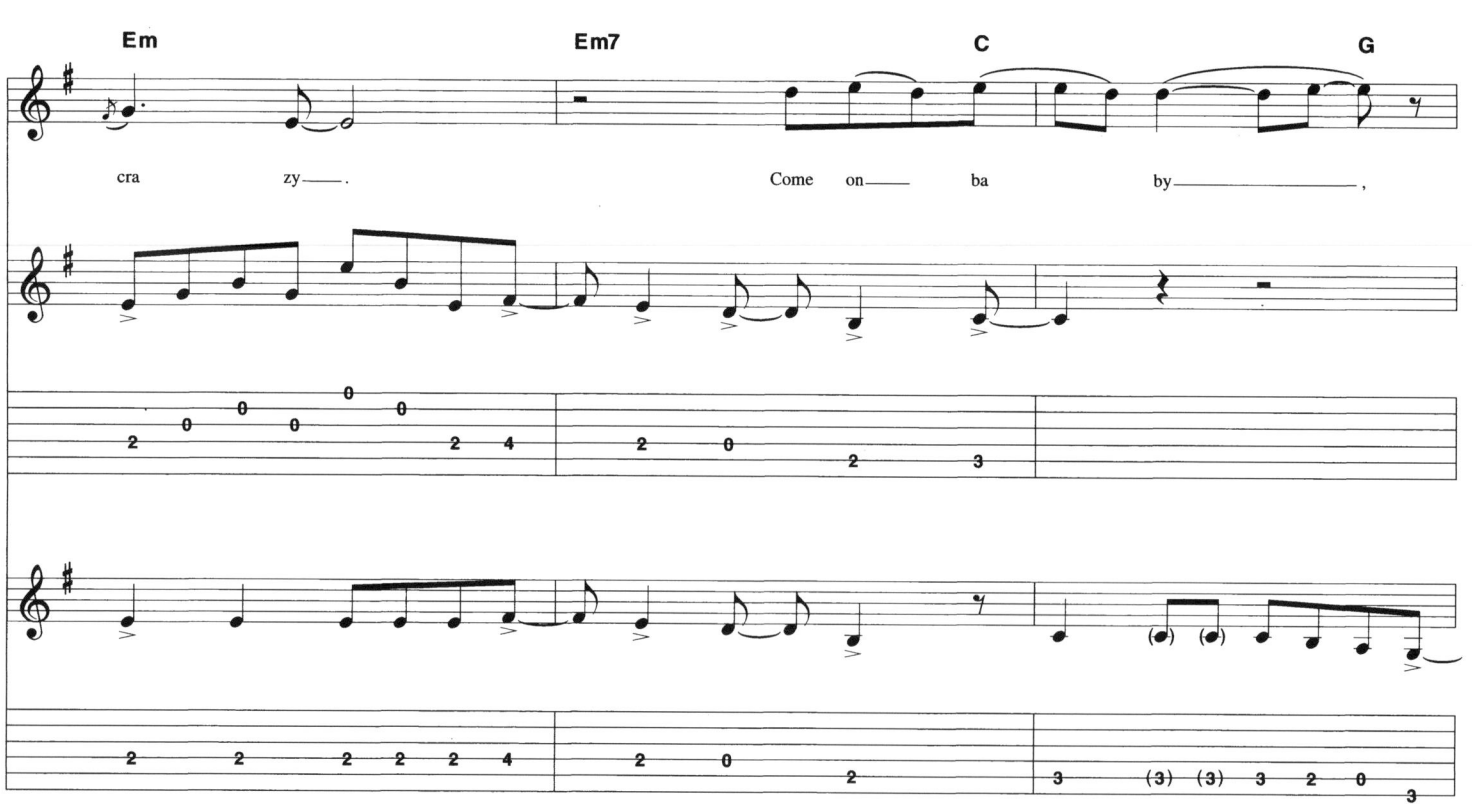

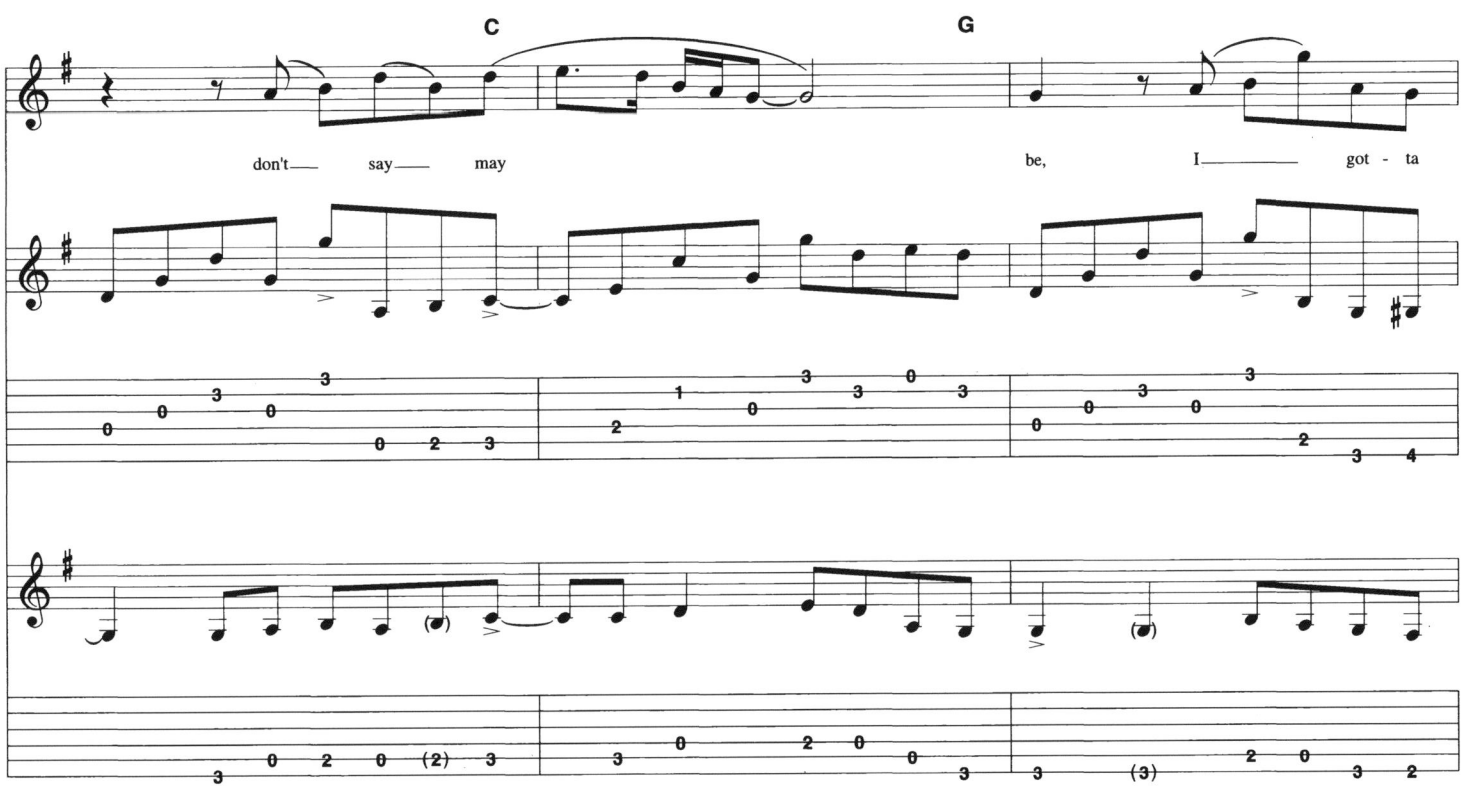
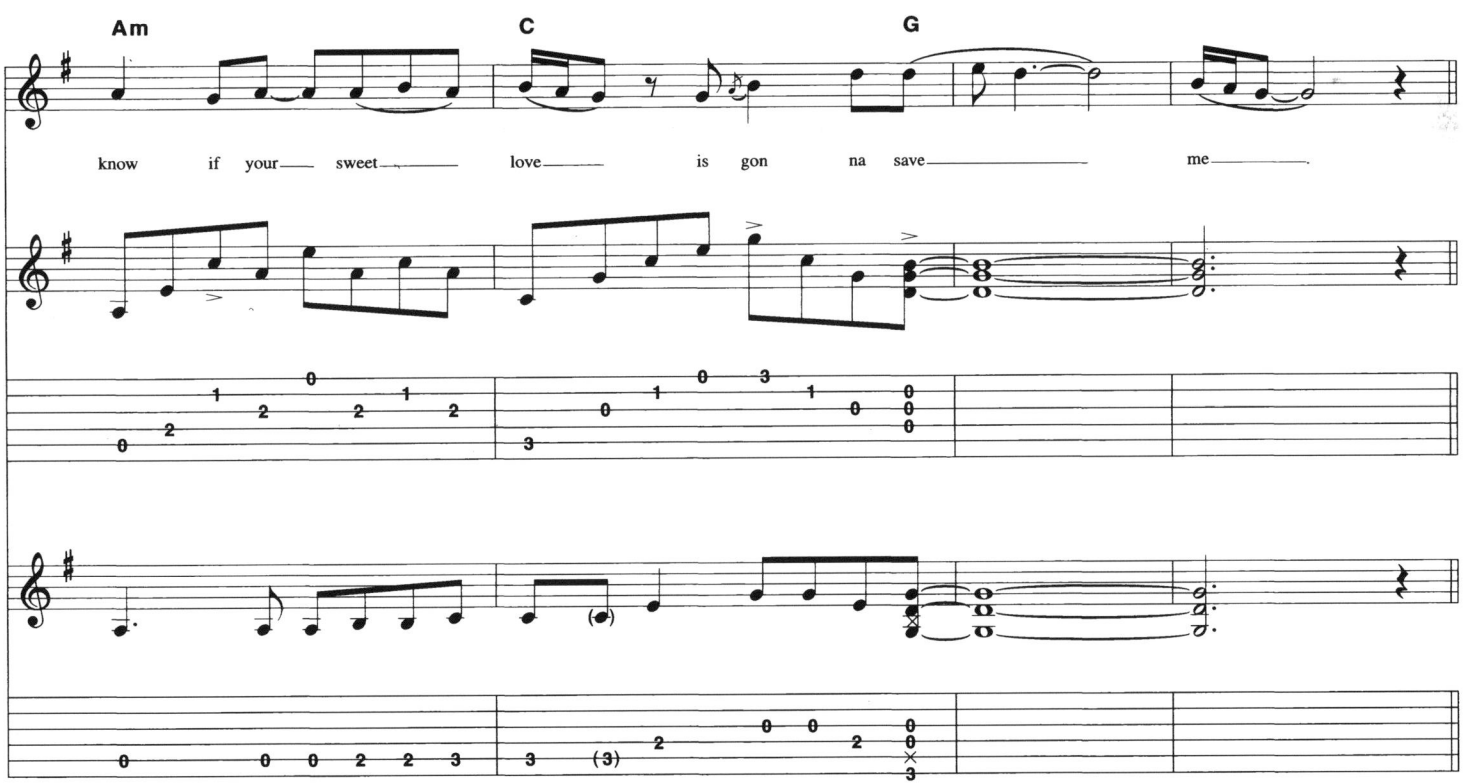

Outro:

Best Of My Love

Words and Music by DAVID JOHN SOUTHER, DON HENLEY and GLENN FREY

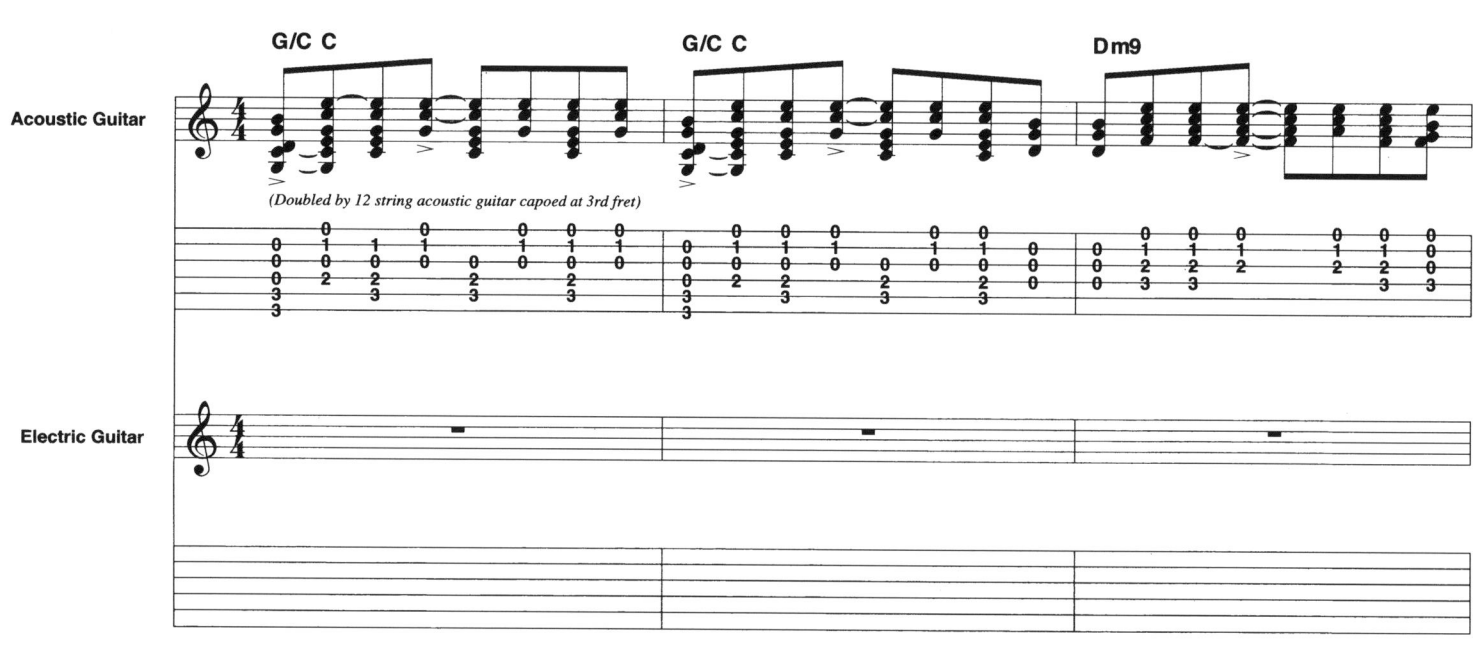

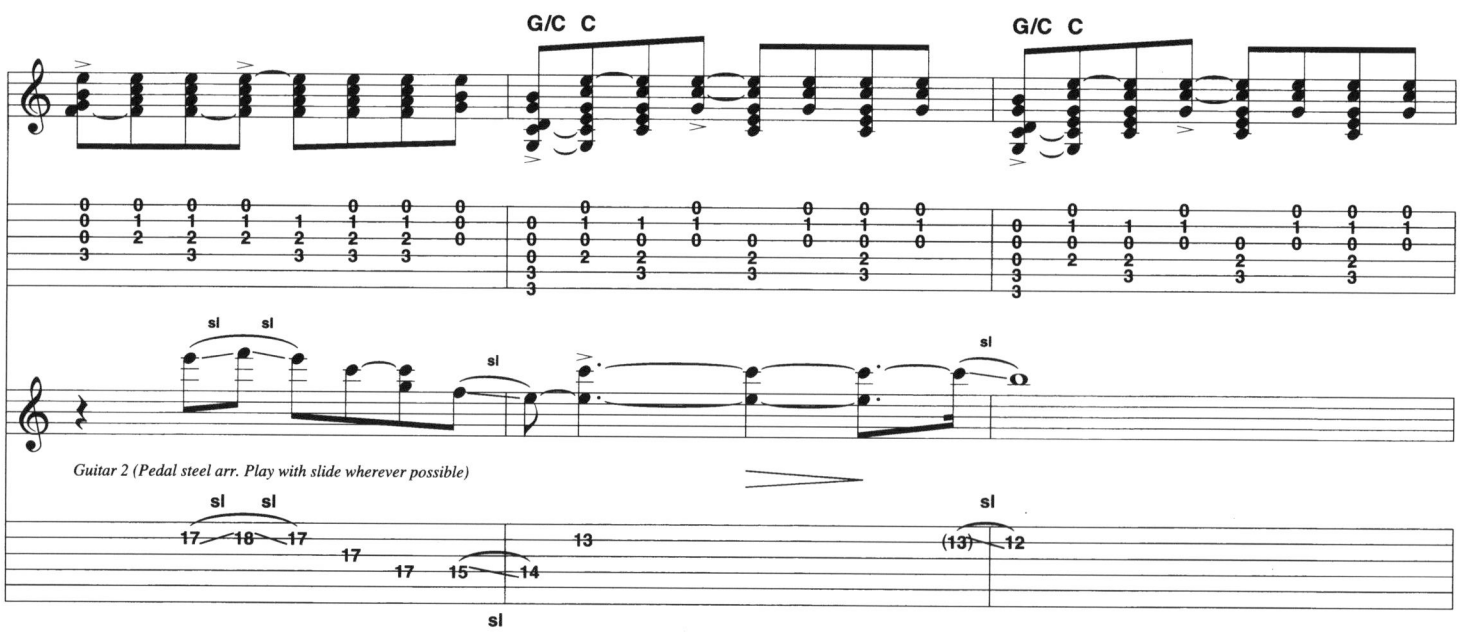

© 1975 & 1996 EMI Blackwood Music Inc, Cass County Music and Red Cloud Music, WB Music Corp and Ice Age Music, USA
Warner/Chappell Music Ltd, London W1Y 3FA and EMI Music Publishing Ltd, London WC2H 0EA

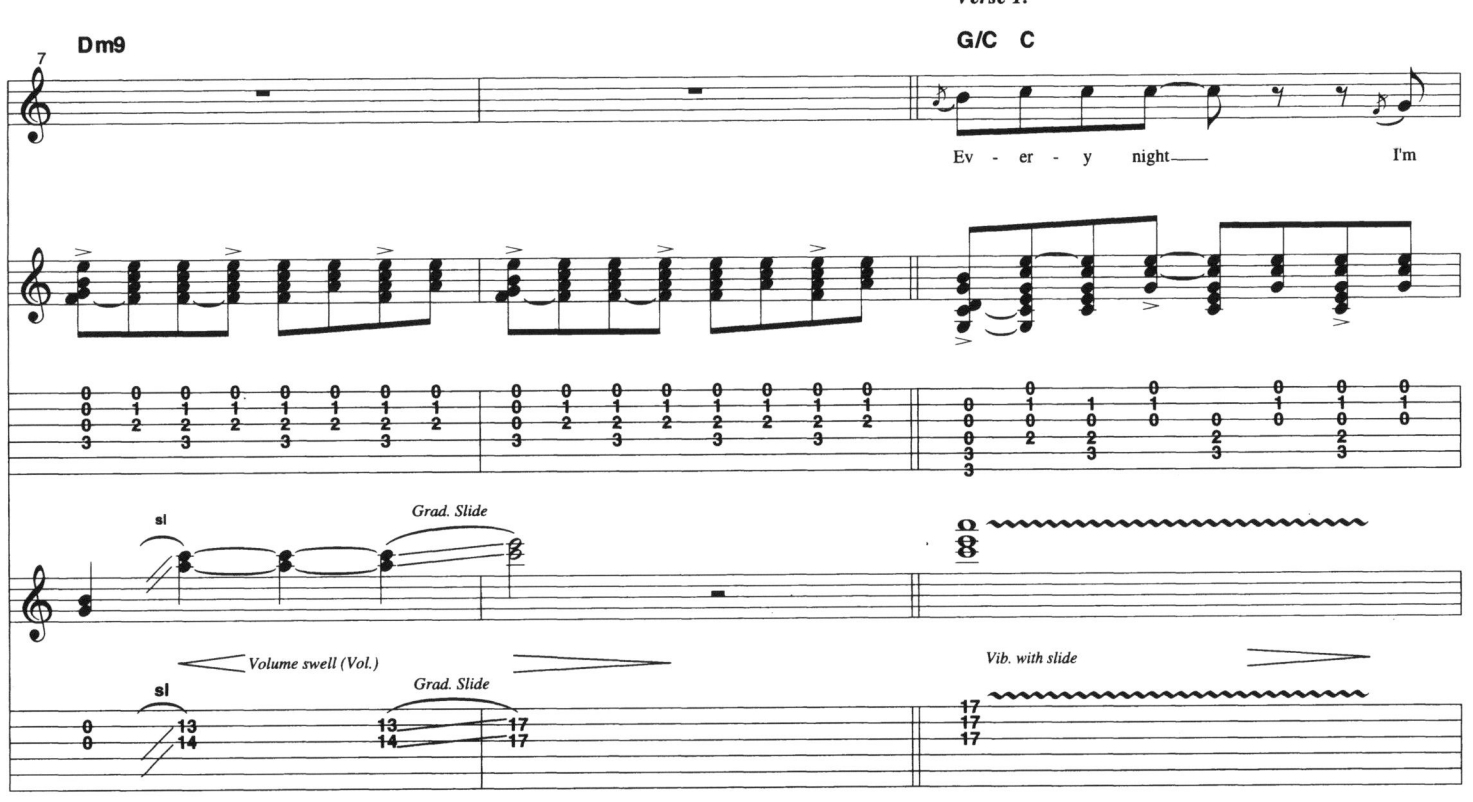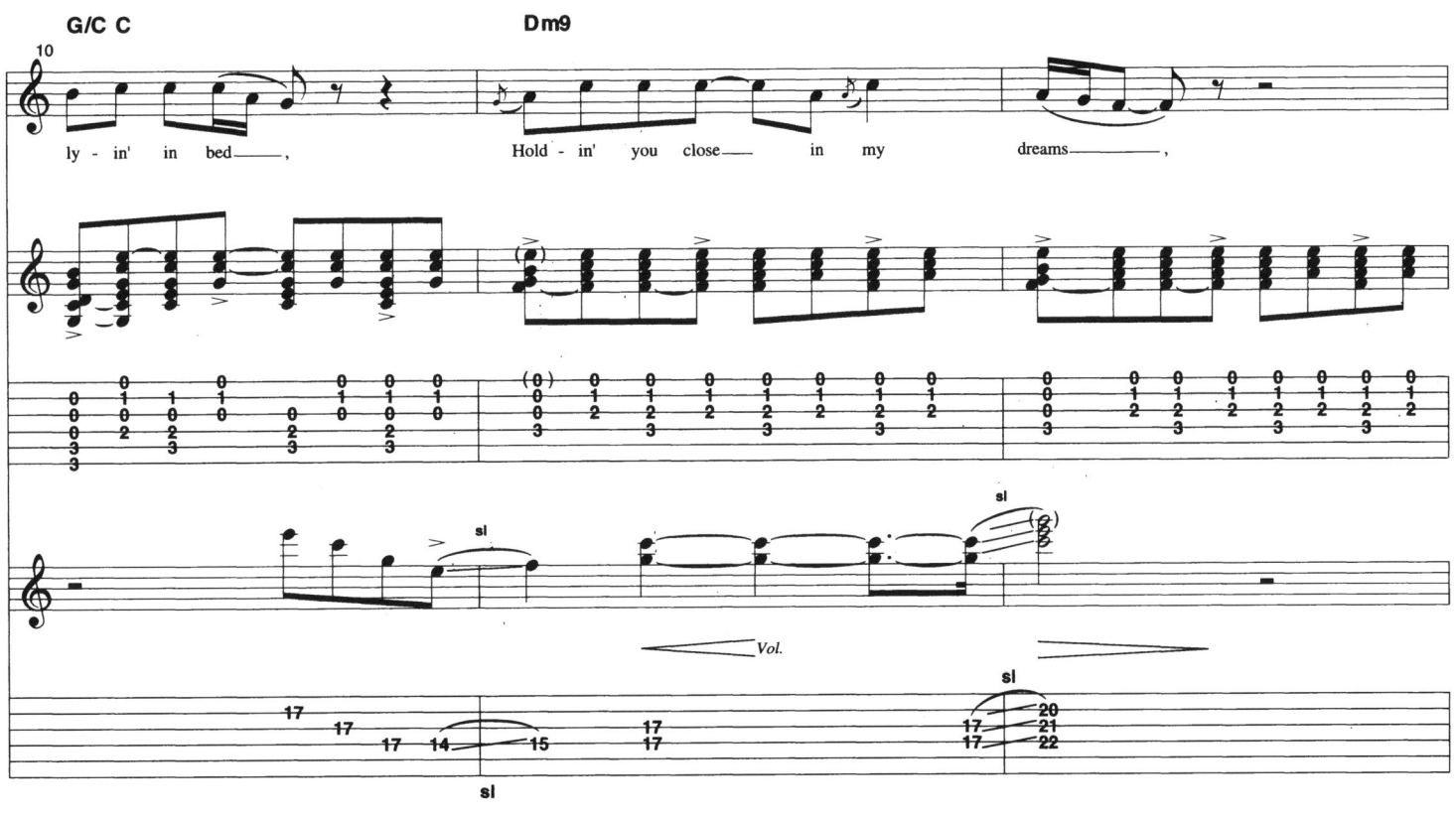

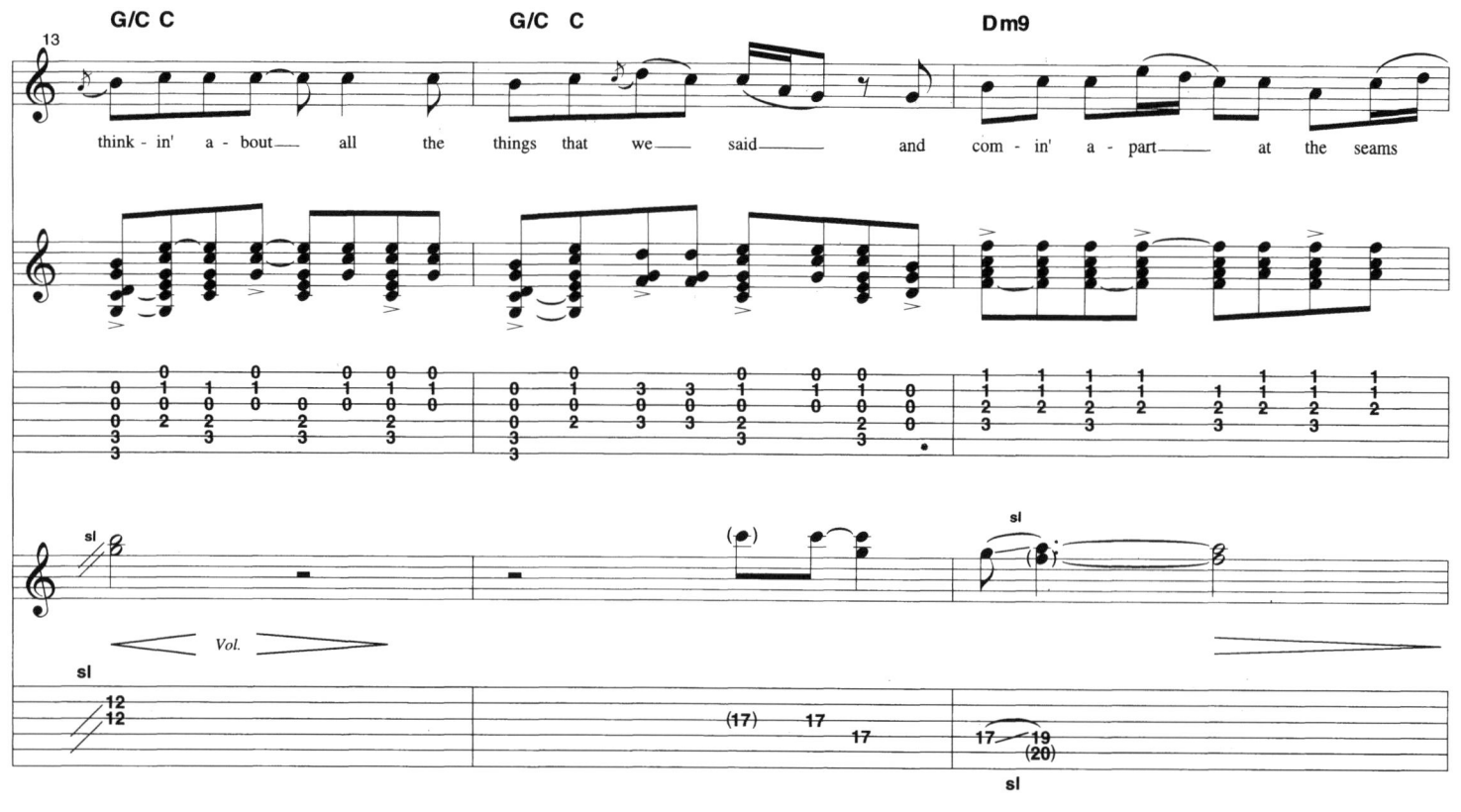
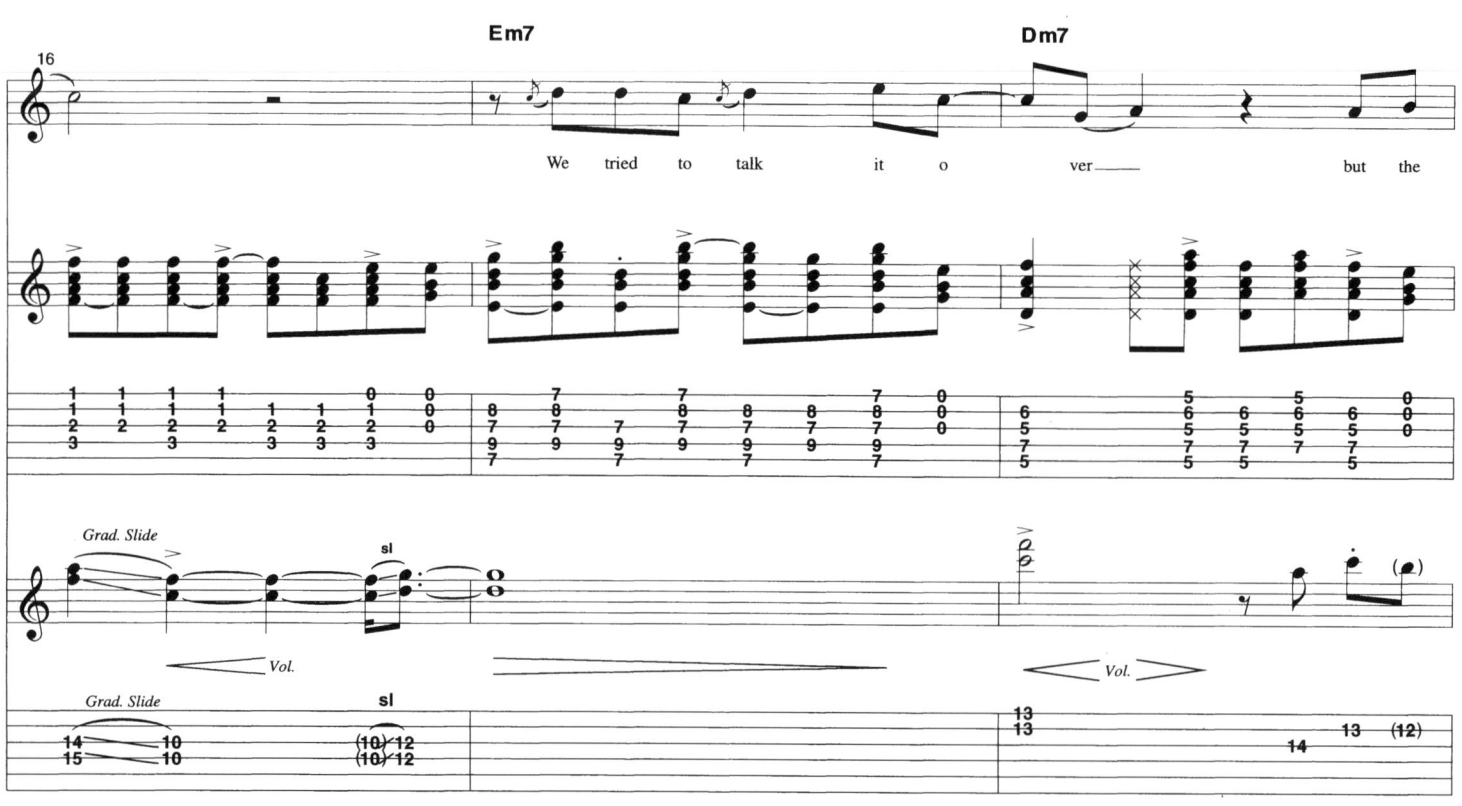

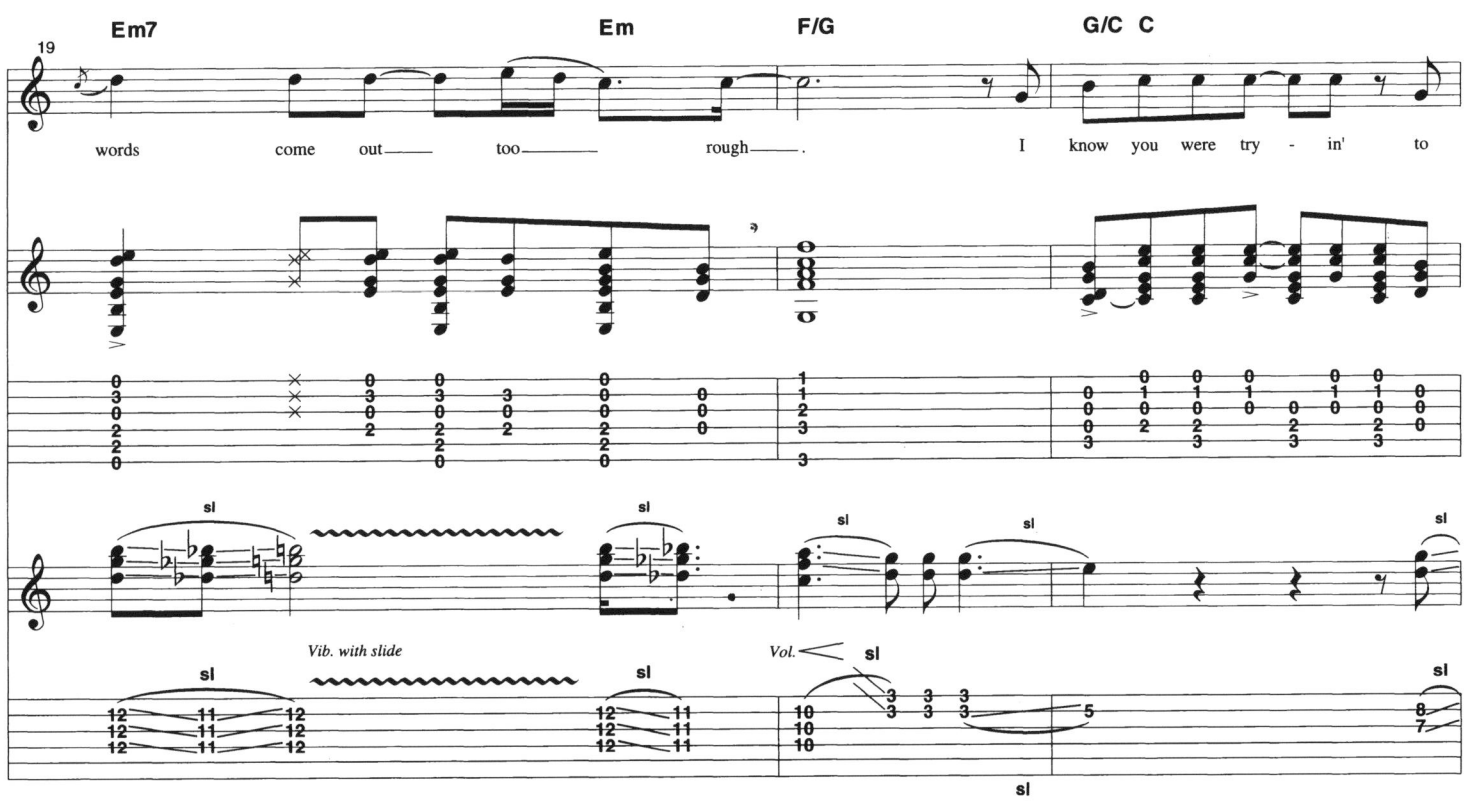
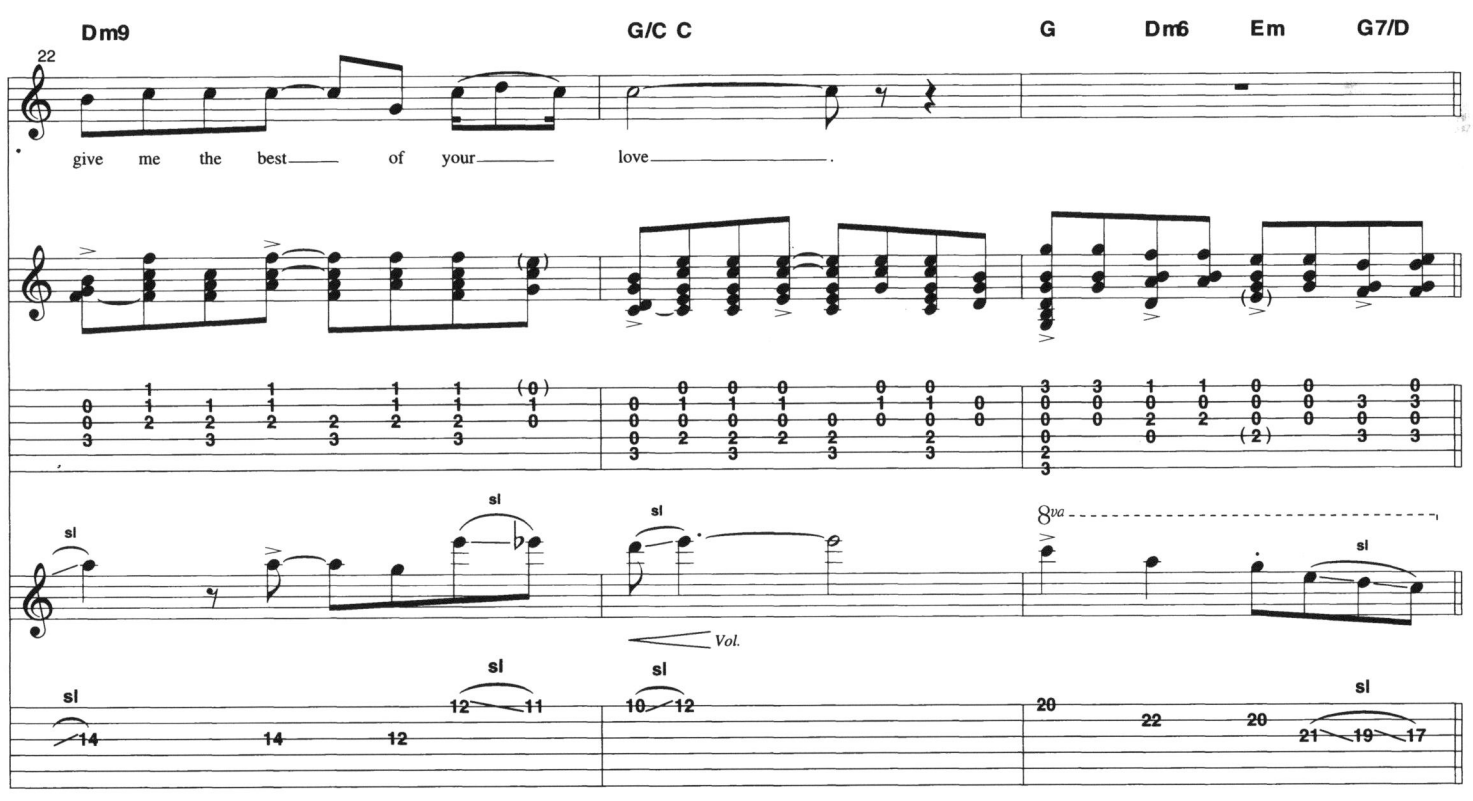

Verse 2:

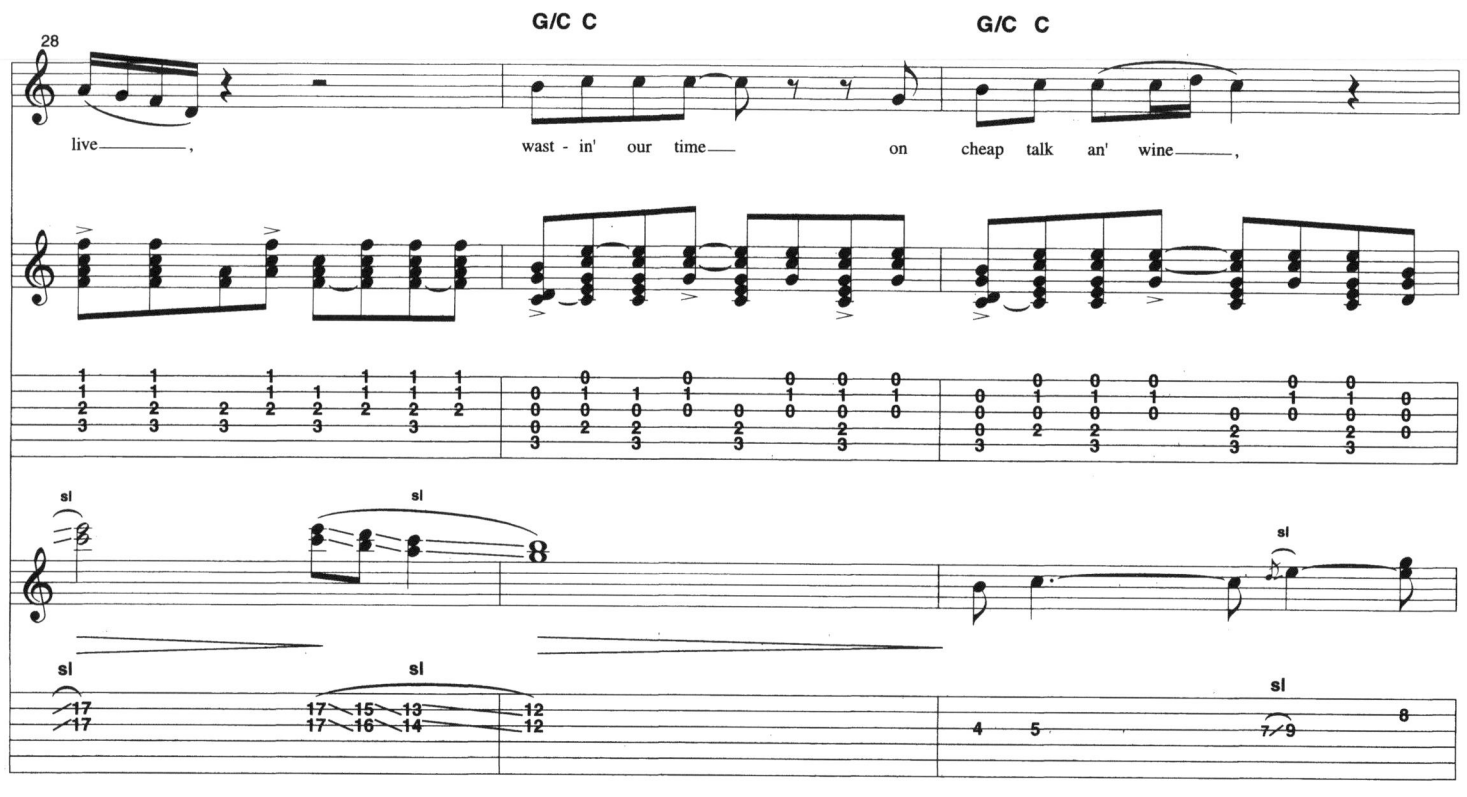

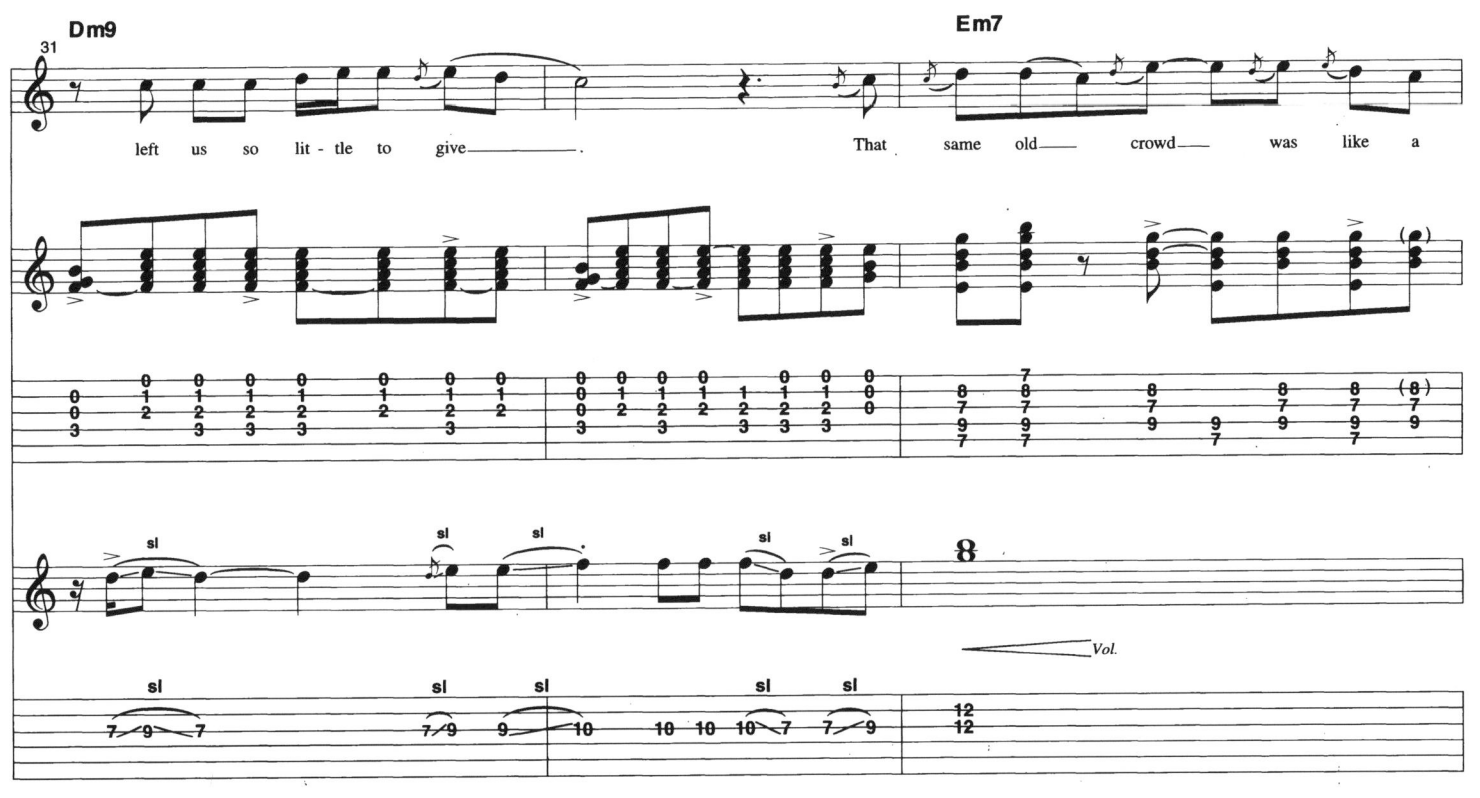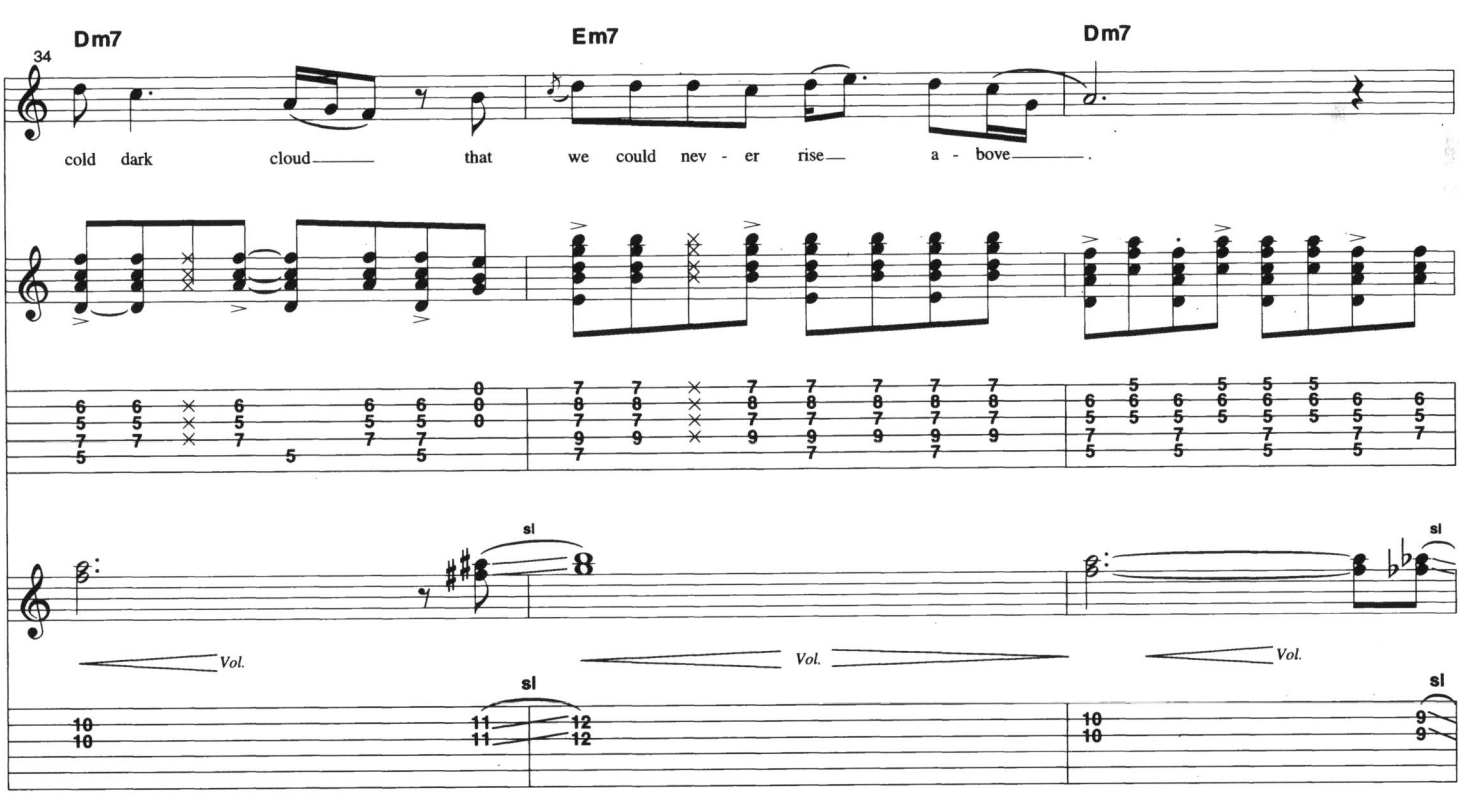

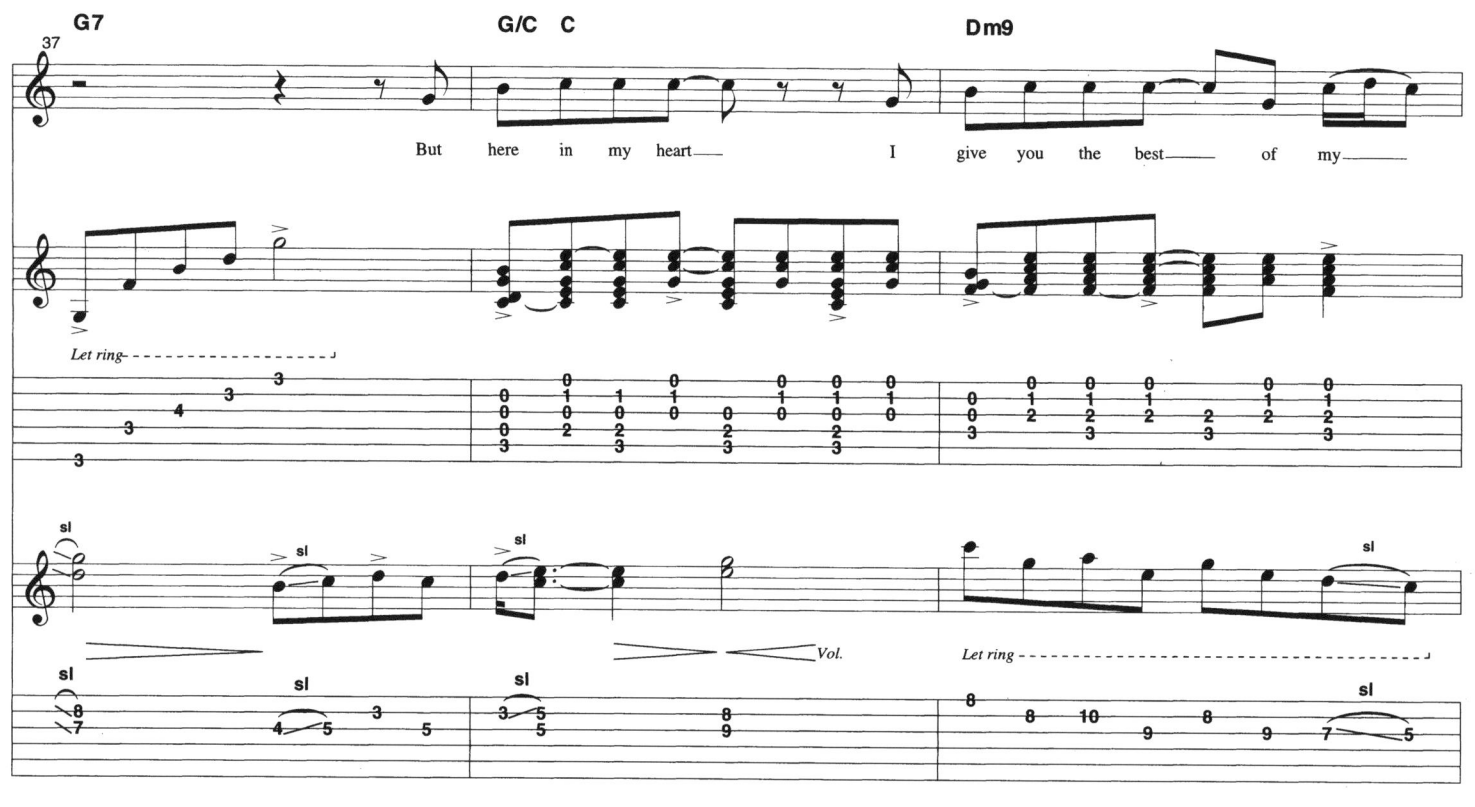

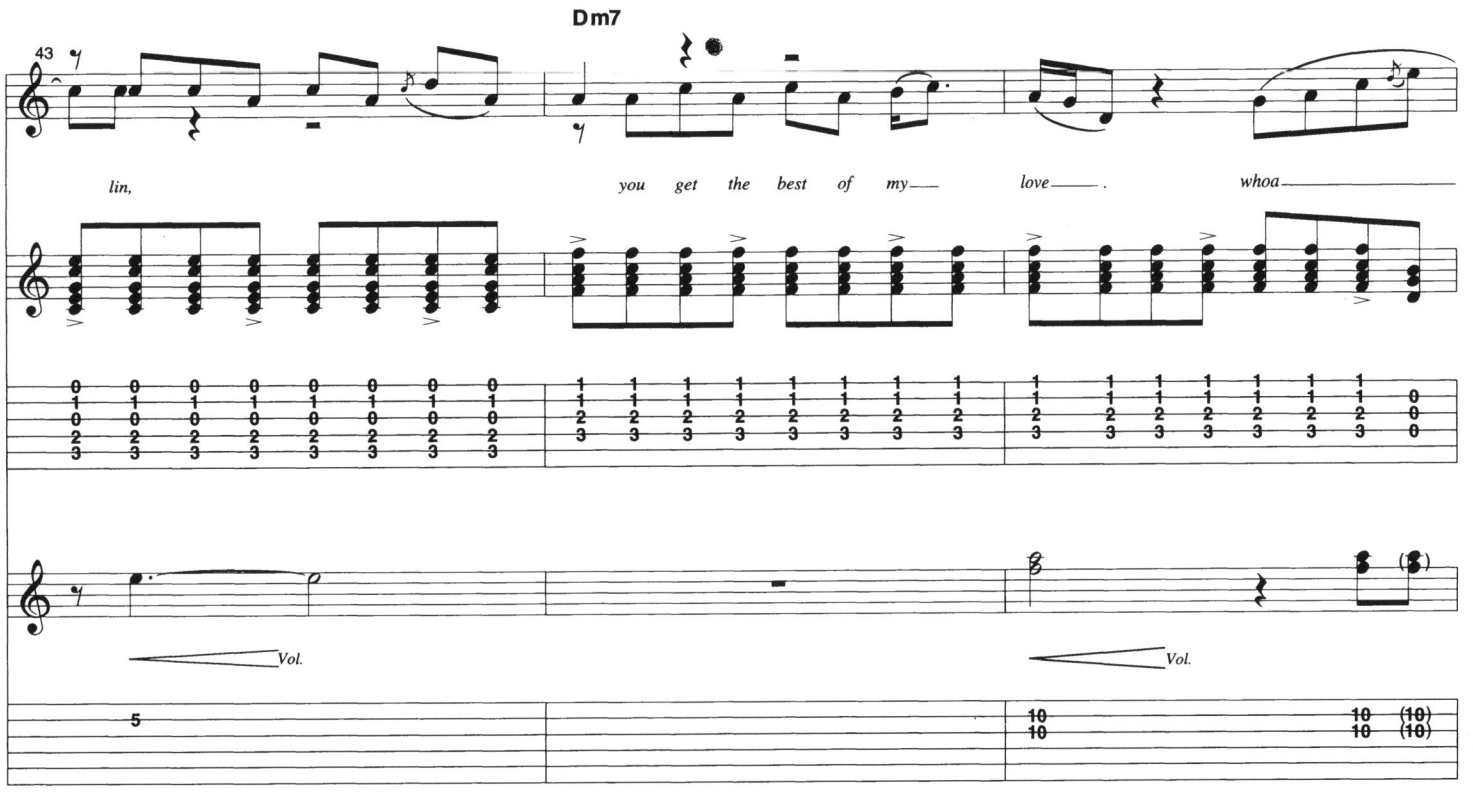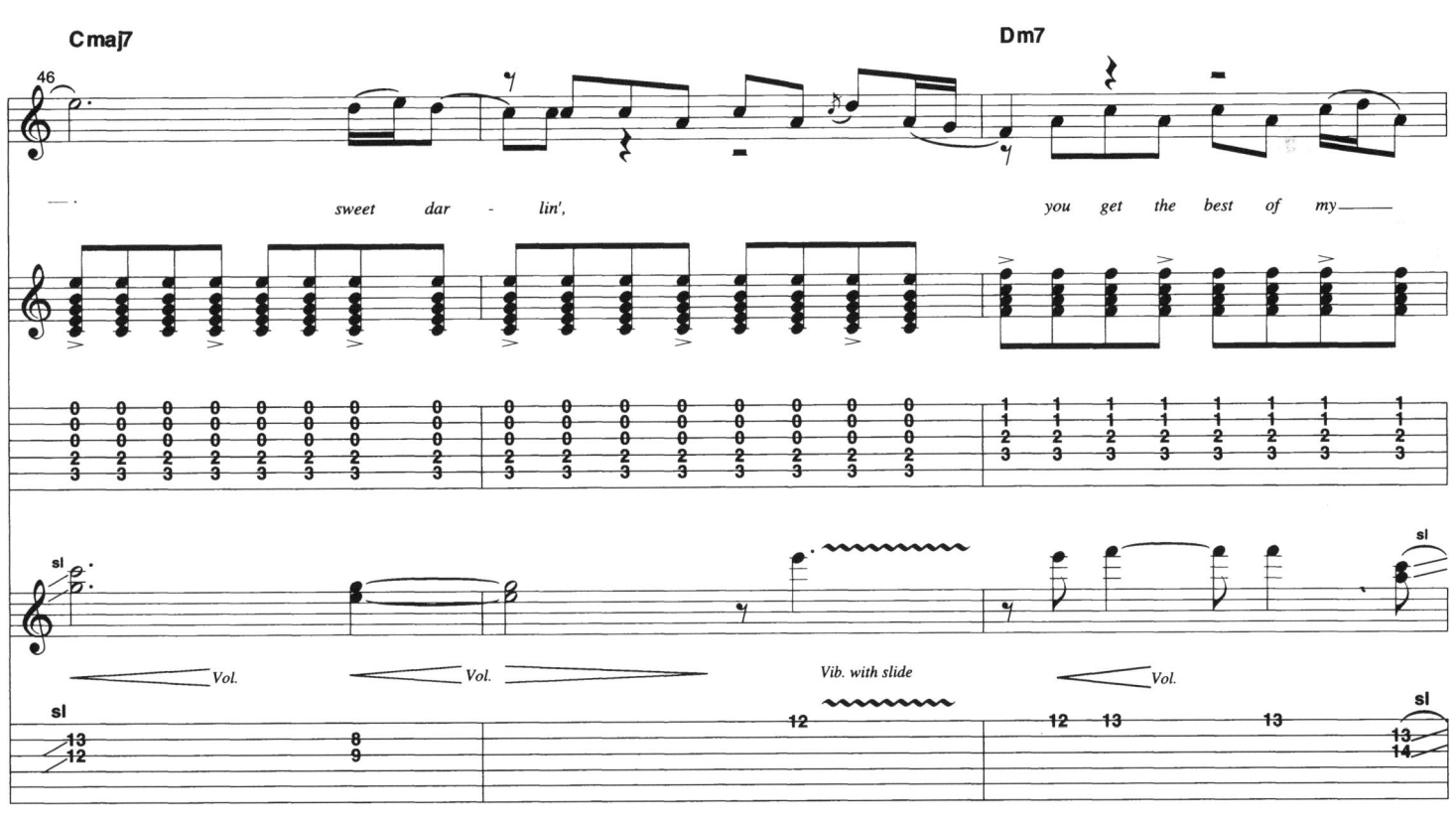

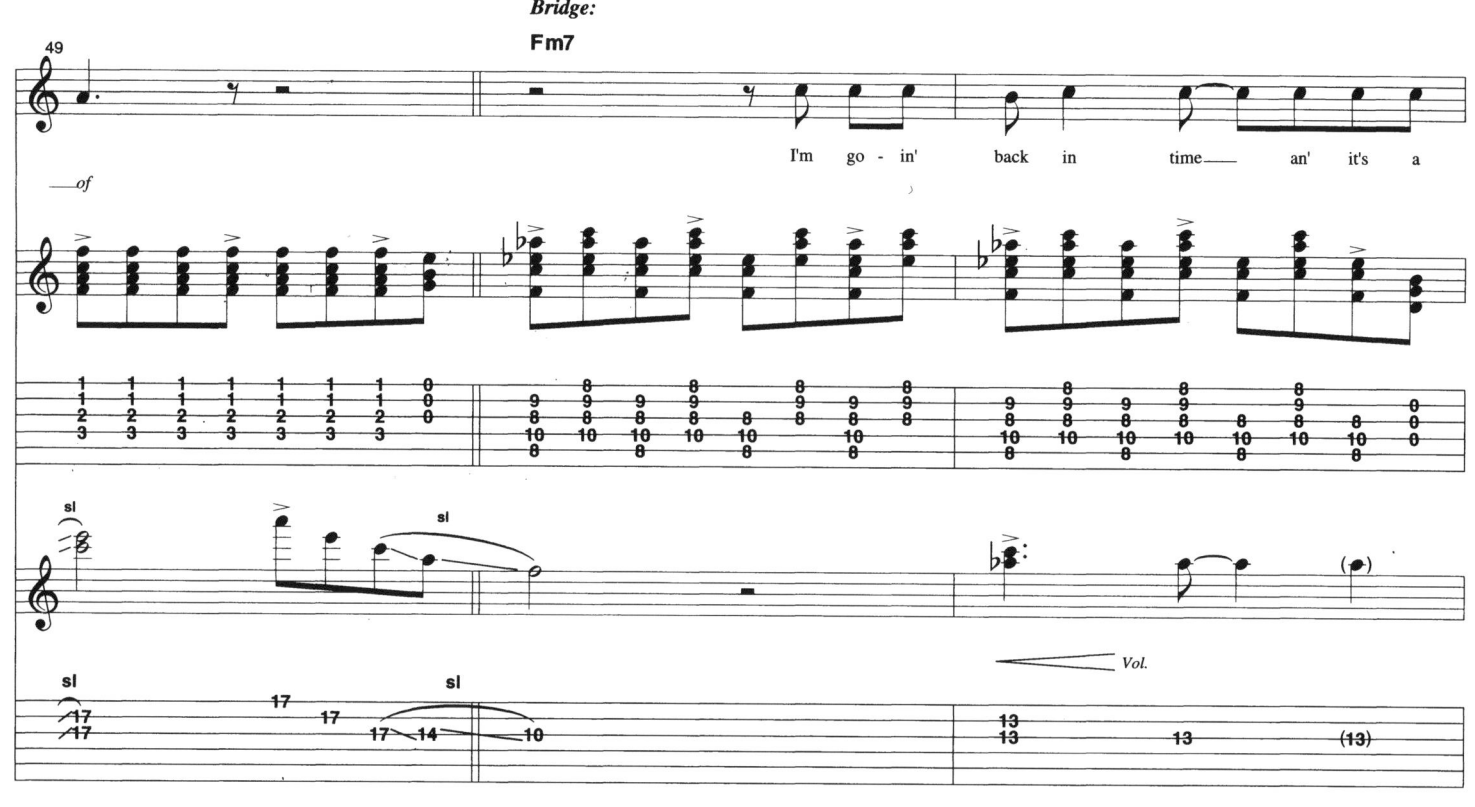
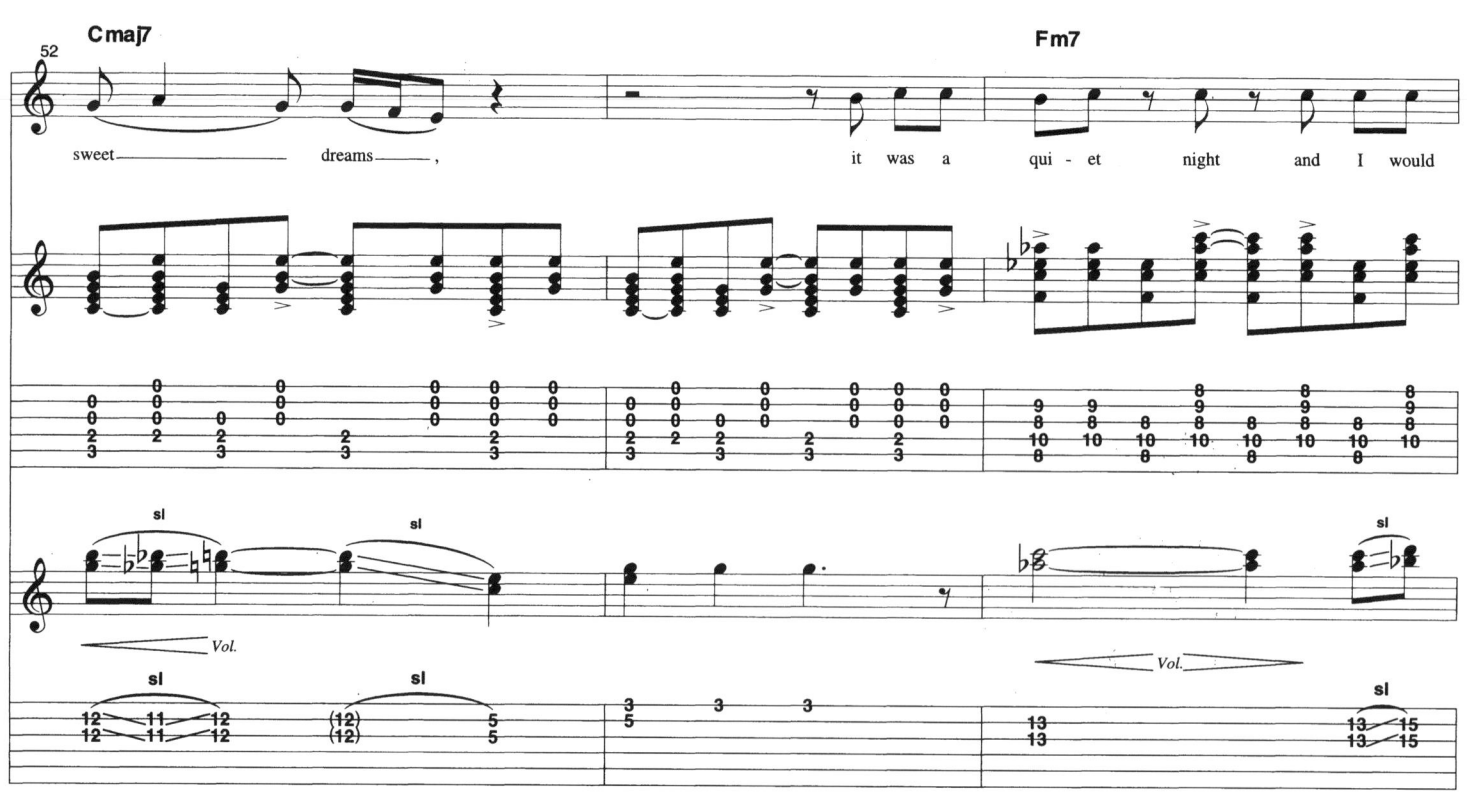

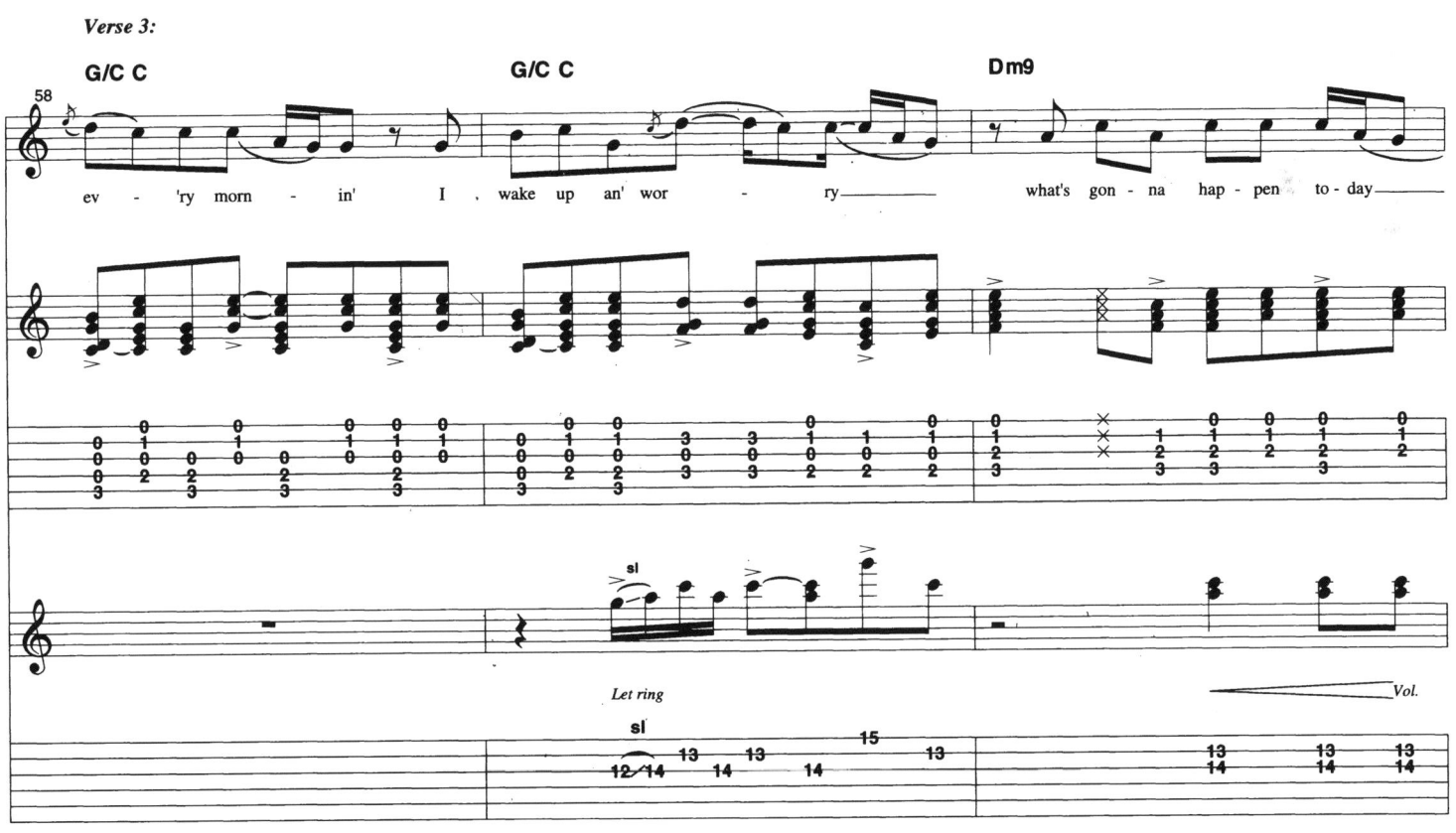

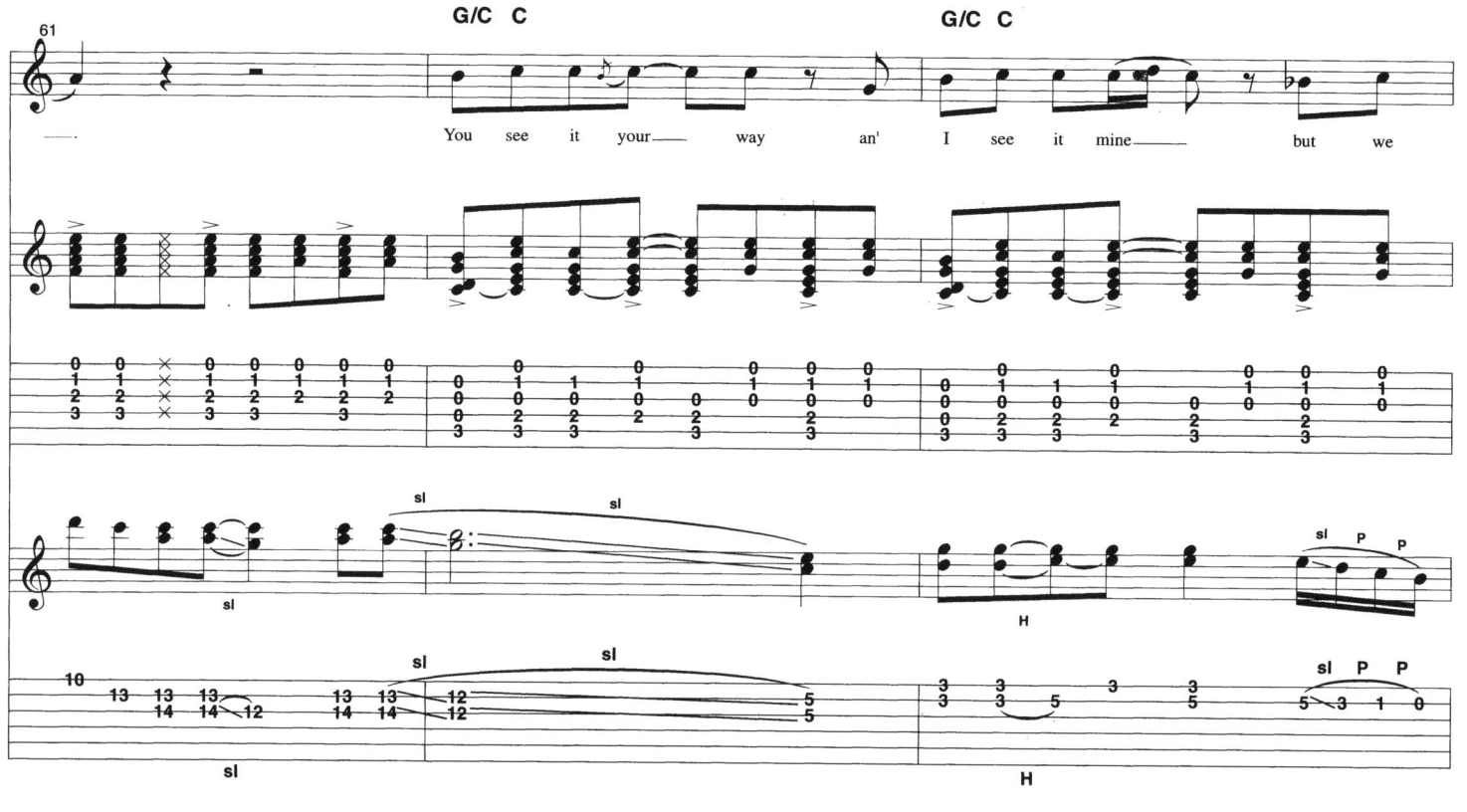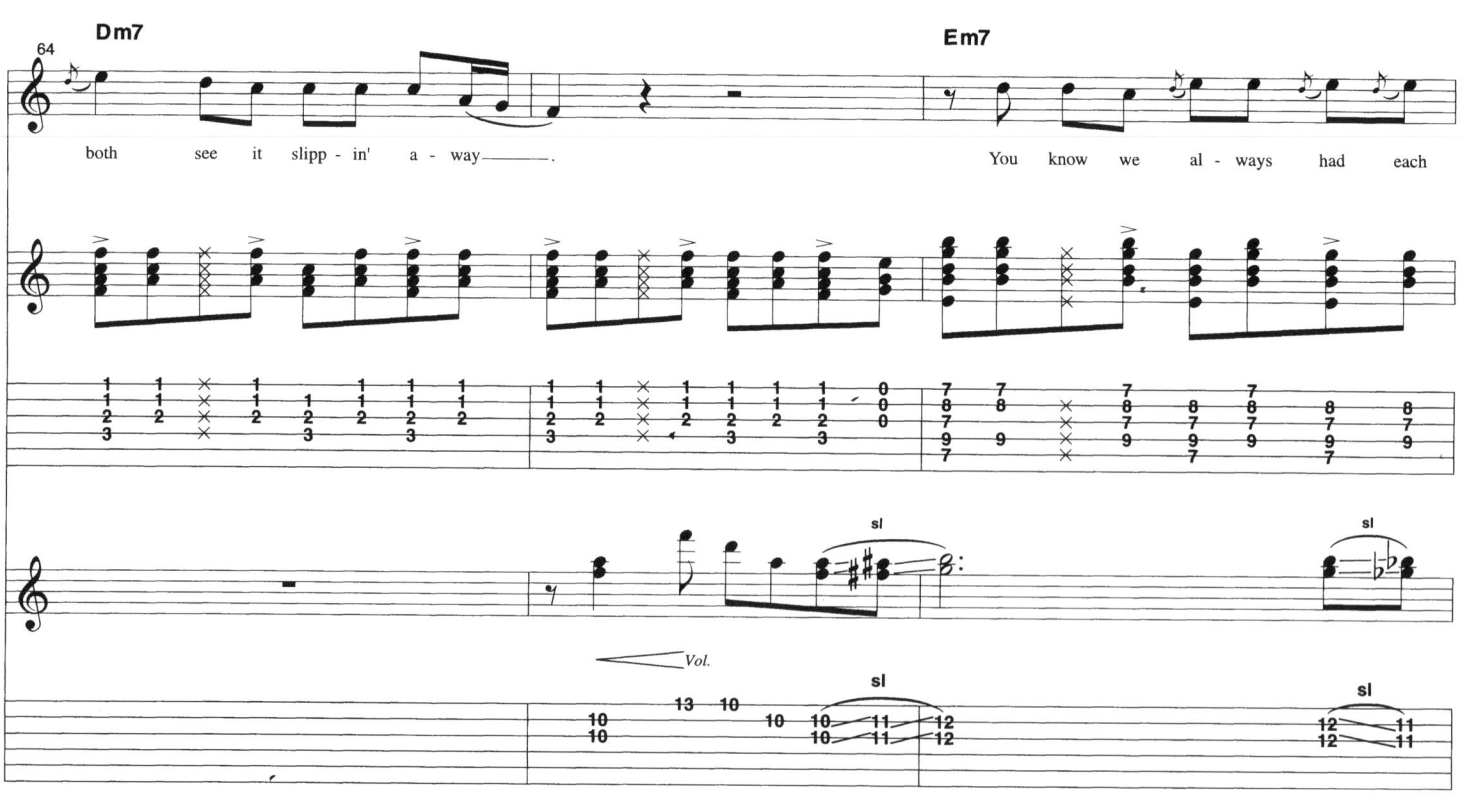

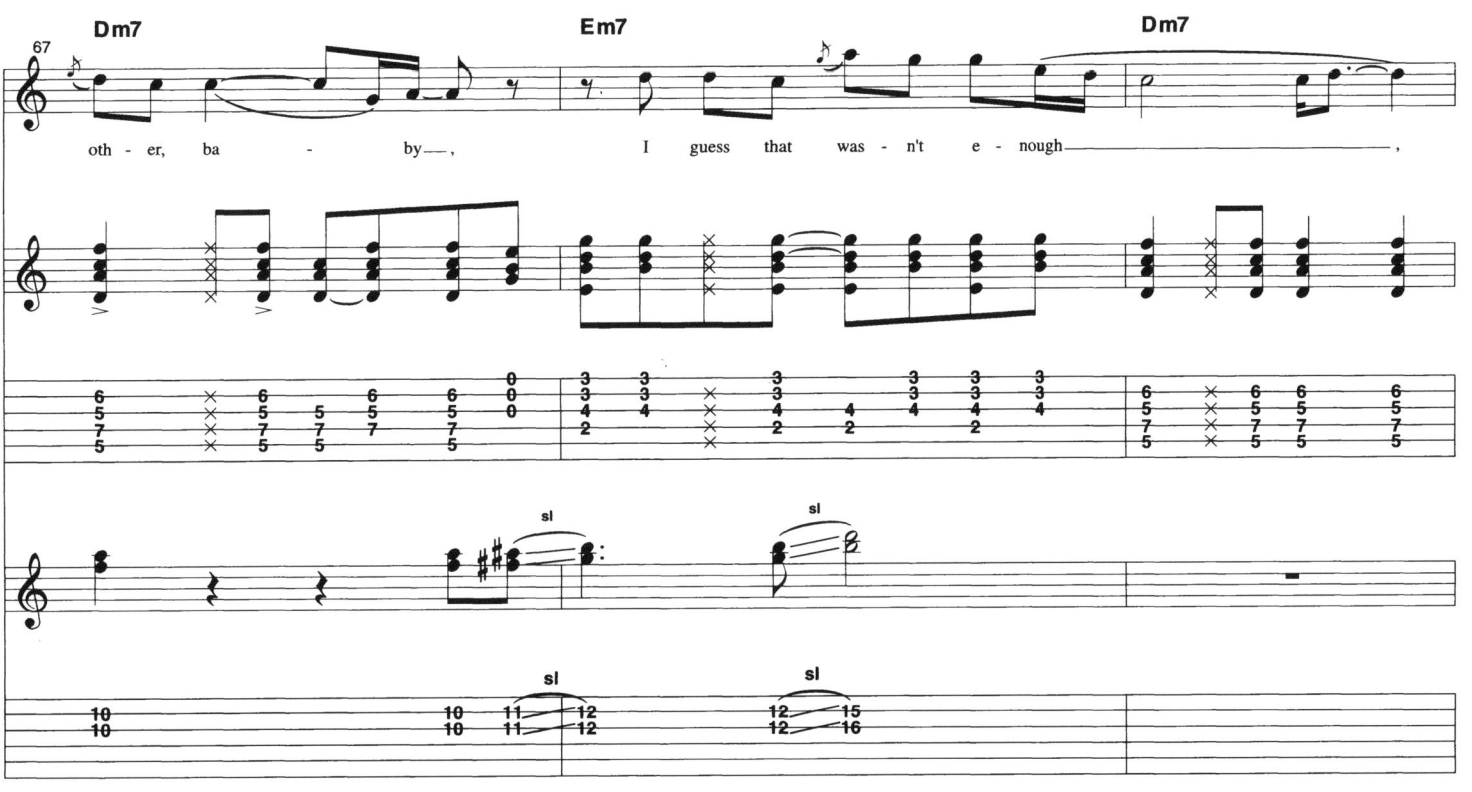
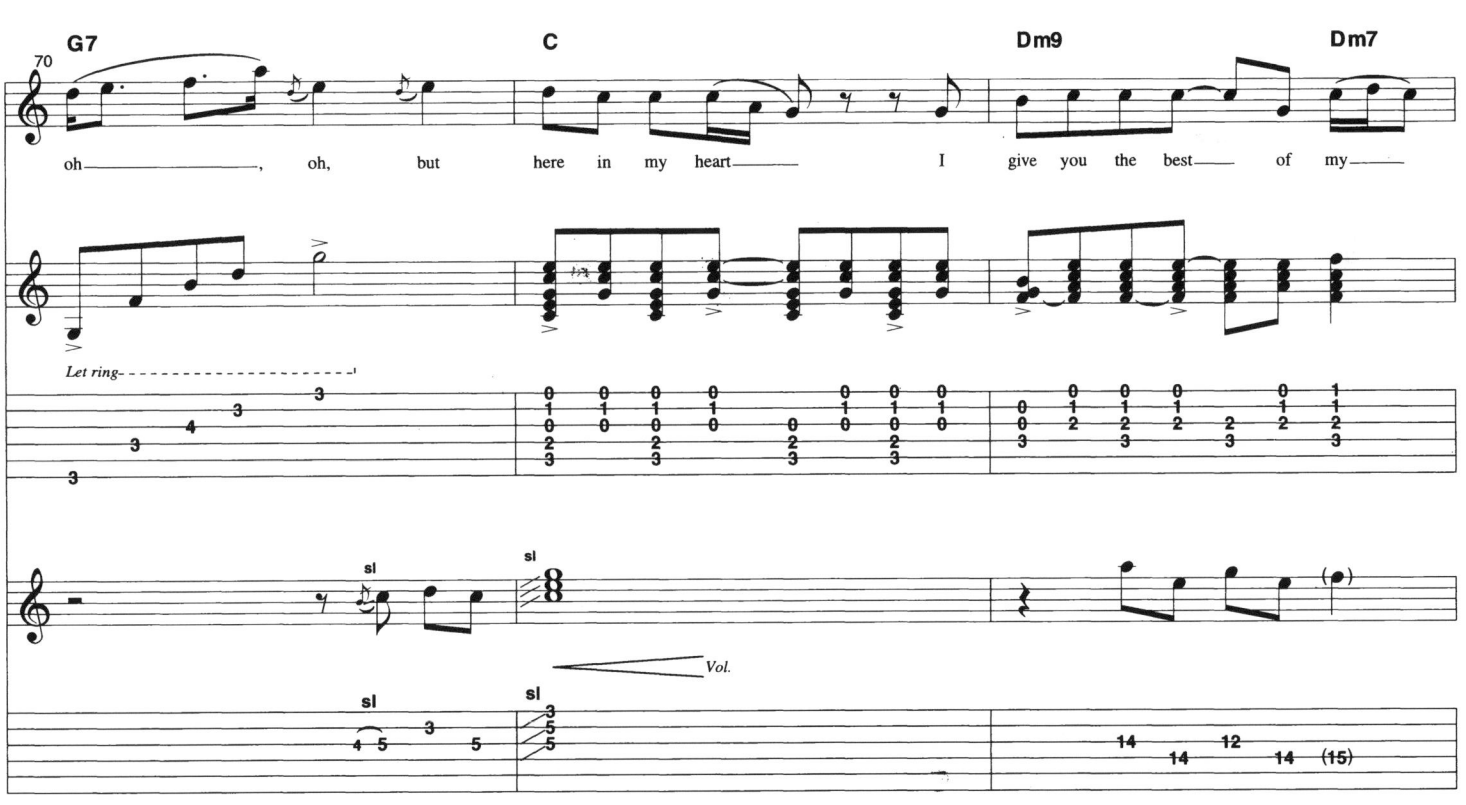

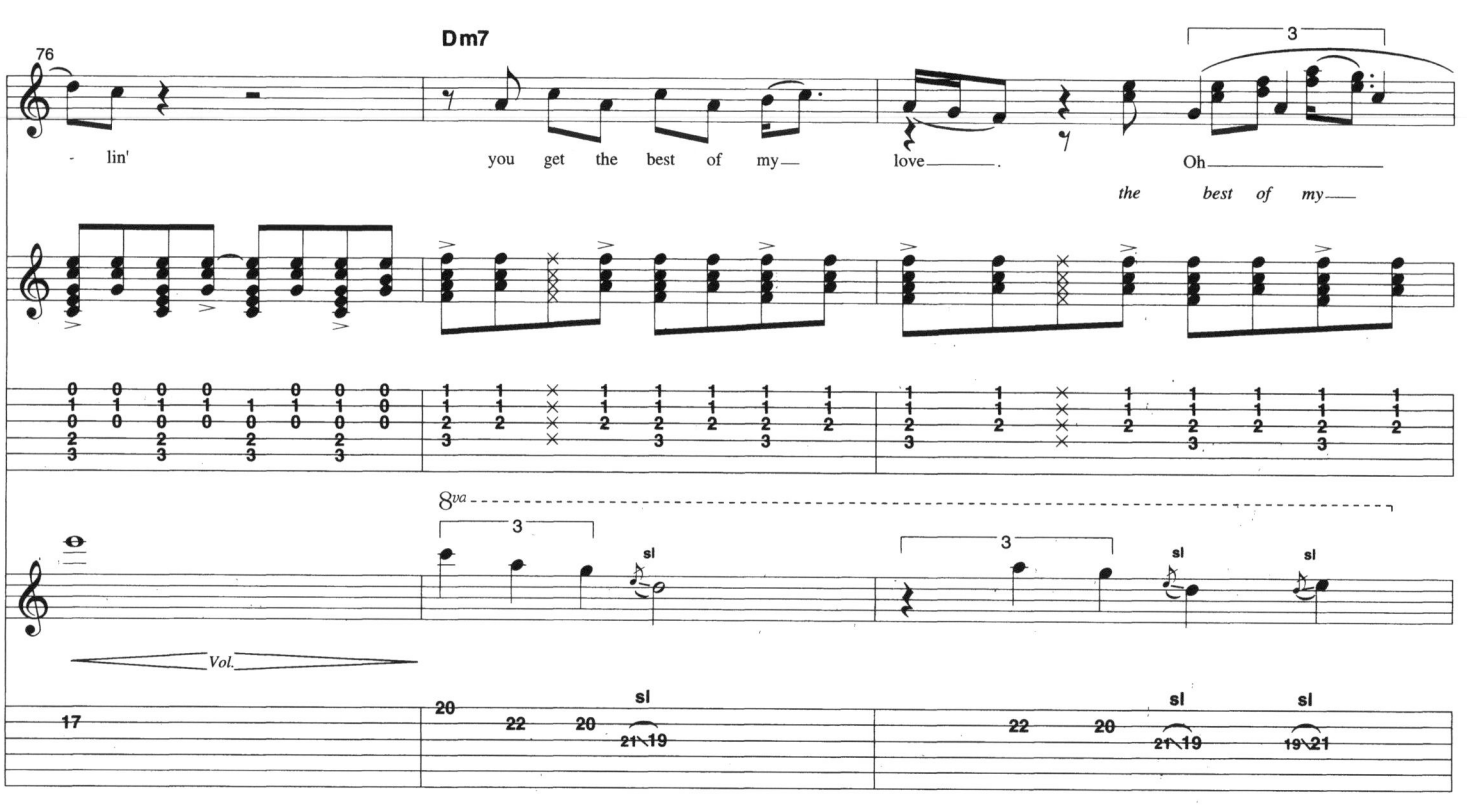

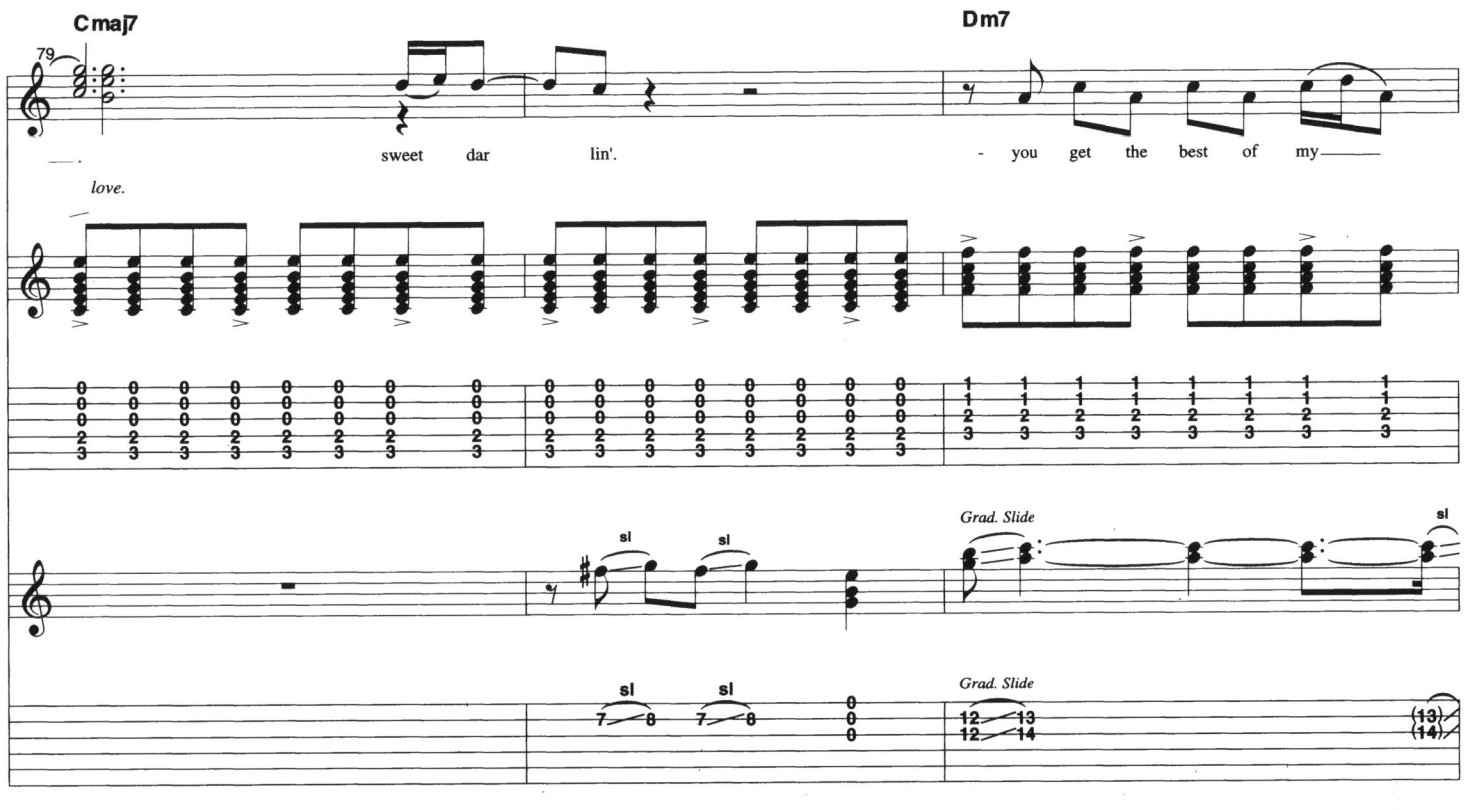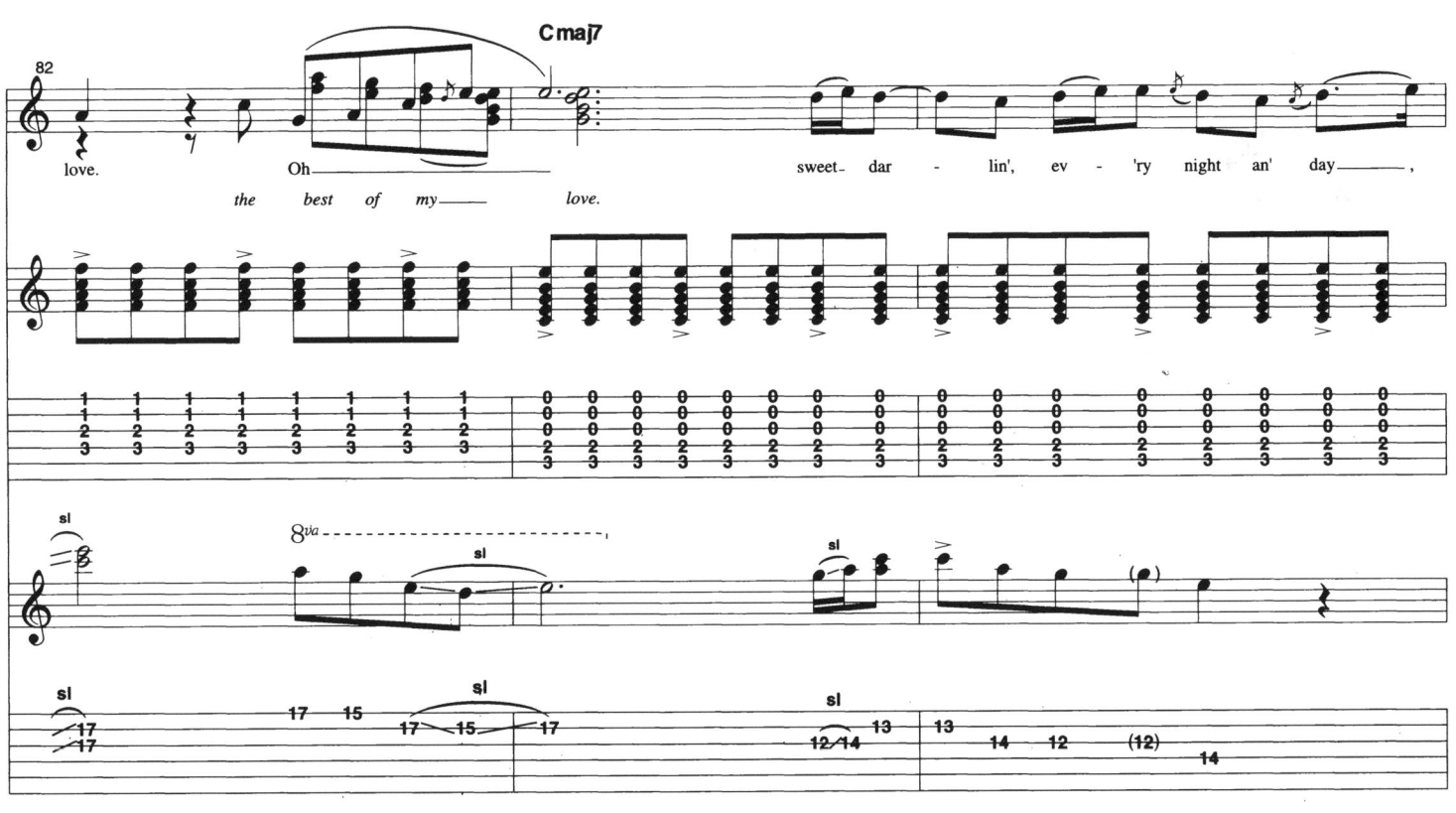

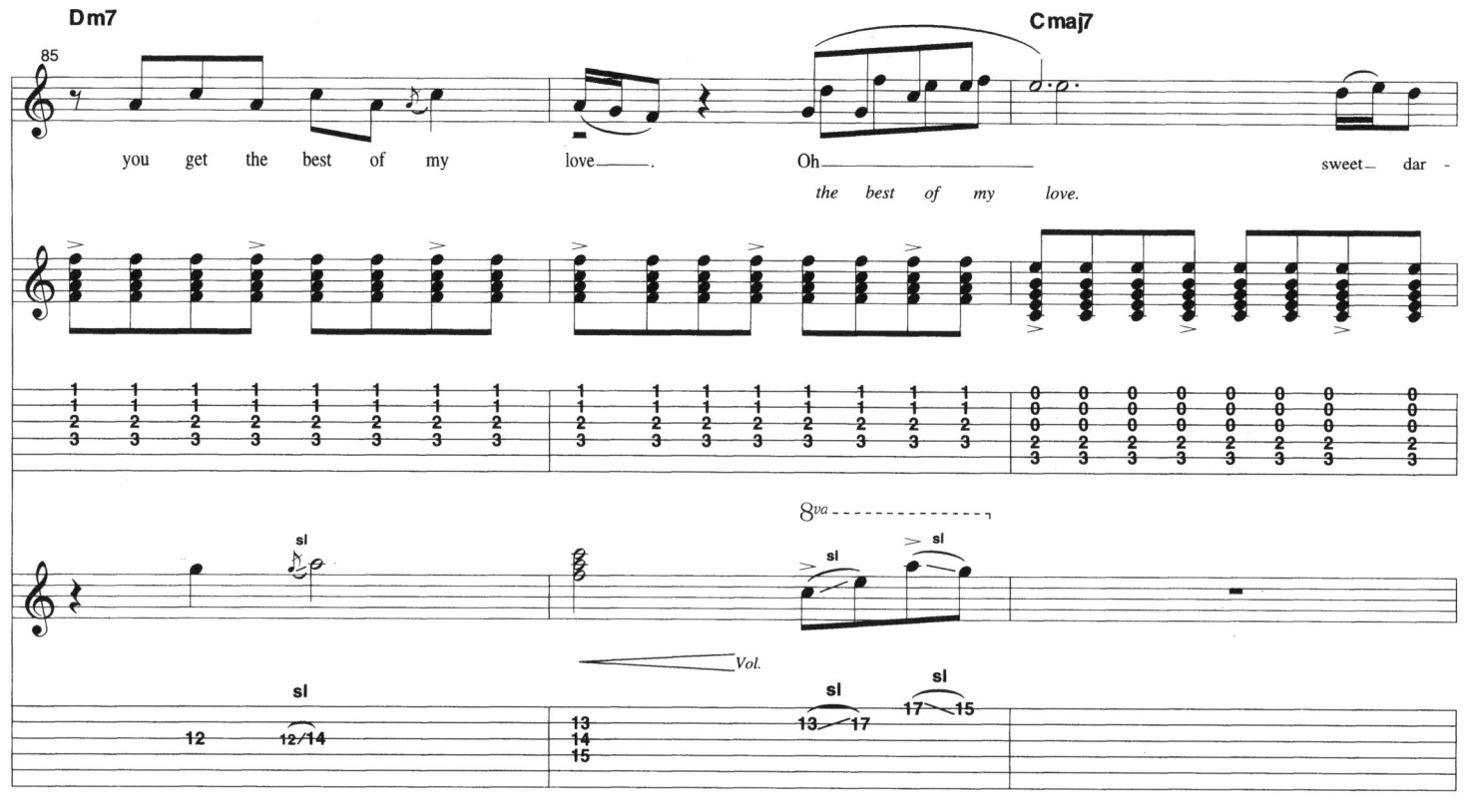
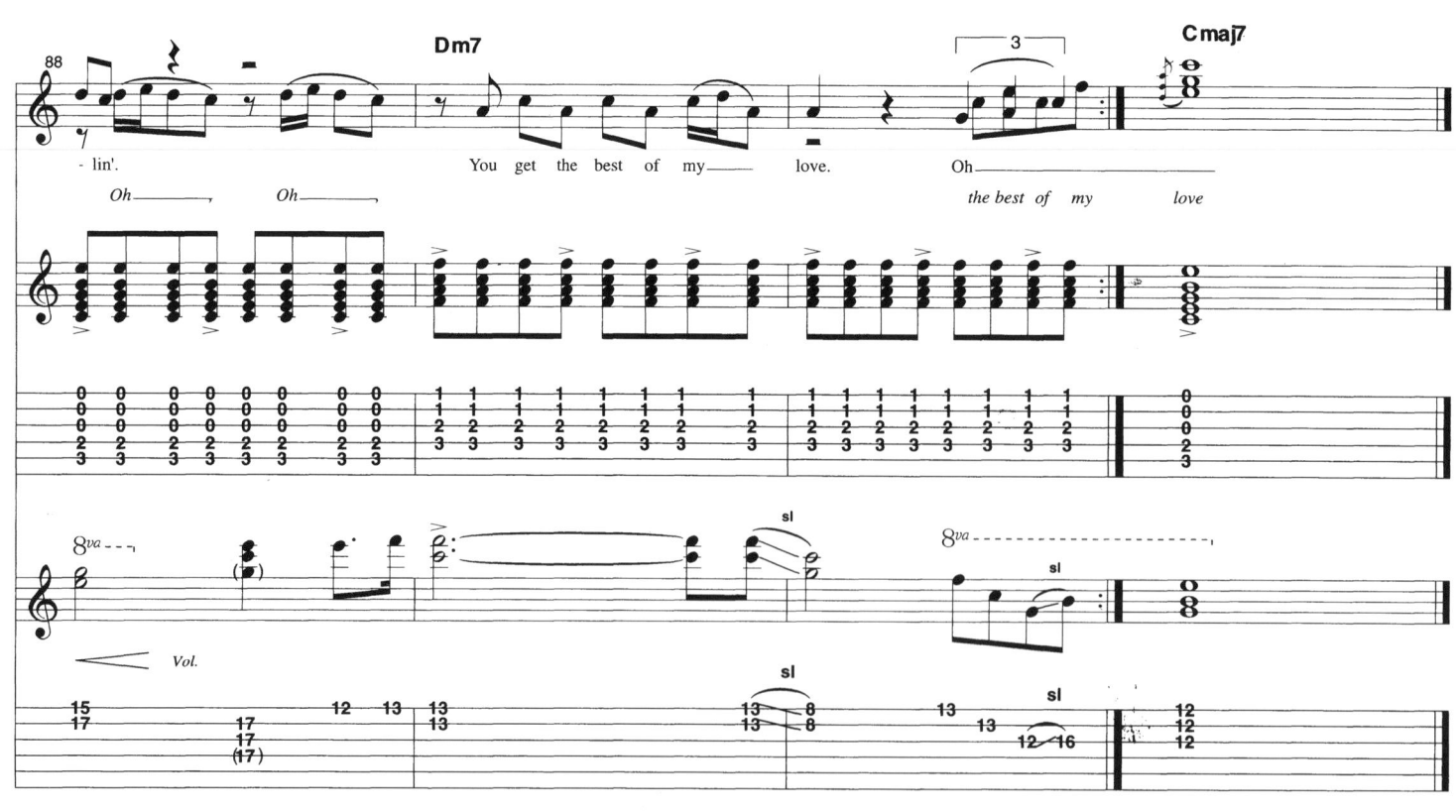